P9-DVQ-693

40	**vierzig**	feer-tsik
50	**fünfzig**	fewnf-tsik
60	**sechzig**	zek-tsik
70	**siebzig**	zeep-tsik
80	**achtzig**	ahkt-tsik
90	**neunzig**	noin-tsik
100	**hundert**	hoon-dairt
101	**hunderteins**	hoon-dairt-<u>eye-ns</u>
102	**hundertzwei**	hoon-dairt-<u>tsvigh</u>
110	**hundertzehn**	hoon-dairt-<u>tsane</u>
111	**hundertelf**	hoon-dairt-<u>elf</u>
120	**hundertzwanzig**	hoon-dairt-<u>tsvahn</u>-tsik
200	**zweihundert**	<u>tsvigh</u>-hoon-dairt
300	**dreihundert**	<u>dry</u>-hoon-dairt
400	**vierhundert**	<u>feer</u>-hoon-dairt
437	**vierhundertsiebenunddreißig**	
	feer-hoon-dairt-zee-ben-oont-<u>dry</u>-sik	
500	**fünfhundert**	<u>fewnf</u>-hoon-dairt
600	**sechshundert**	<u>sex</u>-hoon-dairt
700	**siebenhundert**	<u>zee</u>-ben-hoon-dairt
800	**achthundert**	<u>ahkt</u>-hoon-dairt
900	**neunhundert**	<u>noin</u>-hoon-dairt
1000	**(ein)tausend**	(eye-n) <u>tauw</u>-zunt
2000	**zweitausend**	<u>tsvigh</u>-tauw-zunt
10.000	**zehntausend**	<u>tsane</u>-tauw-zunt
100.000	**hunderttausend**	<u>hoon</u>-dairt-tauw-zunt
1.000.000	**(eine) Million**	(eye-nuh) mil-<u>yohn</u>

info On the phone, **zwo** (tsvoh) is often used instead of **zwei** (tsvigh) because **zwei** and **drei** sound alike. In large numbers, periods, <u>not</u> commas, are used, e.g. 3.500.

The Basics

Good afternoon!	**Guten Tag!** goo-ten tahk
Good evening!	**Guten Abend!** goo-ten ah-bent
Goodbye!	**Auf Wiedersehen!** owf vee-duh-zay-en
..., please!	**..., bitte!** bit-tuh
Thank you!	**Danke!** dahn-kuh
Yes.	**Ja.** yah
No.	**Nein.** nine
Sorry!	**Entschuldigung!** ent-shool-dee-goong
Get a *doctor* / *an ambulance*, quick!	**Rufen Sie schnell einen *Arzt* / *Krankenwagen*!** roo-fen zee shnel eye-nen *ahtst* / *krahnk-en-vah-gen*
Where are the restrooms?	**Wo ist die Toilette?** vo ist dee toi-let-tuh
When?	**Wann?** vahn
What?	**Was?** vahs
Where?	**Wo?** vo
Here.	**Hier.** here
There.	**Dort.** dawt
On the right.	**Rechts.** rex
On the left.	**Links.** linx
Do you have ...?	**Haben Sie ...?** hah-ben zee
I'd like ...	**Ich möchte ...** ish mush-tuh
How much is that?	**Was kostet das?** wahs kaws-tet dahs
Where is ...?	**Wo ist ...?** vo ist
Where can I get ...?	**Wo gibt es ...?** vo gheept es

III

Langenscheidt

Pocket Phrasebook
German

with Travel Dictionary
and Grammar

Langenscheidt

Berlin · Munich · Vienna · Zurich · New York

Graphic Design: Kathrin Mosandl
Editorial: Emily Bernath, Christiane Heil, Gabriela Lindner, Juergen Lorenz

Photo Credits:
Corbis Images: p.15; Ebentheuer, H.: p.31, 172; EyeWire Images: p.65, 152;
Jupiter Image Corporation: 25, 32, 37, 40, 44, 56, 121, 123, 132, 138,
153, 155, 165, 198; Kusche, M.: p. 189; MEV: p.59, 61, 64, 141, 144, 147,
201; PhotoAlto: p. 22, 69; PhotoDisc: p.73; Salzburger Land Tourismus: p.
103, 109, 135, 147, 195; Stockbyte: p.95, 105, 171, 178, 186

ISBN 1-58573-508-6
Printed in Germany
www.langenscheidt.com

10 09 08 07 06

1. 2. 3. 4. 5.

Table of Contents

Numbers I
The Basics III

How to Use This Book 8
Pronunciation 10

Meeting People ———————————————— 15

Communication
Difficulties 16

Greetings 16

Getting to Know Each
Other 18
   Introductions 18
   Asking Someone Out....19

Accepting / Declining
an Invitation 20
   Flirting 20

Polite Expressions 21
   Expressing Likes and
   Dislikes 21
   Expressing Requests
   and Thanks...................21
   Apologies 22

Meeting People:
Additional Words..........23

Accommodations ———————————————— 25

Lodging...........................26
   Looking For a Room 26
   Arriving 26
   Service..........................28
   Departure 30

Rentals 30

Camping 32

Accommodations:
Additional Words 34

Travel ———————————————— 37

Asking for Directions 38
   Where Is It? 39

Luggage / Baggage 39
   Additional Words..........40
At the Airport..................41
   Additional Words..........42

Travel by Train 42
   On the Train 44
   At the Train Station......45
   Additional Words.........45

Travel by Bus 46

Travel by Boat.................47
  Information and
  Reservations 47
  Aboard.........................48
  Additional
  Words 48

Travel by Car and
Motorcycle 49
  Car Rental 49
  At the Gas / Petrol
  Station 50
  Breakdown...................50

  Accidents 51
  Getting Your Car
  Fixed 52
  Additional Words..........53

Public Transportation 55

Travel by Taxi 57

Public Transportation and
Taxi: Additional Words.....57

Travel with Children ——————————— 59

Frequently Asked
Questions.......................60

At the Hotel /
Restaurant......................61

Swimming with
Children 62

Childcare and Health.......63

Travel with Children:
Additional Words 63

For the Disabled ——————————— 65

Asking for Help 66

At the Hotel 67

Additional Words 68

Communications——————————— 69

Telephone 70

Internet..........................71

E-mail............................72

——————Table of Contents —

Eating and Drinking———————— 73

Reservations 74

Menu 75
  Breakfast 75
  Soups 76
  Appetizers 77
  Meat Dishes, Poultry,
  Fish, Seafood...............78
  Egg Dishes...................82
  Side Dishes, Vegetables...83
  Ways of Cooking 85
  Cheese, Desserts 86
  Fruit and Nuts...............88

Beverages.......................90
  Wine, Champagne 90

Beer, Other Alcoholic
Drinks............................91
Non-alcoholic Drinks.....92
Hot Drinks 93

Ordering 94

Complaints.....................96

Paying 97

Having Lunch / Dinner
Together.........................98

Eating and Drinking:
Additional Words 99

Shopping——————————— 103

Paying 104

General Requests 104
  Additional Words........106

Shops and Stores...........107

Food 109
  Additional Words........110

Souvenirs 114
  Additional Words........115

Clothing..........................115
  Buying Clothes 115
  Laundry and Dry
  Cleaning....................117

Fabrics and Materials ..117
Colors 117
Additional Words........118

In the Shoe Store...........120
  Additional Words........120

Jewelry and Watches.....121
  Additional Words........122

Health and Beauty.........123

Household Articles 125

Electrical Articles 127

At the Optician..............127

At the Photo Store 128
  Additional Words........130

At the Music Store 131
  Additional Words........131

Books and Stationery.....131
  Additional Words........132

At the Tobacco Shop 133
  Additional Words........134

Sports and Leisure _____ 135

Activities 136
  Beach and Pool...........136
  Additional Words........138

Games 140
  Additional Words........141

Indoor Activities 142

Hiking 143
  Additional Words........144

Bicycling.......................145
  Additional Words........145

Adventure Sports 146

Winter Sports................147
  Additional Words........148

Beauty..........................148
  At the Salon 148
  Additional Words........150
  Beauty Treatments 150
  Additional Words........151
  Well-Being.................152

Things to Do _____ 153

Sightseeing 154
  Tourist Information 154

Excursions and Sights 156
  Additional Words........156

Cultural Events 160

At the Box Office 162
Cultural Events:
  Additional Words........162

Nightlife 164
  Additional Words........164

Money, Mail and Police _____ 165

Money Matters..............166
  Additional Words........167

Post Office 167
  Additional Words........168

Police 169
  Additional Words........170

Table of Contents

Health ————————————————— 171

Pharmacy 172

Medication Information...172

Medicine and
    Medications...............174

Looking for a Doctor 175

Physicians......................176

At the Doctor's Office 177

Body Parts and Organs 180
Illnesses and
    Complaints.................182

At the Hospital 186

At the Dentist's..............187
Additional Words........188

Time and the Calendar————————————189

Time of the Day.............190
Additional Words........191

Seasons.........................192

Date...............................193
Days of the Week 193
Months 193

Holidays 194

Weather and Environment————————— 195

Weather.........................196
Additional Words........197

Environment...................199
Additional Words........199

Grammar 201

Conversion Charts 208

Travel Dictionary 209

Signs 249

Index 253

Appendix:
  Colors and Fabrics
  Fruits and Vegetables

German has a formal and informal way to address people. You'll find a detailed explanation in the grammar section.

How are you?	Wie geht es *Ihnen* / *dir*? vee gate es *ee-nen* / *deer*
Fine, thanks. And you?	Danke, gut. Und *Ihnen* / *dir*?

Sometimes you see two alternatives in italics, separated by a slash. Choose the one that is appropriate for the situation, e.g. bald for soon or morgen for tomorrow.

I'm afraid I h~~ave to~~ go.	
Goodbye!	Auf Wiedersehen! auwf <u>veeder</u>-zay-en
See you *soon* / *tomorrow*!	Bis *bald* / *morgen*! bis *bahlt* / *maw-ghen*
Bye!	Tschüs! chews
It was nice meeting you.	Schön, *Sie* / *dich* kennen gelernt zu haben. shern *zee* / *dish* ken-nen guh- lairnt tsoo hah-ben
Have a good trip!	Gute Reise! goo-te rye-suh

▶ *Accepting* / *Declining an Invitation, p. 22*

The red arrow indicates a cross reference where you find additional words and expressions.

The pronunciation of each word is given. Simply read it as if it were an English word. See also simplified pronunciation guide pages 10-12.

Phrases that you may hear but may never say are shown in reverse, with German on the left side.

Which *bus / subway* goes to …?	*Welcher Bus / Welche U-Bahn* fährt nach … ? *velsh-uh boos / velsh-uh oo-bahn* fairt nahk
Der Bus Nummer …	The bus number …
Die Linie …	The … line.
When's the next *bus / subway* to …?	Wann fährt *der nächste Bus / die nächste U-Bahn* nach … ? *vahn fairt dair nayx-tuh boos / dee nayx-tuh oo-bahn* nahk
Does this bus go to …?	Fährt dieser Bus nach …? *fairt dee-zuh boos nahk*
Where's the nearest …	Wo ist die nächste … *vo ist dee nayx-tuh*
Do you have …	Gibt es … *gheept es*
– one day travel passes?	– Tageskarten? <u>tah</u>-ghes-kah-ten
– multiple-ride tickets?	– Mehrfahrtenkarten? <u>mair</u>-fah-kah-ten
– weekly travel passes?	– Wochenkarten? <u>vaw</u>-khen-kah-ten
– a booklet of tickets?	– Fahrscheinheftchen?

If there is more than one way to continue a sentence, any of the possibilities that follow can be inserted.

You can insert your choice of word(s) from the Additional Words section in place of ellipses marks.

9

Pronunciation

This section will make you familiar with the sounds of German using our simplified phonetic transcription. You'll find the pronunciation of the letters and sounds explained below, together with their "imitated" equivalents. This system is used throughout the phrase book: just read the pronunciation as if it were English, noting any special rules below.

The German Language

German is the national language of Germany and Austria and is one of the four official languages of Switzerland. It is also spoken by groups of Germans in other countries.

Germany Deutschland

German spoken properly, i.e. without a noticeable accent, is called Hochdeutsch. Native speakers often have accents or speak dialects that vary from region to region.

Austria Österreich

German is the national language for over 7.8 million people.

Switzerland Schweiz

German is spoken by 70% of the population, mainly in the north and east. Other languages: French (20% of the population) in the west; Italian in the south; and the much rarer Romansh.

German is also one of the languages spoken in eastern France (Alsace-Lorraine), northern Italy (Alto Adige), eastern Belgium, Luxembourg and Liechtenstein. There are also about 1.5 million German speakers in the U.S., 500,000 in Canada and sizeable groups in South America, Namibia and Kazakhstan.

Pronunciation

The German alphabet is the same as English, with the addition of the letter ß. It also uses the Umlaut on the vowels ä, ü, ö (see below for pronunciation).

Consonants

Letter	Approximate Pronunciation	Symbol	Example	Pronunciation
b	1. at the end of a word or between a vowel and a consonant, like p in up	p	ab	ahp
	2. elsewhere as in English	b	bis	biss
c	1. before e, i, ö and ä, like ts in hits	ts	Celsius	tsel-see-oos
	2. elsewhere like c in cat	k	Café	kahfay
ch	1. after back vowels (e.g. ah, o, oo) like ch in Scottish loch, otherwise more like h in huge	kh	doch	dokh
	2. sometimes, especially before s, like k in kit	k	Wachs	vahks
	3. somtimes like sh, especially when followed by a t or a vowel.	sh	echt	esht
d	1. at the end of a word or between a vowel and a consonant, like t in eat	t	Rad	raht
	2. elsewhere like d in do	d	danke	dahn-kuh
g	1. always hard as in go, but at the end of a word often like sh in finish	g/gh	geben	gay-ben
		k	weg	vek
		sh	fertig	fer-tish
j	like y in yes	y	ja	yah
qu	like k followed by v as in vat	kv	Quark	kvahrk
r	generally rolled in the back of the mouth	r	warum	vah-room
w	usually like v in voice	v	Wagon	vah-gong

s	1. before or between vowels like z in zoo	z	sie	zee
	2. before p and t at the beginning of a syllable like sh in shut	sh	Sport	shport
	3. elsewhere, like s in sit	s/ss	es ist	es ist
ß	always like s	s/ss	groß	grohs
sch	like sh in shut	sh	schnell	shnel
tsch	like ch in chip	tch	deutsch	doitch
tz	like ts in hits	ts	Platz	plahts
v	1. like f in for	f	vier	fear
	2. in most words of foreign origin, like v in vice	v	Vase	vah-se
w	like v in vice	v	wie	vee
z	like ts in hits	ts	zeigen	tsigh-ghen

Letters f, h, k, l, m, n, p, t, x are pronounced as in English.

Vowels

Letter	Approximate Pronunciation	Symbol	Example	Pronunciation
a		ah	Tag	tahk
ä	1. short like e in let	e/eh	Lärm	lehrm
	2. long like ai in hair	ai	spät	shpayt
e	1. short like e in let	e	schnell	shnel
	2. long like a in late, but pronounced without moving tongue or lips	ay/eh	sehen	say-en
	3. at the end of a word,	uh	bitte	bit-tuh
	4. sometimes almost silent		gehen	gain
i	1. short like i in hit	i	billig	bil-ig
	2. long like ee in meet	ee	ihm	eem
ie	like ee in bee	ee	Bier	beer

o	short like o in cord	o/oh	voll	fol
ö	like er in fern	er	schön	shern
u	short like oo in foot	oo	Nuss	nooss
ü	like ew in new; round your lips	ew	über	ew-ber
y	like ew in new	ew	typisch	tew-pish

Diphthongs

ai, ay, ei, ey	like ey in eye	eye/igh	einen	eye-nen
au	like ow in now	ow/au	auf	owf
äu, eu	like oy in boy	oi	neu	noi

Stress

Generally, as in English, the first syllable is stressed in German, except when short prefixes are added to the beginning of the word. Then the second syllable is stressed (e.g. bewegen to move, gesehen seen).

In exceptions or longer words, stress has been indicated in the phonetic transcription: underlined letters should be pronounced with more stress than the others, e.g. ah-dress uh.(**Adresse**)

Pronunciation of the German Alphabet

A	ah	O	oh
Ä	ai	Ö	er
B	bay	P	pay
C	tsay	Q	koo
D	day	R	ehr
E	eh	S	ess
F	ef	T	tay
G	gay	U	oo
H	hah	Ü	ew
I	ee	V	fow
J	yot	W	vay
K	kah	X	eeks
L	el	Y	ewp-sillon
M	em	Z	tset
N	en		

Meeting
People

How are you?
Wie geht es Ihnen?

It was nice meeting you.
Schön, Sie kennen gelernt zu haben.

Communication Difficulties

Do you speak English?	Sprechen Sie Englisch? shpre-shen zee ayng-lish
Does anyone here speak English?	Spricht hier jemand Englisch? shprisht here yay-mahnt ayng-lish
Did you understand that?	Haben Sie das verstanden? hah-ben zee dahs fair-stahn-den
I understand.	Ich habe verstanden. ish hah-beh fair-stahnd-den
I didn't understand that.	Ich habe das nicht verstanden. ish hah-beh dahs nisht fair-stahnd-den
Could you speak a bit more slowly, please?	Könnten Sie bitte etwas langsamer sprechen? kern-ten zee bit-tuh et-vahs lahng-zahmer shpre-shen
Could you please repeat that?	Könnten Sie das bitte wiederholen? kern-ten zee dahs bit-tuh veeder-ho-len
What's that in German?	Wie heißt das auf Deutsch? vee highst dahs owf doitch
What does … mean?	Was bedeutet …? vahs buh-doi-tet …
Could you write it down for me, please?	Könnten Sie es mir bitte aufschreiben? kern-ten zee es meer bit-tuh owf-shry-ben

Greetings

Good morning!	Guten Morgen! goo-ten maw-ghen
Good afternoon!	Guten Tag! goo-ten tahk
Good evening!	Guten Abend! goo-ten ah-bent

16

— Meeting People —

Goodnight!	**Gute Nacht!** goo-te nakht
Hello!	**Hallo!** <u>hah</u>-lo

info Greetings vary according how well you know someone. It's polite to shake hands, both when you meet and say good-bye. Good friends sometimes give each other a hug, and women kiss each other on the cheeks.

How are you?	**Wie geht es** *Ihnen / dir*? vee gate es *ee-nen / deer*
Fine, thanks. And you?	**Danke, gut. Und** *Ihnen / dir*? dahn-kuh goot oont *eenen / deer*
I'm afraid I have to go.	**Es tut mir Leid, aber ich muss gehen.** es toot meer lite ah-buh ish moos gay-en
Goodbye!	**Auf Wiedersehen!** owf <u>veeder</u>-zay-en
See you *soon / tomorrow*!	**Bis** *bald / morgen*! bis *bahlt / maw-ghen*
Bye!	**Tschüs!** chews
It was nice meeting you.	**Schön,** *Sie / dich* **kennen gelernt zu haben.** shern *zee / dish* ken-nen guh-lairnt tsoo hah-ben
Have a good trip!	**Gute Reise!** goo-te rye-suh

info There are three forms of "you" (taking different verb forms): du (informal / singular) and ihr (informal / plural) are used when talking to relatives, children, close friends and among young people. Sie (formal) is used in all other cases (singular and plural). For more information see the grammar section.

17

Getting to Know Each Other

Introductions

What's your name?	**Wie** *heißen Sie / heißt du*? vee *high-sen zee / highst doo*
My name is …	**Ich heiße** … ish high-suh
May I introduce …	**Darf ich bekannt machen?** **Das ist** … dahf ish buh-<u>kahnt</u> mah-ken dahs ist …
– my husband.	– **mein Mann.** mine mahn
– my wife.	– **meine Frau.** mine-uh frow
– my boyfriend.	– **mein Freund.** mine froint
– my girlfriend.	– **meine Freundin.** mine-uh froin-din

info The terms Freund (male) and Freundin (female) generally define a friend, not necessarily boyfriend or girlfriend.

Where are you from?	**Woher sind Sie?** vo-hair zind *zee*
I'm from …	**Ich komme aus** … ish kom-uh ows …
– the US.	– **den USA.** dane oo-es-<u>ah</u>
– Canada.	– **Kanada.** <u>kah</u>-nah-dah
– the UK.	– **Großbritannien.** gross-brit-<u>tahn</u>-ee-en
Are you married?	**Sind Sie verheiratet?** zind zee fair-<u>high</u>-rah-tet
Do you have any children?	**Haben Sie Kinder?** hah-ben zee kin-duh

Asking Someone Out

► *Accepting / Declining an Invitation, page 20*

Would you like to go out *tonight* / *tomorrow*?	Treffen wir uns heute *Abend* / *morgen*? tref-fen veer oons hoi-tuh *ah-bent* / *maw-ghen*
We could do something together, if you like.	Wir könnten etwas zusammen machen, wenn *Sie möchten* / *du möchtest*. veer <u>kern</u>-ten et-vahs tsu-<u>zahm</u>-men mah-ken ven zee *mersh-ten* / *doo mersh-test*
Would you like to have dinner together tonight?	Wollen wir heute Abend zusammen essen? vo-len veer hoi-tuh ah-bent tsoo-<u>zahm</u>-men ess-en

► *Nightlife, page 164*

I'd like to take you out.	Ich möchte Sie einladen. ish mersh-tuh zee <u>eye-n</u>-lah-den
Would you like to go dancing?	Möchten Sie tanzen gehen? mersh-ten zee tahn-tsen gay-en
What time / *Where* should we meet?	*Wann* / *Wo* treffen wir uns? *vahn* / *vo* treff-en veer oons
Let's meet at …	Treffen wir uns um … Uhr. treff-en veer oons oom … oor
I'll take you home.	Ich bringe *Sie* / *dich* nach Hause. ish bring-uh zee / dish nakh how-zuh
Could we meet again?	Sehen wir uns noch einmal? say-en veer oons nawkh eye-n-mal

Accepting / Declining an Invitation

I'd love to.	Sehr gerne. zair gair-nuh
OK.	In Ordnung. in ord-noong
I don't know yet.	Ich weiß noch nicht. ish vice nawkh nisht
Maybe.	Vielleicht. fee-<u>leysht</u>
I'm sorry, I'm afraid I can't.	Es tut mir Leid, aber ich kann nicht. es toot meer lite ah-buh ish kahn nisht

Flirting

▶ *Asking Someone Out, page 19*

Did you come by yourself?	*Sind Sie / Bist du* allein hier? *zind zee / bist doo* uh-<u>line</u> here
Do you have a *boyfriend / girlfriend*?	Hast du *einen Freund / eine Freundin*? hahst doo *eye-nen froint / eye-nuh froin-din*
You're very beautiful.	Du bist wunderschön. doo bist <u>voon</u>-duh-shern
I like the way you look.	Du gefällst mir. doo guh-<u>felst</u> meer
I like you.	Ich mag dich. ish mahk dish
I love you.	Ich liebe dich. ish lee-buh dish
When will I see you again?	Wann sehe ich dich wieder? vahn say-uh ish dish vee-duh
Are you coming back to my place?	Kommst du mit zu mir? comst doo mit tsoo meer
Leave me alone!	Lass mich in Ruhe! lahss mish in roo-uh

Polite Expressions

Expressing Likes and Dislikes

Very good!	Sehr gut! zair goot
I'm very happy.	Ich bin sehr zufrieden! ish bin zair tsoo-<u>free</u>-den
I like that.	Das gefällt mir. dahs guh-<u>felt</u> meer
What a shame!	Wie schade! vee shah-duh
I'd rather …	Ich würde lieber … ish vewr-duh lee-buh …
I don't like it.	Das gefällt mir nicht. dahs guh-<u>felt</u> meer nisht
I'd rather not.	Das möchte ich lieber nicht. dahs mersh-tuh ish lee-buh nisht
Certainly not.	Auf keinen Fall. auwf keye-nen fahl

Expressing Requests and Thanks

Thank you very much.	Vielen Dank. feel-en dahnk
Thanks, you too.	Danke, gleichfalls. dahn-kuh gl-eye-sh-fahls
May I?	Darf ich? dahf ish
Please, …	Bitte, … bit-tuh …
No, thank you.	Nein, danke. nine dahn-kuh
Could you help me, please?	Könnten Sie mir bitte helfen? kern-ten zee meer bit-tuh hel-fen

21

Thank you, that's very nice of you.	Vielen Dank, das ist sehr nett von Ihnen. feel-en dahnk dahs ist zair net fun ee-nen
Thank you very much for all your *trouble / help*.	Vielen Dank für Ihre *Mühe / Hilfe*. feel-en dahnk fur ee-ruh *mew-uh / hil-fuh*
You're welcome.	Gern geschehen. guern guh-<u>shay</u>-en

info Another way of saying "You're welcome" is Bitte, (also meaning "please"), often said twice as in Bitte, bitte.

Apologies

Sorry!	Entschuldigung! ent-<u>shool</u>-di-goong
Excuse me!	Entschuldigen Sie! ent-<u>shool</u>-di-ghen zee
I'm sorry about that.	Das tut mir Leid. dahs toot meer lite

22

Don't worry about it!	**Macht nichts!** mahkt nishts
How embarrassing!	**Das ist mir sehr unangenehm.** dahs ist meer zair <u>oon</u>-ahn-guh-name
It was a misunderstanding.	**Das war ein Missverständnis.** dahs vah eye-n <u>miss</u>-fair-shtent-niss

Meeting People: Additional Words

address	**die Adresse** dee ah-<u>dress</u>-uh
alone	**allein** uh-<u>line</u>
boy	**der Junge** dair yoong-uh
boyfriend, partner	**der Freund** dair froint
brother	**der Bruder** dair broo-duh
brothers and sisters	**die Geschwister** guh-<u>shvis</u>-tuh
to be called; my name is	**heißen; ich heiße** high-sen ish high-suh
child	**das Kind** dahs kint
country	**das Land** dahs lahnt
daughter	**die Tochter** dee tok-tuh
engaged	**verlobt** fair-<u>lohpt</u>
father	**der Vater** dair fah-tuh
free	**frei** fry
friend	**der Freund** dair froint
(female) friend, girl-friend	**die Freundin** dee froin-din
to be from	**sein aus** zeye-n ows
girl	**das Mädchen** dahs made-shen
to go dancing	**tanzen gehen** tahn-tsen gay-en
to go out to eat	**essen gehen** ess-en gay-en
husband	**der Mann** dair mahn
to invite	**einladen** <u>eye-n</u>-lah-den
to make a date	**sich verabreden** zish fair-<u>ahp</u>-ray-den
married	**verheiratet** fair-<u>high</u>-rah-tet

23

to meet	kennen lernen ken-nen lair-nen
mother	die Mutter dee moo-tuh
Mr.	Herr hair
Ms.	Frau frow
partner (male)	der Partner dair pahrt-nuh
partner (female)	die Partnerin dee <u>pahrt</u>-nuh-rin
photo	das Foto dahs foh-toh
please	bitte bit-tuh
to repeat	wiederholen vee-duh-<u>ho</u>-len
to return	wiederkommen <u>vee</u>-duh-kom-en
school	die Schule shoo-luh
to see (someone) again	(jdn.) wiedersehen
	(<u>yay</u>-mahn-den) <u>vee</u>-duh-say-en
sister	die Schwester dee shves-tuh
slowly	langsam lahng-zahm
son	der Sohn dair zone
to speak	sprechen shpre-shen
student (male)	der Student dair shtoo-<u>dent</u>
student (female)	die Studentin dee shtoo-<u>dent</u>-in
to study	studieren shtoo-<u>dee</u>-ren
to take out to eat	einladen <u>eye-n</u>-lah-den
thank you	danke dahn-kuh
to understand	verstehen fair-<u>shtay</u>-en
vacation	der Urlaub dair oor-lauwp
to wait	warten vah-ten
wife	die Frau dee frow

Accommodations

I have a reservation.
Für mich ist bei Ihnen ein Zimmer reserviert.

The key to room ..., please.
Bitte den Schlüssel für Zimmer ...

Lodging

Looking for a Room

Where's the tourist information office?	**Wo ist die Touristeninformation?** vo ist dee too-<u>ris</u>-ten-in-for-mah-tsi-ohn
Can you recommend …	**Können Sie mir … empfehlen?** ker-nen zee mere … emp-<u>fay</u>-len
– a good hotel?	– **ein gutes Hotel** eye-n goo-tes ho-<u>tel</u>
– a reasonably priced hotel?	– **ein preiswertes Hotel** eye-n <u>price</u>-vair-tes ho-<u>tel</u>
– a bed & breakfast?	– **eine Pension** eye-nuh pahn-zee-<u>ohn</u>
Could you make a reservation for me?	**Können Sie für mich reservieren?** kern-ten zee fur mish ray-zair-<u>veer</u>-en
Is it far from here?	**Ist es weit von hier?** ist es vite fun here
How do I get there?	**Wie komme ich dorthin?** vee kom-muh ish dort-<u>hin</u>

Arriving

I have a reservation.	**Für mich ist bei Ihnen ein Zimmer reserviert.** fur mish ist by ee-nen eye-n tsim-muh ray-zair-<u>veert</u>
Do you have a *double / single* room …	**Haben Sie ein *Doppelzimmer / Einzelzimmer* frei …** hah-ben zee eye-n <u>dup</u>-pel-tsim-muh / <u>eye-n</u>-tzel-tsim-muh fry …
– for one night?	– **für eine Nacht?** fur eye-nuh nakht
– for … nights?	– **für … Nächte?** fur … nash-tuh
– with a bathroom?	– **mit Bad?** mit baht

26

– with a balcony?	– mit Balkon? mit bahl-<u>kone</u>
– with air conditioning?	– mit Klimaanlage?
	mit <u>klee</u>-muh-ahn-lah-guh
– with a fan?	– mit Ventilator? mit ven-tee-<u>lah</u>-taw
– with an ocean view?	– mit Blick aufs Meer?
	mit blik auwfs mair
– facing the back?	– nach hinten hinaus?
	nakh hin-ten hin-<u>auws</u>

info Look for signs Fremdenzimmer (guest rooms) or Zimmer frei (vacancy). These are often similar to bed and breakfasts, with meals served to house guests only.

Wir sind leider ausgebucht.	I'm afraid we're booked.
Morgen / Am ... wird ein Zimmer frei.	There's a vacancy *tomorrow / from ... (day)*.
How much is it ...	Wie viel kostet es ...
	vee-feel kaws-tet es ...
– with breakfast?	– mit Frühstück? mit frew-shtewk
– without breakfast?	– ohne Frühstück?
	oh-nuh frew-shtewk
– with breakfast and lunch or dinner?	– mit Halbpension?
	mit <u>hahlp</u>-pahn-zee-ohn
– with all meals included?	– mit Vollpension?
	mit <u>fol</u>-pahn-zee-ohn
Do you offer a discount if I stay ... nights?	Gibt es eine Ermäßigung, wenn man ... Nächte bleibt? gheept es eye-nuh air-<u>macy</u>-goong ven mahn... nash-tuh blighpt

Can I see the room?	**Kann ich mir das Zimmer ansehen?** kahn ish mere dahs tsim-muh <u>ahn</u>-zay-en
Could you put in an extra bed?	**Könnten Sie ein zusätzliches Bett aufstellen?** kern-ten zee eye-n <u>tsoo</u>-zets-lish-es bet <u>owf</u>-shtel-len
Do you have another room?	**Haben Sie noch ein anderes Zimmer?** hah-ben zee nawk eye-n <u>ahn</u>-duh-res tsim-muh
It's very nice. I'll take it.	**Es ist sehr schön. Ich nehme es.** es ist zair shern ish nay-muh es
Could you take my luggage up to the room?	**Könnten Sie mir das Gepäck aufs Zimmer bringen?** kern-ten zee mere dahs guh-<u>peck</u> owfs tsim-muh bring-en
Where's the bathroom?	**Wo ist das Bad?** vo ist dahs baht
Where can I park my car?	**Wo kann ich meinen Wagen abstellen?** vo kahn ish my-nen vah-ghen <u>ahp</u>-shtel-en
Between what hours is breakfast served?	**Von wann bis wann gibt es Frühstück?** fon vahn bis vahn gheept es frew-shtewk
Where's the dining room?	**Wo ist der Speisesaal?** vo ist dair <u>shpy</u>-zuh-zahl

Service

Can I leave my valuables with you for safekeeping?	**Kann ich Ihnen meine Wertsachen zur Aufbewahrung geben?** kahn ish ee-nen my-nuh <u>vairt</u>-zah-khen tsoor <u>owf</u>-buh-vah-roong gay-ben

The key to room ..., please.	Bitte den Schlüssel für Zimmer ... bit-tuh dane shlew-sel fur tsim-muh
Can I call from my room?	Kann ich von meinem Zimmer aus telefonieren? kahn ish fon my-nem tsim-muh ows tel-eh-fo-<u>nee</u>-ren

► Communications, page 69

Are there any messages for me?	Ist eine Nachricht für mich da? ist eye-nuh nak-risht fur mish da
Could I have ... please?	Könnte ich bitte ... haben? kern-tuh ish bit-tuh ... hah-ben
– an extra blanket	– noch eine Decke nawk eye-nuh dek-uh
– an extra towel	– noch ein Handtuch nawk eye-n hahn-tookh
– a few more hangers	– noch ein paar Kleiderbügel nawk eye-n pah <u>kly</u>-duh-bew ghel
– an extra pillow	– noch ein Kopfkissen nawk eye-n <u>kopf</u>-kiss-en
The window won't *open / close*.	Das Fenster geht nicht *auf / zu*. dahs fen-stuh gayt nisht *owf / tsoo*
... doesn't work.	... funktioniert nicht. ... foonk-tsee-o-<u>neert</u> nisht
– The shower	– Die Dusche dee doo-shuh
– The TV	– Der Fernseher dair <u>fairn</u>-say-uh
– The heat	– Die Heizung dee high-tsoong
– The internet connection	– Der Internetanschluss dair <u>internet</u>-ahn-shloos
– The air conditioning	– Die Klimaanlage dee <u>klee</u>-muh-ahn-lah-guh
– The light	– Das Licht dahs lisht

The toilet won't flush (properly).	Die Wasserspülung funktioniert nicht (richtig). dee *vas*-suh-shpee-loong foonk-tsee-o-*neert* nisht (rish-tish)
The *drain* / *toilet* is clogged.	*Der Abfluss* / *Die Toilette* ist ver-stopft. *dair ahp-floos* / *dee toi-let-tuh* ist fair-*shtopft*

Departure

Please wake me at … (tomorrow morning).	Wecken Sie mich bitte (morgen früh) um … Uhr. vek-ken zee mish bit-tuh (maw-ghen frew) oom … oor
We're leaving tomorrow.	Wir reisen morgen ab. veer rye-zen maw-ghen ahp
May I have my bill, please?	Machen Sie bitte die Rechnung fertig. mah-ken zee bit-tuh dee resh-noong fair-tish
It was very nice here.	Es war sehr schön hier. es vah zair shern here
Can I leave my luggage here until …?	Kann ich mein Gepäck noch bis … Uhr hier lassen? kahn ish mine guh-peck nawk bis … oor here lahss-en
Please call me a taxi.	Rufen Sie bitte ein Taxi. roo-fen zee bit-tuh eye-n tahk-see

Rentals

We've rented apartment …	Wir haben die Wohnung … gemietet. veer hah-ben dee vo-noong … guh-mee-tet
Dürfte ich bitte Ihren Gutschein haben?	Could I have your coupon, please?

Where do we get the keys?	Wo bekommen wir die Schlüssel? vo buh-<u>kom</u>-en veer dee shlew-sel
What's the voltage here?	Wie ist hier die Netzspannung? vee ist here dee <u>nets</u>-shpahn-noong
Where's the fusebox?	Wo ist der Sicherungskasten? vo ist dair <u>zisher</u>- oongs-kah-sten

info The 220-volt / 50-cycle AC is universal in Germany, Austria, and Switzerland. Buy an adapter with round pins, not square if you bring electrical appliances. If your appliances cannot be switched to 220 volts you'll also need a transformer with the appropriate wattage.

Could we please have some (extra) bed linens / dish towels?	Könnten wir bitte noch (zusätzliche) *Bettwäsche / Geschirrtücher* bekommen? kern-ten veer bit-tuh nawk (tso-zets-lish-uh) <u>bet</u>-wesh-uh / guh-<u>sheer</u>-tew-shuh boh-<u>kom</u>-en
Where does the garbage go?	Wohin kommt der Müll? vo-hin komt dair mewl

Could you show us how ... works?	Könnten Sie uns bitte erklären, wie ... funktioniert? kern-ten zee oons bit-tuh air-<u>klair</u>-en vee ... foonk-tsee-o-<u>neert</u>
– the dishwasher	– die Spülmaschine dee <u>speel</u>-muh-sheen-uh
– the washing machine	– die Waschmaschine dee <u>vahsh</u>-muh-sheen-uh
– the dryer	– der Wäschetrockner dair <u>wesh</u>-uh-trok-ner
Where's the nearest bus stop?	Wo ist die nächste Bushaltestelle? vo ist dee nex-tuh <u>boos</u>-hahl-tuh-shtel-uh
Where's a supermarket?	Wo ist ein Lebensmittelgeschäft? vo ist eye-n <u>lay</u>-bens-mittel-guh-sheft

Camping

Is there room for ...?	Haben Sie noch Platz für ...? hah-ben zee nawk plahts fur ...
We'd like to stay for *one day / ... days*.	Wir möchten *einen Tag / ... Tage* bleiben. veer mush-ten *eye-nen tahk / ... tah-guh* bligh-ben

How much is it for …	Wie hoch ist die Gebühr für … vee hokh ist dee guh-<u>bewr</u> fur …
– adults and children? – a car with a trailer?	– Erwachsene und … Kinder? air-<u>vahx</u>-en-uh oont … kin-duh – einen PKW mit Wohnwagen? eye-nen pay-kah-vay mit <u>wone</u>-vah-ghen
– an RV (recreational vehicle)? – a tent?	– ein Wohnmobil? eye-n <u>wone</u>-mo-beel – ein Zelt? eye-n tzelt
Do you also rent out *bungalows / trailers*?	Vermieten Sie auch *Bungalows / Wohnwagen*? fair-<u>mee</u>-ten zee auwk <u>boon</u>-gah-los / <u>wone</u>-wah-ghen
Where can we *put up our tent / park our trailer*?	Wo können wir *unser Zelt / unseren Wohnwagen* aufstellen? vo kern-en veer oon-zer tselt / <u>oon</u>-zer-en <u>wone</u>-wah-ghen owf-shtel-en
Where are the *bath- rooms / restrooms*?	Wo sind die *Waschräume / Toiletten*? vo sint dee <u>wahsh</u>-roi- muh / toi-<u>let</u>-ten
Where can I empty the chemical toilet?	Wo kann ich das Chemieklo entsorgen? vo kahn ish dahs shay-<u>mee</u>-klo ent-<u>zor</u>-ghen
Is there an electric hookup?	Gibt es hier Stromanschluss? gheept es here <u>shtrom</u>-ahn-shloos
Can I *buy / exchange* propane tanks here?	Kann ich hier Gasflaschen *kaufen / umtauschen*? kahn ish here <u>gahs</u>- flah-shen *cow-fen / <u>oom</u>-tauw-shen*

Rentals, page 30

33

Accommodations: Additional Words

adapter	der Adapter dair ah-<u>dahp</u>-tuh
advance booking	die Voranmeldung dee <u>faw</u>-ahn-mel-doong
air mattress	die Luftmatratze dee <u>looft</u>-mah-trah-tsuh
armchair	der Sessel dair zes-sel
ashtray	der Aschenbecher dair <u>ahsh</u>-en-besh-uh
bathtub	die Badewanne dee <u>bah</u>-duh-vahn-nuh
bed	das Bett dahs bet
bed linen	die Bettwäsche dee <u>bet</u>-vesh-uh
bedspread	die Bettdecke dee <u>bet</u>-dek-uh
bill	die Rechnung dee resh-noong
blanket	die Decke dee dek-uh
broom	der Besen dair bay-zen
bulb	die Glühbirne dee <u>glew</u>-beer-nuh
to camp	zelten tselt-en
chair	der Stuhl dair shtool
check-in	die Anmeldung dee <u>ahn</u>-mel-doong
coffee-maker	die Kaffeemaschine dee <u>kah</u>-fay-muh-shee-nuh
cot (for a child)	das Kinderbett dahs <u>kin</u>-duh-bet
deposit	die Kaution dee cow-tsee-<u>ohn</u>
detergent	das Waschmittel dahs <u>vahsh</u>-mit-tel
dirty	schmutzig shmoo-tsish
dishes	das Geschirr dahs guh-<u>sheer</u>
dormitory	der Schlafsaal dair shlahf-zahl
double bed	das Doppelbett dahs <u>dup</u>-pel-bet
down payment	die Anzahlung dee <u>ahn</u>-tsahl-oong
drain	der Abfluss dair ahp-floos
drinking water	das Trinkwasser dahs <u>trink</u>-vas-suh

dryer	der Wäschetrockner
	dair <u>vehsh</u>-uh-trok-nuh
elevator	der Aufzug dair owf-tsook
emergency exit	der Notausgang
	dair <u>noht</u>-auws-gong
extension cord	das Verlängerungskabel
	dahs fair-<u>leng</u>-air-oongs-kah-bel
faucet	der Wasserhahn dair <u>vahs</u>-suh-hahn
fireplace	der Kamin dair kah-<u>meen</u>
firewood	das Kaminholz dahs kah-<u>meen</u>-holts
floor	die Etage dee eh-<u>tah</u>-juh
fuse	die Sicherung dee <u>zish</u>-air-oong
garbage can	der Mülleimer dair <u>mewl</u>-igh-muh
gas canister	die Gaskartusche
	dee <u>gahs</u>-kah-too-shuh
gas stove	der Gaskocher dair <u>gahs</u>-kaw-khuh
glass	das Glas dahs glahs
hammer	der Hammer dair hah-muh
hanger	der Kleiderbügel
	dair <u>kligh</u>-duh-bew-ghel
heat	die Heizung dee high-tsoong
to iron	bügeln bew-gheln
lamp	die Lampe dee lahm-puh
to do the laundry	Wäsche waschen vesh-uh vahsh-en
laundry room	der Waschraum dair vahsh-rauwm
to leave	abreisen <u>ahp</u>-rise-en
light	das Licht dahs lisht
lobby	das Foyer dahs foi-<u>yay</u>
lounge	der Aufenthaltsraum
	dair <u>owf</u>-ent-hahlts-rauwm
mattress	die Matratze dee mah-<u>trah</u>-tsuh
mirror	der Spiegel dair shpee-ghel
off-peak season	die Nachsaison dee <u>nakh</u>-say-song
outlet	die Steckdose dee <u>shtek</u>-do-zuh

peak season	die Hauptsaison
	dee <u>hauwpt</u>-say-song
pillow	das Kopfkissen dahs <u>kopf</u>-kis-sen
plug	der Stecker dair shtek-uh
range/stove	der Herd dair hairt
refrigerator	der Kühlschrank dair <u>kewl</u>-shrahnk
rent	die Miete dee mee-tuh
to rent	mieten meet-en
to reserve	reservieren ray-zair-<u>veer</u>-en
reserved	reserviert ray-zair-<u>veert</u>
restroom	die Toilette dee toi-<u>let</u>-tuh
room	das Zimmer dahs tsim-muh
sheet	das Bettlaken dahs <u>bet</u>-lah-ken
shower	die Dusche dee doo-shuh
single bed	das Einzelbett dahs <u>eye-n</u>-tsel-bet
sink	das Waschbecken
	dahs <u>vahsh</u>-bek-ken
sleeping bag	der Schlafsack dair shlahf-zahk
stove	der Kocher dair kaw-khuh
table	der Tisch dair tish
tent	das Zelt dahs tselt
tent peg	der Hering dair hair-ring
toilet paper	das Toilettenpapier
	dahs toi-<u>let</u>-ten-pah-peer
towel	das Handtuch dahs hahn-tookh
trailer	der Wohnwagen dair <u>vone</u>-vah-ghen
TV	der Fernseher dair <u>fairn</u>-zay-uh
vacation apartment / rental	die Ferienwohnung
	dee <u>fair</u>-ee-en-<u>vo</u>-noong
washing machine	die Waschmaschine
	dee <u>vahsh</u>-muh-shee-nuh
water	das Wasser dahs vahs-suh
window	das Fenster dahs fen-stuh

Travel

Excuse me, where is …?
Entschuldigung, wo ist …?

How much is a ticket to …?
Was kostet die Fahrkarte nach …?

Asking for Directions

Excuse me, where's …?	**Entschuldigung, wo ist …?** ent-<u>shool</u>-di-goong vo ist …
How do I get to …?	**Wie komme ich *nach* / *zu* …?** vee kom-muh ish *nahk* / *tsoo* …
Could you please show me on the map?	**Können Sie mir das bitte auf der Karte zeigen?** kern-en zee mere dahs bit-tuh owf dair kah-tuh tsigh-ghen
How far is it?	**Wie weit ist es?** vee white ist ess
How many minutes *on foot* / *by car*?	**Wie viele Minuten *zu Fuß* / *mit dem Auto*?** vee fee-luh min-<u>oo</u>-ten *tsoo foos* / *mit dame ow-toe*
Is this the road to …?	**Ist das die Straße nach… ?** ist dahs dee shtrah-suh nahk …
How do I get onto the expressway to …?	**Wie komme ich zur Autobahn nach …?** vee kom-uh ish tsoor <u>ow</u>-toe-bahn nahk …
Das weiß ich nicht.	I don't know.
Die *erste* / *zweite* Straße *links* / *rechts*.	The *first* / *second* road on the *left* / *right*.
An der nächsten *Ampel* / *Kreuzung* …	At the next *traffic lights* / *intersection* …
Überqueren Sie *den Platz* / *die Straße*.	Cross the *square* / *street*.
Dann fragen Sie noch einmal.	Then ask again.
Sie können *den Bus* / *die U-Bahn* nehmen.	You can take the *bus* / *subway*.

38

Where Is It?

die Ampel	traffic lights
dort (hinten)	(over) there
gegenüber	opposite
geradeaus	straight ahead
hier	here
hier entlang	this way
hinter	after / behind
die Kurve	bend
links	left
nach *links* / *rechts*	to the *left* / *right*
nahe bei	nearby
neben	beside / next to
nicht weit	not far
rechts	right
die Straße	road
die Treppe hinauf	up the steps
die Treppe hinunter	down the steps
vor	before / in front of
ziemlich weit	quite a long way
zurück	back

Luggage / Baggage

I'd like to leave my luggage here.	**Ich möchte mein Gepäck hier lassen.** ish mush-tuh mine guh-<u>peck</u> here lahs-sen
I'd like to pick up my luggage.	**Ich möchte mein Gepäck abholen.** ish mush-tuh mine guh-<u>peck</u> <u>ahp</u>-ho-len
My luggage hasn't arrived (yet).	**Mein Gepäck ist (noch) nicht angekommen.** mine guh-<u>pek</u> ist (nawk) nisht <u>ahn</u>-guh-kom-en

Where's my luggage?	Wo ist mein Gepäck?
	vo ist mine guh-<u>pek</u>
My suitcase has been damaged.	Mein Koffer ist beschädigt worden.
	mine kaw-fuh ist buh-<u>shay</u>-dikt <u>vaw</u>-den
Whom should I speak to?	An wen kann ich mich wenden?
	ahn vehn cahn ish mish ven-den

Luggage / Baggage: Additional Words

backpack	der Rucksack dair rook-zahk
bag	die Tasche dee tah-shuh
baggage claim	die Gepäckausgabe
	dee guh-<u>pek</u>-ows-gah-buh
baggage storage	die Gepäckaufbewahrung
	dee guh-<u>pek</u>-owf-buh-vah-roong
carry-on	das Handgepäck dahs <u>hahnt</u>-guh-pek
to check in / hand in	aufgeben <u>owf</u>-gay-ben
duffle bag	der Seesack dair say-zahk
excess baggage	das Übergepäck dahs <u>ew</u>-buh-guh-pek
locker	das Schließfach dahs shlees-fahk
luggage counter	die Gepäckannahme
	dee guh-<u>pek</u>-ahn-nah-muh
luggage ticket	der Gepäckschein dair guh-<u>pek</u>-shine
travel bag	die Reisetasche dee <u>rise</u>-uh-tah-shuh

At the Airport

Where's the … desk?	Wo ist der Schalter der Fluggesellschaft …? vo ist dair shahl-tuh dair <u>flook</u>-guh-zel-shahft …
When's the next flight to …?	Wann fliegt die nächste Maschine nach …? vahn fleegt dee nayx-tuh mah-<u>shee</u>-nuh nahk …
Are there any seats left?	Sind noch Plätze frei? zint nawk plets-uh fry
How much is a flight to …?	Wie viel kostet ein Flug nach …? vee feel kaws-tet eye-n flook nahk
A … ticket, please.	Bitte ein Flugticket … bit-tuh eye-n <u>flook</u>-ticket …
– one-way	– einfach. eye-n-fahk
– round-trip	– hin und zurück. hin oont tsoo-<u>rewk</u>
– business class	– Businessklasse. business-clahs-uh
I'd like a *window seat* / *an aisle seat*.	Ich hätte gern einen *Fensterplatz* / *Platz am Gang*. ish het-tuh gairn eye-nen <u>fen</u>-stair-plats / plats ahm gahng
Can I take this as a carry-on?	Kann ich das als Handgepäck mitnehmen? kahn ish dahs ahls <u>hahnt</u>-guh-pek <u>mit</u>-nay-men
I'd like to … my flight.	Ich möchte meinen Flug … ish mush-tuh my-nen flook …
– confirm	– rückbestätigen lassen. <u>rewk</u>-buh-stay-tee-ghen lahs-sen
– cancel	– stornieren. shtaw-<u>nee</u>-ren
– change	– umbuchen. <u>oom</u>-boo-khen

Airport: Additional Words

airport	der Flughafen dair <u>flook</u>-hah-fen
arrival	die Ankunft dee ahn-koonft
boarding pass	die Bordkarte dee <u>bawt</u>-kah-tuh
check-in desk	der Schalter dair shahl-tuh
connecting flight	der Anschlussflug dair <u>ahn</u>-shlooss-flook
delay	die Verspätung dee fair-<u>shpeh</u>-toong
departure	der Abflug dair ahp-flook
exit	der Ausgang dair ows-gong
flight attendant (male)	der Steward dair stoo-art
flight attendant (fem- male)	die Stewardess dee <u>stoo</u>-art-dess
flying time	die Flugzeit dee flook-tsight
landing	die Landung dee lahn-doong
local time	die Ortszeit dee awts-sight
plane	das Flugzeug dahs flook-tsoik
return flight	der Rückflug dair rewk-flook
sick bag	die Spucktüte dee <u>shpook</u>-tew-tuh
stopover	die Zwischenlandung dee <u>tsvish</u>-en-lahn-doong

Travel by Train

What time do trains leave for …?	Wann fahren Züge nach … ? vahn fah-ren tsew-guh nahk …
When's the next train to …?	Wann fährt der nächste Zug nach … ? vahn fairt dair <u>nayx</u>-tuh tsook nahk …
When does it arrive in …?	Wann ist er in … ? vahn ist air in …

Do I have to change trains?	**Muss ich umsteigen?** moos ish <u>oom</u>-shty-ghen
Which track does the train to … leave from?	**Von welchem Gleis fährt der Zug nach … ab?** fun vel-shem glais fairt dair tsook nahk … ahp
How much is a ticket to …?	**Was kostet die Fahrkarte nach … ?** vas kaws-tet dee <u>fah</u>-kah-tuh nahk …
Are there discounts for …?	**Gibt es eine Ermäßigung für … ?** gheept es eye-nuh air-<u>may</u>-see-goong fur …
A(n) … ticket please.	**Bitte eine Karte …** bit-tuh eye-nuh kah-tuh …
– first-class	– **erster Klasse.** airs-tuh klahs-suh
– second-class	– **zweiter Klasse.** tsveye-tuh klahs-suh
– child-fare	– **für Kinder.** fur kin-duh
– adult-fare	– **für Erwachsene.** fur air-<u>vahx</u>-en-uh
I'd like to reserve a seat on the train to … at … o'clock.	**Bitte eine Platzkarte für den Zug nach … um … Uhr.** bit-tuh eye-nuh <u>plats</u>-kah-tuh fur dane tsook nahk … oom … oor
I'd like …	**Ich hätte gern …** ish het-tuh gairn …
– a window seat.	– **einen Fensterplatz.** eye-nen <u>fen</u>-stuh-plahts
– an aisle seat.	– **einen Platz am Gang.** eye-nen plahts ahm gahng
– a non-smoking seat.	– **einen Platz für Nichtraucher.** eye-nen plahts fur <u>nisht</u>-rauw-kher
– a smoking seat.	– **einen Platz für Raucher.** eye-nen plahts fur rauw-kher

43

| Will there be refreshments on the train? | Gibt es im Zug etwas zu essen und zu trinken? gheept es im tsook et-vahs tsoo es-sen oont tsoo trink-en |
| Where can I find the *baggage storage / lockers*? | Wo finde ich die *Gepäckaufbewahrung / Schließfächer*? vo fin-duh ish dee guh-pek-owf-buh-vah-roong / shlees-fesh-uh |

On the Train

Is this the train to ...?	Ist das der Zug nach ...? ist dahs dair tsook nahk ...
Excuse me, that's my seat.	Entschuldigen Sie, das ist mein Platz. ent-shool-di-ghen zee dahs ist mine plahts
Do you mind if I *open / close* the window?	Darf ich das Fenster *öffnen / schließen*? dahf ish dahs fens-tuh ewf-nen / shlees-en
How many more stops to ...?	Wie viele Stationen sind es noch bis ...? vee feel-uh shtah-tsee-o-nen sint es nawk bis ...

At the Train Station

Ausgang	Exit
Duschen	Showers
Gepäckaufbewahrung	Baggage Storage
Gleis	Track
Kein Trinkwasser	Water not Potable
Schließfächer	Lockers
Toiletten	Restrooms
Wartesaal	Waiting Room
Zu den Bahnsteigen	To the Platforms

Travel by Train: Additional Words

arrival	die Ankunft dee ahn-koonft
to arrive	ankommen ahn-com-en
car	der Waggon dair vah-gong
to change trains	umsteigen oom-shteye-ghen
compartment	das Abteil dahs ahp-tile
conductor	der Schaffner dair shahf-nuh
connection	der Anschluss dair ahn-shloos
departure	die Abfahrt dee ahp-faht
dining car	der Speisewagen
	dair shpy-zuh-vah-ghen
exit	der Ausgang dair ows-gahng
fare	der Fahrpreis dair fah-price
to get off	aussteigen ows-shtai-ghen
to get on	einsteigen eye-n-shtai-ghen
luggage car	der Gepäckwagen
	dair guh-pek-vah-ghen
non-smoking	das Nichtraucherabteil
compartment	dahs nisht-rauw-kher-ahp-tile
reserved	reserviert ray-zair-veert
schedule	der Fahrplan dair fah-plahn

45

sleeper car	**der Schlafwagen**
	dair <u>shlahf</u>-vah-ghen
smoking compartment	**das Raucherabteil**
	dahs <u>rauwk</u>-er-ahp-tile
surcharge	**der Zuschlag** dair tsoo-shlahk
train station	**der Bahnhof** dair bahn-hoaf

Travel by Bus

Where do the buses leave?	**Wo fahren die Busse ab?** vo fah-ren dee boo-suh ahp
When does the next bus to … leave?	**Wann fährt der nächste Bus nach … ab?** vahn fairt dair nayx-tuh boos nahk … ahp
A ticket / Two tickets to …, please.	**Bitte *eine Karte / zwei Karten* nach …** bit-tuh *eye-nuh kah-tuh / tsweye kah-ten* nahk …
Is … the last stop?	**Ist … die Endstation?** ist … dee <u>ent</u>-shtah-tsee-ohn
Could you tell me where I have to get off, please?	**Sagen Sie mir bitte, wo ich aussteigen muss?** zah-ghen zee mere bit-tuh vo ish <u>ows</u>-shteye-ghen moos
How long does the trip last?	**Wie lange dauert die Fahrt?** vee lahng-uh dow-airt dee faht

info Validate your ticket in the machine marked with the sign **Hier Fahrschein entwerten**. If you get caught without a ticket you'll have to pay a hefty fine.

Travel by Boat

Information and Reservations

When does the next *boat* / *ferry* leave for …?	**Wann fährt das nächste *Schiff* / *die nächste Fähre* nach … ab?** vahn fairt dahs nayx-tuh shif / dee nayx-tuh fair-uh nahk… ahp
How long is the trip to …?	**Wie lange dauert die Überfahrt nach …?** vee lahng-uh dow-airt dee <u>ew</u>-buh-faht nahk …
When do we dock in …?	**Wann legen wir in … an?** vahn lay-ghen veer in… ahn
When do we have to be on board?	**Wann müssen wir an Bord sein?** vahn mews-en veer ahn bawt zeye-n
I'd like a *first* / an *economy* class boat ticket to …	**Ich möchte eine Schiffskarte *erster Klasse* / *Touristenklasse* nach …** ish mush-tuh eye-nuh <u>shifs</u>-kah-tuh *airs-tuh klahs-uh* / *too-<u>rist</u>-en-klahs-uh* nahk …
I'd like …	**Ich möchte …** ish mush-tuh
– a single cabin.	**– eine Einzelkabine.** eye-nuh <u>eye-n</u>-tsel-kah-bee-nuh
– a twin cabin.	**– eine Zweibettkabine.** eye-nuh <u>tsveye</u>-bet-kah-<u>bee</u>-nuh
– an outside cabin.	**– eine Außenkabine.** eye-nuh <u>ows</u>-sen-kah-<u>bee</u>-nuh
– an inside cabin.	**– eine Innenkabine.** eye-nuh <u>in</u>-nen-kah-bee-nuh
Where is the … docked?	**An welcher Anlegestelle liegt die …?** ahn vel-shuh <u>ahn</u>-lay-guh-shtel-uh leekt dee …

47

Aboard

I'm looking for cabin number ...	**Ich suche die Kabine Nummer ...** ish zoo-kuh dee kah-<u>bee</u>-nuh noom-muh ...
Could I have another cabin?	**Kann ich eine andere Kabine bekommen?** kahn ish eye-nuh <u>ahn</u>-duh-ruh kah-<u>bee</u>-nuh buh-<u>kom</u>-en
Do you have anything for seasickness?	**Haben Sie ein Mittel gegen Seekrankheit?** hah-ben zee eye-n mit-tel gay-ghen <u>zay</u>-krahnk-hight

Travel by Boat: Additional Words

captain	**der Kapitän** dair kah-pee-<u>tane</u>
car ferry	**die Autofähre** dee <u>ow</u>-toe-fair-uh
coast	**die Küste** dee kew-stuh
cruise	**die Kreuzfahrt** dee <u>kroits</u>-faht
deck	**das Deck** dahs deck
deckchair	**der Liegestuhl** dair <u>lee</u>-guh-shtool
dock	**die Anlegestelle** dee <u>ahn</u>-lay-guh-<u>shtel</u>-uh
land excursion	**der Landausflug** dair <u>lahnt</u>-ows-flook
life jacket	**die Schwimmweste** dee <u>shvim</u>-ves-tuh
lifeboat	**das Rettungsboot** dahs <u>ret</u>-toongs-boat
rough seas	**der Seegang** dair zay-gahng
seasick	**seekrank** zay-krahnk
ship	**das Schiff** dahs shif
ship's doctor	**der Schiffsarzt** dair shifs-ahtst
sightseeing tour	**die Rundfahrt** dee roont-faht
steward	**der Steward** dair steward

Travel by Car and Motorcycle

Car Rental

I'd like to rent …

Ich möchte … mieten.
ish mush-tuh … mee-ten

– a car.
– an automatic car.

– ein Auto. eye-n ow-toe
– ein Auto mit Automatik.
eye-n ow-toe mit ow-toe-<u>mah</u>-tik

– an off-road vehicle.

– einen Geländewagen
eye-nen guh-<u>len</u>-duh-wah-ghen

– a motorbike.
– an RV (recreational
vehicle).

– ein Motorrad eye-n mo-<u>taw</u>-raht
– ein Wohnmobil
eye-n <u>wone</u>-mo-beel

I'd like to rent it for …

Ich möchte es für … mieten.
ish mush-tuh es fur … mee-ten

– tomorrow.
– one day.
– two days.
– a week.

– morgen maw-ghen
– einen Tag eye-nen tahk
– zwei Tage tsveye tah-guh
– eine Woche eye-nuh vaw-khuh

How much does that
cost?

Wie viel kostet das?
vee feel kaws-tet dahs

How many kilometers
are included in the
price?

Wie viele Kilometer sind im Preis
enthalten? vee feel-uh kee-lo-<u>may</u>-
tuh zint im price ent-<u>hahl</u>-ten

What fuel does it take?

Was muss ich tanken?
vahs moos ish tahn-ken

Is full comprehensive
insurance included?

Ist eine Vollkaskoversicherung
eingeschlossen? ist eye-nuh <u>fawl</u>kahs-
ko-fair-sish-uh-roong <u>eye-n</u>-ghe-shloss-en

Can I return the car
in …?

Kann ich das Auto in … abgeben?
kahn ish dahs ow-too in … <u>ahp</u>-gay-ben

| Could you please give me a crash helmet as well? | Bitte geben Sie mir auch einen Sturzhelm. bit-tuh gay-ben zee mere auwk eye-nen shtoorts-helm |

At the Gas / Petrol Station

Where's the nearest gas station?	Wo ist die nächste Tankstelle? vo ist dee nayx-tuh <u>tahnk</u>-shtel-uh
Fill it up, please.	Bitte volltanken. bit-tuh <u>fawl</u>-tahnk-en
… euros' worth of …, please.	Bitte für … Euro … bit-tuh fur … oi-ro
– regular gas	– Normalbenzin. nor-<u>mahl</u>-ben-tseen
– premium gas	– Super. super
– diesel	– Diesel. diesel
I'd like one liter *one liter / two liters* of oil.	Ich möchte *1 Liter / 2 Liter* Öl. ish mush-tuh *eye-nen lee-tuh / tsvai lee-tuh* erl

Breakdown

I've run out of gas.	Ich habe kein Benzin mehr. ish hah-buh kine ben-<u>tseen</u> mare
I've got a flat tire.	Ich habe eine Reifenpanne. ish hah-buh eye-nuh <u>rye</u>-fen-pahn-nuh
Could you lend me …, please?	Können Sie mir bitte … leihen? ker-nen zee mere bit-tuh … ligh-en
Could you …	Könnten Sie … kern-ten zee …
– give me a jump-start?	– mir Starthilfe geben? mere <u>shtaht</u>-hil-fuh gay-ben
– give me a ride?	– mich ein Stück mitnehmen? mish eye-n shtewk <u>mit</u>-nay-men

– tow my car?   – meinen Wagen abschleppen?
                       my-nen vah-ghen <u>ahp</u>-shlep-pen

– send me a tow truck?   – mir einen Abschleppwagen
                       schicken? mere eye-nen <u>ahp</u>-shlep-
                       vah-ghen shik-en

Accidents

Please call …, quick!	**Rufen Sie bitte schnell …** roof-en zee bit-tuh shnel …
– an ambulance	**– einen Krankenwagen!** eye-nen <u>krahnk</u>-en-vah-ghen
– the police	**– die Polizei!** dee poly-<u>tsigh</u>
– the fire station	**– die Feuerwehr!** dee <u>foi</u>-uh-vair
There's been an accident!	**Es war ein Unfall passiert!** es vah eye-n oon-fahl pas-<u>seert</u>
… people have been (seriously) hurt.	**… Personen sind (schwer) verletzt.** … pair-<u>zone</u>-en zind (shvair) fair-<u>letst</u>
It wasn't my fault.	**Es war nicht meine Schuld.** es vah nisht my-nuh shoolt
I'd like to call the police.	**Ich möchte, dass wir die Polizei holen.** ish mesh-tuh dahs veer dee poly-<u>tsigh</u> ho-len
I had right of way.	**Ich hatte Vorfahrt.** ish haht-tuh for-faht
You were driving too fast.	**Sie sind zu schnell gefahren.** zee sint tsoo shnel guh-<u>fah</u>-ren
Give me your name and address, please.	**Bitte geben Sie mir Ihren Namen und Ihre Adresse.** bit-tuh gay-ben zee mere ee-ren nah-men oont ee-ruh ah-<u>dress</u>-suh

Give me *the name of your insurance / insurance number*, please.	**Bitte geben Sie mir *Ihre Versicherung / Versicherungsnummer*.** bit-tuh gay-ben zee mere ee-ruh vair-_sish_-uh-roong / vair-_sish_-uh-roongs-noo-muh
Would you act as my witness?	**Können Sie eine Zeugenaussage machen?** ker-nen zee eye-nuh _zoi_-ghen-ows-zah-guh mahk-en

Getting Your Car Fixed

Where's the nearest garage?	**Wo ist die nächste Werkstatt?** vo ist dee nayx-tuh vairk-shtaht
My car's (on the road to) …	**Mein Wagen steht (an der Straße nach) …** mine vah-ghen shtayt (ahn dair strahs-suh nahk) …
Can you tow it?	**Können Sie ihn abschleppen?** ker-nen zee een _ahp_-shlep-en
Could you have a look at it?	**Können Sie mal nachsehen?** ker-nen zee mahl _nahk_-zay-en
… isn't working.	**… funktioniert nicht.** … foonk-tsee-o-_neert_ nisht
My car won't start.	**Mein Auto springt nicht an.** mine ow-toe shpringt nisht ahn
The battery's dead.	**Die Batterie ist leer.** dee baht-uh-_ree_ ist lair
The engine sounds funny.	**Der Motor klingt merkwürdig.** dair mo-tor *klinkt* _mairk_-wewr-dish
Can I still drive the car?	**Kann ich mit dem Auto noch fahren?** kahn ish mit daym ow-toe nawk fah-ren

52

Just do the essential repairs, please.	**Machen Sie bitte nur die nötigsten Reparaturen.** mahk-en zee bit-tuh noor dee <u>ner</u>-tigs-ten rep-ah-rah-<u>toor</u>-en
About how much will the repairs cost?	**Wie viel wird die Reparatur un gefähr kosten?** vee feel veert dee rep-ah-rah-<u>toor</u> <u>oon</u>-guh-fair kaws-ten
When will it be ready?	**Wann ist es fertig?** vahn ist es fair-tish

Travel by Car / Motorcycle: Additional Words

accident report	**das Unfallprotokoll** dahs <u>oon</u>-fahl-pro-toe-kawl
air filter	**der Luftfilter** dair looft-filter
alternator	**die Lichtmaschine** dee <u>lisht</u>-mah-shee-nuh
antifreeze	**das Frostschutzmittel** dahs <u>frawst</u>-shoots-mit tel
brake	**die Bremse** dee brem-suh
brake fluid	**die Bremsflüssigkeit** dee <u>brems</u>-flew-sish-kite
brake light	**das Bremslicht** dahs brems-lisht
broken	**kaputt** kah-<u>put</u>
bumper	**die Stoßstange** dee <u>shtos</u>-stahng-uh
car seat	**der Kindersitz** dair <u>kin</u>-duh-zits
catalytic converter	**der Katalysator** dair kah-tah-lee-<u>zah</u>-tor
clutch	**die Kupplung** dee koop-loong
coolant	**das Kühlwasser** dahs <u>kewl</u>-vahs-suh
driver's license	**der Führerschein** dair <u>few</u>-ruh-shine
emergency brake	**die Handbremse** dee <u>hahnt</u>-brem-zuh
expressway	**die Autobahn** dee <u>ow</u>-toe-bahn
fanbelt	**der Keilriemen** dair <u>kyle</u>-ree-men

fender	der Kotflügel dair <u>coat</u>-flew-gull
fire extinguisher	der Feuerlöscher dair <u>foi</u>-uh-lersh-uh
fuse	die Sicherung dee sish-uh-roong
gear	der Gang dair gahng
headlights	der Scheinwerfer dair <u>shine</u>-vair-fuh
heat	die Heizung dee high-tsoong
hood	die Motorhaube dee <u>mo</u>-tor-how-buh
horn	die Hupe dee hoo-puh
ignition	die Zündung dee tsewn-doong
insurance card	die Versicherungskarte
	dee fair-<u>sish</u>-uh-roongs-kah-tuh
jumper cable	das Starthilfekabel
	dahs <u>shtaht</u>-hil-fuh-kah-bel
light	das Licht dahs lisht
light bulb	die Glühbirne dee <u>glew</u>-beer-nuh
mirror	der Spiegel dair shpee-gull
multi-level parking garage	das Parkhaus dahs <u>pahk</u>-house
neutral	der Leerlauf dair lair-lauwf
no-parking zone	das Parkverbot dahs <u>pahk</u>-fair-boat
oil change	der Ölwechsel dair <u>erl</u>-wex-el
to park	parken pah-ken
parking disc	die Parkscheibe dee <u>pahk</u>-shy-buh
parking lot	der Parkplatz dair pahk-plahts
parking meter	die Parkuhr dee pahk-oor
radiator	der Kühler dair kew-luh
seatbelt	der Sicherheitsgurt
	dair <u>zisher</u>-hites-goort
service area	die Raststätte dee <u>rahst</u>-shtet-tuh
shock absorber	der Stoßdämpfer dair <u>shtos</u>-demp-fuh
snow chains	die Schneekette <u>shnay</u>-ket-ten
spare tire	der Ersatzreifen dair air-<u>zahts</u>-rye-fen
spark plug	die Zündkerze dee <u>tsewnt</u>-kair-tsuh
speedometer	der Tachometer dair tahko-<u>may</u>-tuh

starter	der Anlasser dair <u>ahn</u>-lass-uh
steering	die Lenkung dee lenk-oong
tail light	das Rücklicht dahs rewk-lisht
tow rope	das Abschleppseil dahs <u>ahp</u>-shlep-zile
transmission	das Getriebe dahs guh-<u>tree</u>-buh
turn signal	das Blinklicht dahs blink-lisht
vehicle registration	der Kfz-Schein dair kah-ef-<u>tset</u>-shine
wheel	das Rad dahs raht
windshield wipers	der Scheibenwischer
	dair <u>shy</u>-ben-vish-uh

Public Transportation

info Subway tickets should be purchased from the vending machines at all U-Bahn stations before you board a train. Ticket inspection is common and you'll have to pay a steep fine if you get caught without a valid ticket.

Where's the nearest …	Wo ist die nächste …
	vo ist dee nayx-tuh …
– subway station?	– U-Bahn-Station?
	<u>oo</u>-bahn-shtah-tsee-ohn
– bus stop?	– Bushaltestelle?
	<u>boos</u>-hahl-tuh-stel-uh
– tram stop?	– Straßenbahnhaltestelle?
	<u>shtrah</u>-sen-bahn-hahl-tuh-sthel-uh
Where does the bus to … stop?	Wo hält der Bus nach …?
	vo helt dair boos nahk …
Which *bus / subway* goes to …?	*Welcher Bus / Welche U-Bahn* fährt nach … ? *velsh-uh boos / velsh-uh oo-bahn* fairt nahk …

Der Bus Nummer ...	The bus number ...
Die Linie ...	The ... line.
When's the next *bus / subway* to ...?	**Wann fährt *der nächste Bus / die nächste U-Bahn* nach ... ?** vahn fairt *dair nayx-tuh boos / dee nayx-tuh oo-bahn* nahk ...
Does this bus go to ...?	**Fährt dieser Bus nach ...?** fairt dee-zuh boos nahk ...
Do I have to transfer to get to ...?	**Muss ich nach ... umsteigen?** moos ish nahk ... <u>oom</u>-shty-ghen
Where do I get a ticket?	**Wo bekomme ich einen Fahrschein?** vo buh-<u>kom</u>-uh ish eye-nen fah-shine
A ticket to ..., please.	**Bitte einen Fahrschein nach ...** bit-tuh eye-nen fah-shine nahk ...
Do you have ...	**Gibt es ...** gheept es ...
– one day travel pass?	**– Tageskarten?** <u>tah</u>-ghes-kah-ten
– multiple-ride tickets?	**– Mehrfahrtenkarten?** <u>mair</u>-fah-kah-ten
– weekly travel passes?	**– Wochenkarten?** <u>vaw</u>-khen-kah-ten
– a booklet of tickets?	**– Fahrscheinheftchen?** <u>fah</u>-shine-heft-shen

Travel by Taxi

Could you call a taxi for me (for tomorrow morning)?	Könnten Sie mir (für morgen) ein Taxi bestellen? kern-ten zee mere (fur maw-ghen) eye-n tahx-ee buh-<u>shtel</u>-en
..., please.	Bitte ... bit-tuh ...
– To the train station	– zum Bahnhof. tsoom <u>bahn</u>-hoaf
– To the airport	– zum Flughafen. tsoom <u>flook</u>-hah-hen
– To the ... Hotel	– zum Hotel ... . tsoom ho-<u>tel</u> ...
– To the city center	– in die Innenstadt. in dee <u>in</u>-nen-shtaht
– To ... Street	in die ... Straße. in dee ... shtrah-suh
How much is it to ...?	Wie viel kostet es nach ... ? vee-feel kaws-tet es nahk
Could you *turn on / reset* the meter, please?	Bitte schalten Sie den Taxameter *ein / auf null*. bi-tuh shahl-ten zee dane tahx-ah-<u>may</u>-tuh *eye-n / owf nool*
Keep the change.	Das Wechselgeld ist für Sie. dahs <u>vex</u>-el-ghelt ist fur zee

info Taxis in Germany are beige colored and all have meters. For tipping, round up the bill. Add 10% tip in Austria and 15% in Switzerland.

Public Transportation and Taxi: Additional Words

conductor	der Schaffner dair shahf-nuh
departure	die Abfahrt dee ahp-faht
direction	die Richtung dee rish-toong
driver	der Fahrer dair fah-ruh
fare	der Fahrpreis dair fah-price

to get off	**aussteigen** <u>ows</u>-shty-ghen
last stop	**die Endstation**
	dee <u>end</u>-shtah-tsee-ohn
local train	**die S-Bahn** dee ess-bahn
schedule	**der Fahrplan** dair fah-plahn
stop	**die Haltestelle** dee <u>hahl</u>-tuh-stel-uh
to stop	**halten** hahl-ten
taxi stand	**der Taxistand** dair <u>tahx</u>-ee-shtahnt
ticket inspector	**der Kontrolleur** dair con-tro-<u>lair</u>
ticket machine	**der Fahrkartenautomat**
	dair <u>fah</u>-kah-ten-ow-toe-maht
ticket validation machine	**der Entwerter** dair ent-<u>vair</u>-tuh
to transfer	**umsteigen** <u>oom</u>-shty-ghen
to validate	**entwerten** ent-<u>vair</u>-ten

Travel with Children

Is there a children's playground here?
Gibt es hier einen Kinderspielplatz?

How old is your child?
Wie alt ist Ihr Kind?

Frequently Asked Questions

Is there a children's discount?

Gibt es eine Ermäßigung für Kinder? gheept es eye-nuh air-<u>macy</u>-goong fur kin-duh

From / Up to what age?

Bis / Ab wie viel Jahren? bis / ahp vee feel yah-ren

Tickets for two adults and two children, please.

Bitte Karten für zwei Erwachsene und zwei Kinder. bit-tuh kah-ten fur tsveye air-<u>vahx</u>-en-uh oont tsveye <u>kin</u>-duh

Is there a children's playground here?

Gibt es hier einen Kinderspielplatz? gheept es here eye-nen <u>kin</u>-duh-shpeel-plahts

How old is your child?

Wie alt ist Ihr Kind? vee ahlt ist ear kint

My daughter / My son is ....

Meine Tochter / Mein Sohn ist ... Jahre alt. *my-nuh tawk-tuh / mine zone* ist ... yah-ruh ahlt

Where is there a changing room?

Wo ist ein Wickelraum? vo ist eye-n <u>vik</u>-el-rowm

Where can we buy ...

Wo können wir ... kaufen? vo kern-en veer ... cow-fen

– baby food?
– children's clothes?
– diapers?

– Babynahrung <u>bay</u>-bee-nah-roong
– Kinderkleidung <u>kin</u>-duh-kly-doong
– Windeln vin-deln

Do you have special offers for children?

Haben Sie spezielle Angebote für Kinder? hah-ben zee shpets-ee-<u>elluh</u> <u>ahn</u>-guh-bo-tuh fur kin-duh

Travel with Children

Have you seen a little girl / boy?	**Haben Sie *ein kleines Mädchen / einen kleinen Jungen* gesehen?** hah-ben zee *eye-n kly-nes made-shen / eye-nen kly-nen yoong-en* guh-<u>zayn</u>
Is there a children's section?	**Gibt es ein Kinderabteil?** gheept es eye-n <u>kin</u>-duh-ahp-tile
Do you have a car seat for the rental car?	**Haben Sie für den Leihwagen auch einen Kindersitz?** hah-ben zee fur dane <u>lye</u>-vah-ghen owkh eye-nen <u>kin</u>-duh-zits
Can I rent a child seat for a bicycle?	**Kann ich einen Kinderfahrradsitz ausleihen?** kahn ish eye-nen <u>kin</u>-duh-fah-raht-zits <u>ows</u>-lye-en

At the Hotel / Restaurant

Could you put in a cot?	**Könnten Sie ein Kinderbett aufstellen?** kern-ten zee eye-n <u>kin</u>-duh-bet <u>owf</u>-shtel-en
Do you have an entertainment program for children?	**Haben Sie ein Unterhaltungsprogramm für Kinder?** hah-ben zee eye-n oon-tuh-<u>hahl</u>-toongs-pro-grahm fur kin-duh

61

Do you have a high chair?	**Haben Sie einen Hochstuhl?** hah-ben zee eye-nen hokh-shtool
Could you please warm the bottle?	**Könnten Sie bitte das Fläschchen aufwärmen?** kern-ten zee bit-tuh dahs flesh-shen <u>owf</u>-vair-men
Do you have a children's menu?	**Haben Sie ein Kindermenü?** hah-ben zee eye-n <u>kin</u>-duh-mehn-<u>ew</u>
Could we get half portions for the children?	**Können wir für die Kinder eine halbe Portion bekommen?** kern-ten veer fur dee kin-duh eye-nuh hahl-beh <u>paw</u>-tsee-ohn buh-<u>kom</u>-en
Could we please have another place setting?	**Können wir bitte noch ein Extra-Gedeck bekommen?** kern-ten veer bit-tuh nawk eye-n <u>ex</u>-trah-guh-<u>dek</u> buh-<u>kom</u>-en

Swimming with Children

Is it dangerous for children?	**Ist es für Kinder gefährlich?** ist es fur kin-duh guh-<u>fair</u>-lish
Are there swimming lessons for children?	**Gibt es Schwimmunterricht für Kinder?** gheept es <u>shvim</u>-oon-tuh-risht fur kin-duh
I'd like to rent arm floats.	**Ich möchte Schwimmflügel ausleihen.** ish mush-tuh <u>shvim</u>-flew-gull <u>ows</u>-lye-en
Is there a children's pool as well?	**Gibt es auch ein Kinderbecken?** gheept es auwk eye-n <u>kin</u>-duh-bek-ken

How deep is the water?	**Wie tief ist das Wasser?** vee teef ist dahs vahs-suh

Childcare and Health

Can you recommend a reliable babysitter?	**Können Sie uns einen verlässlichen Babysitter empfehlen?** kern-en zee oons eye-nen fair-<u>less</u>-lish-en baby-sitter emp-<u>fay</u>-len
My child is allergic to milk products.	**Mein Kind ist allergisch gegen Milchprodukte.** mine kint ist ah-<u>lair</u>-gish gay-ghen <u>milsh</u>-pro-dook-tuh

► *Health, page 171*

Travel with Children: Additional Words

allergy	**die Allergie** dee ah-lair-<u>ghee</u>
baby bottle	**das Babyfläschchen** dahs <u>bay</u>-bee-flesh-shen
baby powder	**der Babypuder** dair <u>bay</u>-bee-poo-duh
bottle warmer	**der Fläschchenwärmer** dair <u>flesh</u>-shen-vair-muh
boy	**der Junge** dair young-uh
changing table	**die Wickelkommode** dee <u>vik</u>-el-kom-o-duh
child safety belt	**der Kindersicherheitsgurt** dair <u>kin</u>-duh-sik-uh-hites-goort
children's portion	**der Kinderteller** dair <u>kin</u>-duh-tel-uh
coloring book	**das Malbuch** dahs mahl-bookh
cot	**das Kinderbett** dahs <u>kin</u>-duh-bet
crayon	**der Buntstift** dair boont-shtift

daughter	die Tochter	dee tawk-tuh
girl	das Mädchen	dahs made-shen
insect bite	der Insektenstich	daiř in-šeḱ-ten-shtish
mosquito repellent	der Mückenschutz	
	dair mewken-shoots	
nipple	der Sauger	dair sow-guh
pacifier	der Schnuller	dair shnool-uh
picture book	das Bilderbuch	dahs bil-duh-bookh
playground	der Spielplatz	dair shpeel-plahts
playpen	der Laufstall	dair lauwf-shtahl
rash	der Ausschlag	dair ows-shlahk
son	der Sohn	dair zone
stroller	der Kinderwagen	
	dair kin-duh-vah-ghen	
toy	das Spielzeug	dahs shpeel-tsoik
vaccination card	der Impfpass	dair impf-pahss
visored cap	die Schirmmütze	
	dee sheerm-mewts-uh	

For the Disabled

Does it have wheelchair access?
Gibt es einen Eingang für Rollstuhlfahrer?

Where's the nearest elevator / lift?
Wo ist der nächste Fahrstuhl?

Asking for Help

Could you help me, please?	**Können Sie mir bitte helfen?** kern-en zee meer bit-tuh hel-fen
I have mobility problems.	**Ich bin gehbehindert.** ish bin gay-buh-hin-dairt
I'm disabled.	**Ich bin körperbehindert.** ish bin ker-puh-buh-hin-dairt
I'm visually impaired.	**Ich bin sehbehindert.** ish bin zay-buh-hin-dairt
I'm *hearing impaired* / *deaf*.	**Ich bin *hörgeschädigt* / *taub*.** ish bin her-guh-shay-digt / tauwp
I'm hard of hearing.	**Ich höre schlecht.** ish her-uh shlesht
Could you speak up a bit?	**Können Sie bitte lauter reden?** kern-en zee bit-tuh lauw-tuh ray-den
Could you write that down, please?	**Können Sie das bitte aufschreiben?** kern-en zee dahs bit-tuh owf-shreye-ben
Is it suitable for wheelchair users?	**Ist es für Rollstuhlfahrer geeignet?** ist es fur roll-shtool-fah-ruh guh-ike-net
Is there a wheelchair ramp?	**Gibt es eine Rampe für Rollstuhlfahrer?** gheept es eye-nuh rahm-puh fur roll-shtool-fah-ruh
Is there a wheelchair-accessible restroom around here?	**Gibt es hier eine Behindertentoilette?** gheept es here eye-nuh buh-hin-dair-ten-toi-let-tuh

── For the Disabled ──

Can I bring my (collapsible) wheelchair?

Kann ich meinen (zusammenklappbaren) Rollstuhl mitbringen? kahn ish my-nen tsoo-(<u>zahm</u>-en-klahp-bah-ren) <u>roll</u>-shtool <u>mit</u>-breen-ghen

Could you please help me get *on / off*?

Könnten Sie mir bitte beim *Einsteigen / Aussteigen* helfen? kern-ten zee mere bit-tuh by-m <u>*eye-n-*</u>*shteye-ghen / <u>ows</u>-shteye-ghen* hel-fen

Could you please *open / hold open* the door for me?

Könnten Sie mir bitte die Tür *öffnen / aufhalten*? kern-ten zee mere bit-tuh dee tewr *erf-nen / <u>owf</u>-hahl-ten*

Do you have a seat where I can stretch my legs?

Haben Sie einen Platz, wo ich meine Beine ausstrecken kann? hah-ben zee eye-nen plats vo ish my-nuh by-nuh <u>ows</u>-shtrek-en kahn

At the Hotel

Does the hotel have facilities for the disabled?

Hat das Hotel behindertengerechte Einrichtungen? haht dahs ho-<u>tel</u> buh-<u>hin</u>-dair-ten-guh-resh-tuh <u>eye-n</u>-rish-toong-en

Does it have wheelchair access?

Gibt es einen Eingang für Rollstuhlfahrer? gheept es eye-nen <u>eye-n</u>-gahng fur <u>roll</u>-shtool-fah-ruh

Do you have a wheelchair I could use?

Haben Sie einen Rollstuhl für mich? hah-ben zee eye-nen <u>roll</u>-shtool fur mish

Could you take my luggage *up to my room* / *to the taxi*?	Können Sie mir das Gepäck *aufs Zimmer* / *zum Taxi* tragen? kern-en zee mere dahs guh-<u>pek</u> owfs tsim-muh / tsoom tahx-ee bring-en
Where's the nearest elevator / lift?	Wo ist der nächste Fahrstuhl? vo ist dair nayx-tuh fah-shtool
Could you call for me?	Könnten Sie für mich anrufen? kern-ten zee fur mish ahn-roo-fen

For the Disabled: Additional Words

blind	blind blint
collapsible wheelchair	der Faltrollstuhl dair <u>fahlt</u>-roll-shtool
companion	die Begleitperson dee buh-<u>gleyt</u>-pair-zone
crutch	die Krücke dee krew-kuh
guide dog	der Blindenhund dair <u>blin</u>-den-hoont
hearing impaired	hörgeschädigt <u>her</u>-guh-shay-dikt
level access	ebenerdig <u>ay</u>-ben-air-dish
mobility cane	der Taststock dair tahst-shtok
paraplegic	querschnittgelähmt <u>kvair</u>-shnit-guh-laymt
suitable for the disabled	behindertengerecht buh-<u>hin</u>-dair-ten-guh-resht
to have mobility problems	gehbehindert sein <u>gay</u>-buh-hin-dairt zeyn
wheelchair lift	die Hebebühne dee <u>hay</u>-buh-bew-nuh
without steps	stufenlos <u>shtoo</u>-fen-lohs

Communications

I'd like a telephone card.
Ich hätte gern eine Telefonkarte.

Where is an internet café around here?
Wo gibt es hier ein Internet-Café?

Telephone

info Purchase a **Telefonkarte** at the post office (**Postamt**) since most public phones accept only telephone cards.

Where can I make a phone call around here?	**Wo kann ich hier telefonieren?** vo kahn ish here telefo-<u>nee</u>-ren
A (... euro) phonecard, please.	**Ich hätte gern eine Telefonkarte (zu... Euro).** ish het-tuh gairn eye-nuh tele-<u>fone</u>-kah-tuh (tsoo ... oi-ro)
Excuse me, I need some change for the phone.	**Entschuldigung, ich brauche Münzen zum Telefonieren.** ent-<u>shool</u>-di-goong ish brow-khuh mewnts-en tsoom telefo-<u>nee</u>-ren
What's the area code for ...?	**Wie ist die Vorwahl von ...?** vee ist dee faw-vahl fun ...
Hello? This is	**Hallo? Hier ist ...** <u>hah</u>-lo here ist ...
I'd like to speak to ...	**Ich möchte... sprechen.** ish mush-tuh ... shpre-shen
Am Apparat.	Speaking.
Ich verbinde.	I'll put you through.
... spricht gerade.	... is on the other line.
... ist leider nicht da.	I'm afraid ... isn't here.
Bitte bleiben Sie am Apparat.	Hold on, please.
Kann ich etwas ausrichten?	Can I take a message?

70

Communications

What time does the evening rate start?	**Ab wie viel Uhr gilt der Nachttarif?** ahp vee feel oor guilt dair <u>nahkt</u>-tah-reef
How much is a 3-minute call?	**Was kostet ein 3-Minuten-Gespräch?** vahs kaws-tet eye-n dry-min-<u>oo</u>-ten- guh-shpraysh
A long-distance call to ..., please.	**Bitte ein Ferngespräch nach ...** bit-tuh eye-n <u>fairn</u>-guh-spraysh nahk
A collect call to ..., please.	**Bitte ein R-Gespräch nach ...** bit-tuh eye-n <u>air</u>-guh-shpraysh nahk ...
Bitte, gehen Sie in Kabine ...	Please go to booth number ...
Die Leitung ist besetzt.	The line's busy.
Es meldet sich niemand.	There's no reply.

Internet

Where's an internet café around here?	**Wo gibt es hier ein Internet-Café?** vo gheept es here eye-n in-ter-net-kah-<u>fay</u>
I'd like to send an e-mail.	**Ich möchte eine E-Mail senden.** ish mush-tuh eye-nuh e-mail zen-den
Which computer can I use?	**Welchen Computer kann ich benutzen?** velsh-en computer kahn ish buh-<u>noots</u>-en
How much is it for 15 minutes?	**Was kostet eine Viertelstunde?** vahs kaws-tet eye-nuh feer-tel-<u>shtoon</u>-duh

71

| Could you help me, please? | Könnten Sie mir bitte helfen? |
| | kern-ten zee meer bit-tuh hel-fen |

E-mail

Abmelden	Logout
Antwort	Reply
Antwort an alle	Reply all
Drucken	Print
Entwürfe	Draft
Löschen	Delete
Mail verfassen	Compose
Neue Mail	New mail
Papierkorb	Trash
Posteingang	Inbox
Senden	Send
Speichern	Save
Versendete Mails	Sent mails
Weiterleiten	Forward
Zurück	Back

Eating and Drinking

What do you recommend?
Was empfehlen Sie mir?

What are the regional specialities here?
Was sind die Spezialitäten aus dieser Region?

Reservations

Is there ... around here?	Wo gibt es hier in der Nähe ... *vo gheept es here in dair nay-uh ...*
– a café	– ein Café? *eye-n cah-fay*
– a bar	– eine Kneipe? *eye-nuh kuh-nigh-puh*
– a reasonably priced restaurant	– ein preiswertes Restaurant? *eye-n price-vair-tes rest-ow-rahng*
– a typical German restaurant	– ein typisch deutsches Restaurant? *eye-n tee-pish doitch-es rest-ow-rahng*
A table for ..., please.	Einen Tisch für ... Personen bitte. *eye-nen tish fur... pair-zone-en bit-tuh*
I'd like to reserve a table for *two / six* people for ... o'clock.	Ich möchte einen Tisch für *zwei / sechs* Personen um ... Uhr reservieren. *ish mush-tuh eye-nen tish fur tsveye / sex pair-zone-en oom ... oor ray-zair-vee-ren*
We've reserved a table for ... people.	Wir haben einen Tisch für ... Personen reserviert. *veer hah-ben eye-nen tish fur ... pair-zone-en ray-ziar-veert*
Is this *table / seat* free?	Ist dieser *Tisch / Platz* noch frei? *ist dee-zair tish / plahts nawk fry*
Where are the restrooms?	Wo sind hier die Toiletten? *vo sint here dee toi-let-ten*
Raucher-oder Nichtraucher(zone)?	Smoking or non-smoking (area)?

info Many restaurants in Germany have separate non-smoking areas. Since you don't wait to be seated, you may have to ask about the non-smoking area.

Menu

FRÜHSTÜCK
Breakfast

Kaffee cah-feh	coffee
Tee tay	tea
Tee mit Zitrone	tea with lemon
tay mit tsee-<u>tro</u>-nuh	
Tee mit Milch tay mit milsh	tea with milk
Kräutertee <u>kroi</u>-tuh-tay	herbal tea
Ei eye	egg
hart gekochtes Ei	hard-boiled egg
heart guh-<u>kokh</u>-tes eye	
weich gekochtes Ei	soft-boiled egg
why-sh guh-<u>kokh</u>-tes eye	
Rührei rewr-eye	scrambled egg
Spiegelei <u>shpee</u>-ghel-eye	fried egg
Käse kay-zuh	cheese
Wurst woorst	sausage
Speck shpek	bacon
Aufschnitt owf-shnit	cold cuts
Vollkornbrot	whole grain bread
<u>fawl</u>-korn-broht	
Roggenbrot <u>roh</u>-ghen-broht	rye bread
Toast toast	toast
Müsli mews-lee	cereal
Croissant krwoah-<u>sohn</u>	croissant
Marmelade	jam
mahr-may-<u>lah</u>-duh	
Honig ho-neegh	honey

Suppen

Soups

Champignoncremesuppe <u>shahm</u>-peen-yone-krem-zoo-puh	cream of mushroom soup
Erbsensuppe <u>airp</u>-sen-zoo-puh	pea soup
Fischsuppe <u>fish</u>-zoo-puh	fish soup
Fleischbrühe <u>flysh</u>-brew-uh	bouillon
Gemüsesuppe guh-<u>mew</u>-zuh-zoo-puh	vegetable soup
Hühnersuppe <u>hewn</u>-uh-zoo-puh	chicken soup
klare Brühe klah-ruh brew-uh	consommé
klare Gemüsebrühe klah-ruh guh-<u>mew</u>-suh-brew-uh	vegetable broth
Linsensuppe <u>lin</u>-zen-zoo-puh	lentil soup
Nudelsuppe <u>noo</u>-del-zoo-puh	noodle soup
Ochsenschwanzsuppe <u>oxen</u>-shvahntz-zoo-puh	oxtail soup
Tomatensuppe to-<u>mah</u>-ten-zoo-puh	tomato soup
Zwiebelsuppe <u>tsvee</u>-bel-zoo-puh	onion soup

VORSPEISEN

Appetizers

Aufschnittplatte owf-shnit-plah-tuh	cold cuts served with bread
Fleischpastete flysh-pah-stay-tuh	meat paté
gemischter Salat guh-mish-tuh zah-laht	mixed salad
Gänseleberpastete ghen-suh-lay-buh-pah-stay-tuh	pâté de foie gras
italienische Vorspeisen ee-tahl-yane-ish-uh faw-shpy-zen	antipasti
Knoblauchbrot kuh-nope-lauwk-broht	garlic bread
Krabbencocktail krah-ben-cock-tail	shrimp cocktail
Lothringer Speckkuchen / Quiche Lorraine lo-tring-uh shpek-koo-khen / quiche lor-raine	ham quiche
Matjesfilet nach Hausfrauenart maht-yes-fee-lay nahk house-frow-en-aht	filets of herring with apples and onions
Rohkost ro-kawst	crudités
Russische Eier roos-ish-uh eye-uh	hard-boiled eggs with mayonnaise
Räucherlachs roish-uh-lahx	smoked salmon
Salat zah-laht	salad
Tomatensalat to-mah-ten-zah-laht	tomato salad

FLEISCHGERICHTE

Meat Dishes

Braten brah-ten	roast
Eisbein ice-bine	pickled pig's knuckle
Filet fee-<u>lay</u>	filet
Fleischeintopf <u>flysh</u>-eye-n-topf	stew
Fleischklößchen <u>flysh</u>-klers-shen	meatballs
Fleischkäse <u>flysh</u>-kay-zuh	meatloaf
Frankfurter Würstchen <u>frahnk</u>-foor-tuh <u>vewrst</u>-shen	frankfurters
Frikadelle frik-ah-<u>del</u>-luh	burger
gemischte Grilltellerplatte guh-<u>mish</u>-tuh <u>grill</u>-tel-luh-plah-tuh	mixed grill
Hackfleisch hahk-flysh	ground meat
Hamburger <u>hahm</u>-boor-guh	hamburger
Hammelfleisch <u>hahm</u>-el-flysh	mutton
Hammelkeule <u>hahm</u>-mel-koi-luh	leg of mutton
Herz hairts	heart
Kalbfleisch kahlp-flysh	veal
Kalbsschnitzel <u>kahlps</u>-shnit-tsel	veal filet, breaded
Kaninchen kah-<u>neen</u>-shen	rabbit
Keule koi-luh	leg
Kotelett <u>kaw</u>-tuh-let	pork chop
Lammfleisch lahm-flysh	lamb
Lammkeule <u>lahm</u>-koi-luh	leg of lamb
Leber lay-buh	liver

Nieren neer-en	kidneys
Pfeffersteak <u>fef</u>-uh-steak	steak au poivre
Reh ray	venison
Rinderbraten <u>rin</u>-duh-brah-ten	roast beef
Rinderfilet <u>rin</u>-duh-fee-lay	filet of beef
Rindergulasch in Rotweinsoße <u>rin</u>-duh-goo- lahsh in <u>roht</u>-vine-zoh-suh	beef bourguignon
Rinderlende <u>rin</u>-duh-len-duh	sirloin
Rindfleisch rint-flysh	beef
Rippenstück <u>rip</u>-pen-stewk	ribs
Rouladen roo-<u>lah</u>-den	beef slices filled, rolled, and braised in brown gravy
Sauerbraten <u>sour</u>-brah-ten	beef roast, marinated with herbs and in a rich sauce
Schmorbraten <u>shmor</u>-brah-ten	pot roast
Schweinebraten <u>shvine</u>-nuh-brah-ten	roast pork
Schweinefleisch <u>shvine</u>-nuh-flysh	pork
Schweinefleischpastete <u>shvine</u>-nuh-flysh-pah-stay-tuh	pork pie
Schweinelende <u>shvine</u>-uh-len-duh	pork loin
Spanferkel <u>shpahn</u>-fair-kel	suckling pig
Steak steak	steak
Tatar tah-<u>tahr</u>	steak tartare

Wiener Schnitzel	veal cutlet
vee-nuh shnit-tsel	
Wild vilt	game
Wildpastete <u>vilt</u>-pah-stay-tuh	game pie
Zunge tsoong-uh	tongue

GEFLÜGEL

Poultry

Brathähnchen	roast chicken
<u>braht</u>-hayn-shen	
Ente en-tuh	duck
Entenbraten <u>en</u>-ten-brah-ten	roast duck
Fasan fah-<u>zahn</u>	pheasant
Gans gahnss	goose
Geflügel guh-<u>flew</u>-gull	poultry
Hähnchen hayn-shen	chicken
Hähnchen in Rotweinsoße	
hayn-shen in <u>roht</u>-vine-zohs-suh	coq au vin
Huhn hoon	chicken
Hühnerbrust <u>hewn</u>-uh-broost	chicken breast
Hühnerflügel	chicken wings
<u>hewn</u>-uh-flew-gull	
Hühnerleber	chicken liver
<u>hewn</u>-uh-lay-buh	
Pute poo-tuh	turkey
Rebhuhn rayp-hoon	partridge
Truthahn troot-hahn	turkey
Wachtel vahk-tel	quail

FISCH

Fish

Aal ahl	eel
Barsch bahsh	perch
Bückling bewk-ling	smoked herring
Fischfrikadelle <u>fish</u>-frik-ah-del-luh	fishcake
Fischstäbchen <u>fish</u>-step-shen	fish fingers
Forelle faw-<u>rel</u>-luh	trout
Heilbutt hile-boot	halibut
Hering hair-ring	herring
Kabeljau <u>kah</u>-bel-yow	cod
Karpfen kahp-ten	carp
Lachs lahx	salmon
Languste lahn-<u>goose</u>-tuh	crayfish
Makrele mah-<u>kray</u>-luh	mackerel
Sardellen zah-<u>del</u>-len	anchovies
Sardinen zah-<u>deen</u>-en	sardines
Schellfisch shell-fish	haddock
Scholle shawl-luh	flounder
Schwertfisch shvairt-fish	swordfish
Seebarsch zay-bahrsh	bass
Seefisch zay-fish	salt-water fish
Seezunge <u>zay</u>-tsoong-uh	sole
Süßwasserfisch <u>zews</u>-vas-suh-fish	fresh-water fish
Thunfisch toon-fish	tuna

MEERESFRÜCHTE

Seafood

Austern ows-tairn	oysters
Garnelen gah-nay-len	shrimp
gebratene Tintenfischringe	calamari
guh-brah-ten-uh tin-ten-fish-rin-gheh	
Hummer hoom-muh	lobster
Jakobsmuscheln	scallops
yah-cups-moosh-eln	
Krebs krayps	crab
Meeresfrüchte	seafood
mair-es-frewsh-tuh	
Muscheln moosh-eln	mussels
Riesengarnelen	jumbo shrimp
ree-zen-gah-nay-len	
Schalentiere	shellfish
shahl-en-tee-ruh	
Venusmuscheln	clams
vay-noos-moosh-eln	

EIERSPEISEN

Egg Dishes

Bauernomelett	diced bacon and onion
bow-airn-om-let	omelet
Käseomelett kay-zuh-om-let	cheese omelet
Omelett om-let	omelet
Spiegeleier mit Vorder-	ham and eggs
schinken shpee-gull-eye-uh	
mit faw-duh-shink-en	

BEILAGEN

Side Dishes

Bratkartoffeln <u>braht</u>-kah-taw-feln	fried potatoes
Frühkartoffeln <u>frew</u>-kah-taw-feln	new potatoes
gekochter Reis guh-<u>kawk</u>-tuh rice	boiled rice
Kartoffelklöße kah-<u>taw</u>-fel-kler-suh	potato dumplings
Kartoffelpüree kah-<u>taw</u>-fel-pew-ray	mashed potatoes
Kartoffelsalat kah-<u>taw</u>-fel-zah-laht	potato salad
Knödel kuh-<u>ner</u>-del	dumplings
Kroketten kro-<u>ket</u>-ten	potato croquettes
Pommes frites pom-<u>frit</u>	French fries
Rösti res-tea	hash browns
Salzkartoffeln <u>zahlts</u>-kah-taw-feln	boiled potatoes
Schwenkkartoffeln <u>shvenk</u>-kah-taw-<u>feln</u>	potatoes tossed in butter

GEMÜSE

Vegeatbles

Aubergine oh-bair-<u>jeen</u>-uh	eggplant
Blumenkohl <u>bloom</u>-en-coal	cauliflower
Blumenkohl mit Käse überbacken <u>bloom</u>-en-coal mit kay-suh ew-buh-<u>bahk</u>-en	cauliflower with cheese

German	Pronunciation	English
Bohnen	bo-nen	beans
Chicoree	<u>shee</u>-kaw-ray	chicory
Eisbergsalat	<u>ice</u>-berg-zah-laht	iceberg lettuce
Erbsen	airp-sen	peas
Fenchel	fen-shel	fennel
Frühlingszwiebeln	<u>frew</u>-lings-tsvee-beln	green onions
grüne Bohnen	grewn-uh bo-nen	green beans
Gurke	goor-kuh	cucumber
Kichererbsen	<u>kish</u>-uh-airp-sen	chickpeas
Kohl	coal	cabbage
Kopfsalat	<u>kopf</u>-zah-laht	lettuce
Krautsalat	<u>kraut</u>-zah-laht	coleslaw
(Brunnen)Kresse	(broon-nen)- kres-suh	watercress
Kürbis	kewr-biss	pumpkin
Linsen	lin-zen	lentils
Mais	mice	corn
Maiskolben	<u>mice</u>-kol-ben	corn on the cob
Paprikaschoten	<u>pahp</u>-ree-kah-shoh-ten	bell peppers
Peperoni	pep-air-<u>oh</u>-nee	chili peppers
Pilze	pilts-uh	mushrooms
Radieschen	rah-<u>dees</u>-shen	radish
Rettich	ret-tish	radish
Rosenkohl	<u>ro</u>-zen-coal	brussels sprouts
Rote Bete	<u>ro</u>-tuh <u>bay</u>-tuh	beets
rote Bohnen	ro-tuh bo-nen	kidney beans
Rotkohl	rote-coal	red cabbage
Rübe	rew-buh	turnip

Schalotte shah-<u>lawt</u>-tuh	shallot
Sellerie <u>sel</u>-uh-ree	celery
Spargel shpah-gull	asparagus
Spinat shpih-<u>naht</u>	spinach
Tomaten to-<u>mah</u>-ten	tomatoes
weiße Bohnen vice-uh bo-nen	lima beans
Zucchini zoo-<u>kee</u>-nee	zucchini
Zuckererbsen <u>tsook</u>-kuh-airp-sen	snow peas
Zwiebel tsvee-bel	onion

ZUBEREITUNGSARTEN

Ways of Cooking

blutig <u>bloo</u>-tik	rare
durchgebraten <u>doorsh</u>-guh-brah-ten	well done
eingelegt <u>eye-n</u>-guh-laygt	marinated
englisch ayng-lish	rare
flambiert flahm-<u>beert</u>	flambé
frittiert frit-<u>teert</u>	deep-fried
gebacken guh-<u>bahk</u>-en	baked
gebraten guh-<u>brah</u>-ten	fried
gedämpft guh-<u>dempft</u>	steamed
gedünstet guh-<u>dewns</u>-tet	steamed
gegrillt guh-<u>grilt</u>	barbecued, grilled
gekocht guh-<u>kawkt</u>	boiled
gepökelt guh-<u>per</u>-kelt	pickled
geräuchert guh-<u>roish</u>-airt	smoked
geröstet guh-<u>rers</u>-tet	roasted
geschmort guh-<u>shmort</u>	braised

in Essig eingelegt   pickled
  in ess-ish <u>eye-n</u>-guh-laygt
mariniert mah-ree-<u>neert</u>   marinated
medium <u>may</u>-dee-oom   medium (rare)
paniert pahn-<u>eert</u>   breaded
überbacken ew-buh-<u>bahk</u>-en   au gratin

KÄSE

Cheese

Appenzeller <u>ah</u>-pen-tsel-uh   hard cheese from
                                    Switzerland
Blauschimmelkäse   blue cheese
  <u>blauw</u>-shim-el-kay-zuh
Emmentaler <u>em</u>-en-<u>tahl</u>-uh   mild Swiss cheese
französischer Ziegenkäse   chèvre
  frahn-<u>tser</u>-sish-uh <u>tsee</u>-ghen-
  kay-zuh
Frischkäse frish-<u>kay</u>-zuh   cream cheese
Handkäse <u>hahnt</u>-kay-zuh   sharp, soft cheese
Käseplatte <u>kay</u>-zuh-plah-tuh   cheese platter
Schafskäse <u>shahfs</u>-kay-zuh   feta
Ziegenkäse   goat cheese
  <u>tsee</u>-ghen-kay-zuh

NACHSPEISEN

Dessert

Apfelkuchen	<u>ahp</u>-fel-kookh-en	apple pie
Baiser	bay-<u>zay</u>	meringue
Eis	ice	ice cream
Eisbecher	<u>ice</u>-besh-uh	sundae
gemischtes Eis		mixed ice cream
	guh-<u>mish</u>-tes ice	
Germknödel		sweet dumpling
	<u>gairm</u>-kuh-ner-del	
Karamellcreme		crème caramel
	kah-rah-<u>mel</u>-krem	
Karamellpudding		crème brûlée
	kah-rah-<u>mel</u>-pudding	
Krapfen	krahp-fen	doughnut
Käsckuchen		cheesecake
	<u>kay</u>-zuh-kookh-en	
Makrone	mah-<u>kro</u>-nuh	macaroon
Milchreis	milsh-rice	rice pudding
Mousse au chocolat		chocolate mousse
	moos oh sho-ko-<u>lah</u>	
Obstsalat	<u>ohpst</u>-zah-laht	fruit salad
Pfannkuchen	<u>fahn</u>-kookh-en	pancake
Plundergebäckstück		Danish pastry
	<u>ploon</u>-duh-guh-bek-shtewk	
Pudding	pudding	pudding
Rote Grütze	ro-tuh greets-uh	red berry compote
(Schlag)Sahne		(whipped) cream
	<u>shlahk</u>-zah-nuh	
Schokoladensoße		chocolate sauce
	sho-ko-<u>lah</u>-den-zos-suh	

Schokoladencreme	chocolate mousse
sho-ko-<u>lah</u>-den-krem	
Schwarzwälder Kirschtorte	Black Forest cake
<u>shvahts</u>-vel-duh <u>keersh</u>-taw-tuh	
Vanillesoße van-<u>nil</u>-zos-suh	(liquid) custard
Zwetschgenkuchen	plum tart
<u>tsvetch</u>-gen-kookh-en	

OBST UND NÜSSE

Fruit and Nuts

Ananas <u>ah</u>-nah-nahs	pineapple
Apfel ahp-fel	apple
Aprikosen ah-pree-<u>koh</u>-zen	apricots
Banane bah-<u>nah</u>-nuh	banana
Birne beer-nuh	pear
Brombeeren <u>brom</u>-bair-en	blackberries
Erdbeeren <u>airt</u>-bair-en	strawberries
Erdnüsse <u>airt</u>-nees-suh	peanuts
Esskastanien	chestnuts
<u>ess</u>-kah-stahn-yen	
Feigen fye-ghen	figs
Haselnüsse <u>hah</u>-zel-news-suh	hazelnuts
Himbeeren <u>him</u>-bair-en	raspberries
Johannisbeeren	currants
yo-<u>hahn</u>-is-bair-en	
Kirschen keer-shen	cherries
Kiwi kee-wee	kiwi
Kokosnuss <u>ko</u>-koss-noos	coconut
Limone lee-<u>mo</u>-nuh	lime

German	Pronunciation	English
Mandarine	mahn-dah-<u>ree</u>-nuh	mandarin
Mandeln	mahn-deln	almonds
Melone	mel-<u>oh</u>-nuh	melon
Nüsse	news-suh	nuts
Obst	ohpst	fruit
Orange	oh-<u>rahn</u>-juh	orange
Paranüsse	<u>pah</u>-rah-news-uh	Brazil nuts
Pfirsich	feer-sish	peach
Pflaume	flauw-muh	plum
Pistazien	pis-<u>tah</u>-tsee-en	pistachios
Preiselbeeren	<u>pry</u>-zel-bair-en	cranberries
Reineclaude	<u>rhine</u>-klauw-duh	(green) plum
Rhabarber	rah-<u>bah</u>-buh	rhubarb
Rosinen	ro-<u>zee</u>-nen	raisins
rote Johannisbeeren	ro-tuh yoh-<u>hah</u>-nis-bair-en	red currants
schwarze Johannisbeeren	shvahts-uh yo-<u>hahn</u>-is-bair-en	black currants
Stachelbeeren	<u>stahk</u>-el-bair-en	gooseberries
Walnüsse	<u>vahl</u>-new-suh	walnuts
Weintrauben	<u>vine</u>-trow-ben	grapes
Zitrone	tsee-<u>tro</u>-nuh	lemon

GETRÄNKE

Beverages

WEIN, SEKT

Wine, Champagne

Burgunder boor-<u>goon</u>-duh	Burgundy
Champagner	champagne
shahm-<u>pahn</u>-yuh	
Dessertwein des-<u>sair</u>-vine	dessert wine
halbtrocken <u>hahlp</u>-trock-en	medium
Hauswein house-vine	house wine
lieblich leep-lish	sweet
offener Wein	wine by the glass
<u>awf</u>-fen-uh vine	
Portwein pawt-vine	port
Rosé ro-<u>zay</u>	rosé
Rotwein rot-vine	red wine
Schaumwein shouwm-vine	sparkling wine
Sekt zekt	sparkling wine
Sherry shair-ree	sherry
Tafelwein <u>tah</u>-fel-vine	table wine
trocken trock-en	dry
Wein vine	wine
Weißwein vice-vine	white wine

BIER

Beer

alkoholarmes Bier ahl-ko-_hole_-ahm-ess beer	low-alcohol beer
alkoholfreies Bier ahl-ko-_hole_-fry-ess beer	non-alcoholic beer
Altbier ahlt-beer	beer with a high hops content, similar to British ale
Berliner Weiße mit Schuss bair-_leen_-uh vice-uh mit shoos	lager with a shot of raspberry syrup
Bier beer	beer
Bier vom Fass beer fom fahss	draught beer
Bockbier bock-beer	beer with a high alcoholic and malt content
Export ex-_pawt_	pale beer, higher in alcohol and less bitter than Pilsener
Hefeweizen, Hefeweißbier _hay_-fuh-white-zen _hay_-fuh-vice-beer	pale beer brewed from wheat
Kölsch kerlsh	lager, brewed in Cologne
Malzbier mahlts-beer	dark and sweet beer, very low in alcohol
Pilsener (Pils) pilss-nuh (pils)	pale and strong beer with an aroma of hops
Starkbier shtahk-beer	beer with a high alcoholic and malt content
Weißbier vice-beer	beer, brewed from wheat

AKOHOLISCHE GETRÄNKE

Other Alcoholic Drinks

Apfelkorn <u>ahp</u>-fel-korn	apple schnapps
Apfelwein <u>ahp</u>-fel-vine	hard cider
Cognac kone-yahk	brandy
Gin-Tonic gin-<u>tonic</u>	gin and tonic
Likör lee-<u>ker</u>	liqueur
Rum room	rum
schottischer Whisky	Scotch
<u>shawt</u>-tish-uh whisky	
Tomatensaft mit Wodka	Bloody Mary
to-<u>mah</u>-ten-zahft mit wodka	
Weinbrand vine-brahnt	brandy
Whisky whisky	
Whisky mit Eis	whisky
whisky mit ice	whisky on the rocks

ALKOHOLFREIE GETRÄNKE

Non-alcoholic Drinks

alkoholfreies Getränk	soft drink
ahl-ko-<u>hol</u>-fry-es guh-<u>trenk</u>	
Apfelsaft <u>ahp</u>-fel-zahft	apple juice
Eiskaffee <u>ice</u>-kah-fay	iced coffee
Fruchtsaft frookt-zahft	fruit juice
Limonade lee-mo-<u>nah</u>-duh	soda
Milch milsh	milk
Milchmixgetränk	milkshake
<u>milsh</u>-mix-guh-trenk	
Mineralwasser	mineral water
min-air-<u>ahl</u>-vas-suh	

Eating and Drinking

Mineralwasser mit Kohlen-
säure min-air-<u>ahl</u>-vas-suh
mit <u>kol</u>-en-soi-ruh
— sparkling mineral water

Mineralwasser ohne Koh-
lensäure min-air-<u>ahl</u>-vas-suh
oh-nuh <u>kol</u>-en-soi-ruh
— non-sparkling mineral water

Orangensaft
aw-<u>rahn</u>-jen-zahft
— orange juice

Saft zahft — juice

Tomatensaft
toe-<u>mah</u>-ten-zahft
— tomato juice

Tonic tonic — tonic water

WARME GETRÄNKE

Hot Drinks

Cappuccino
kah-pu-<u>tshee</u>-no
— cappuccino

Espresso es-<u>press</u>-o — espresso

heiße Schokolade
hice-uh sho-ko-<u>lah</u>-duh
— hot chocolate

Kaffee kah-fay — coffee

Kaffee mit Milch
kah-fay mit milsh
— coffee with milk

Kaffee ohne Milch
kah-fay oh-nuh milsh
— black coffee

Kräutertee <u>kroi</u>-tuh-tay — herbal tea

Tee tay — tea

Tee mit Milch tay mit milsh — tea with milk

Tee mit Zitrone
tay mit tsee-<u>tro</u>-nuh
— tea with lemon

Ordering

The menu, please.

Die Karte bitte. dee kah-tuh bit-tuh

I'd just like something to drink.

Ich möchte nur etwas trinken.
ish mush-tuh noor et-vahs trink-en

Are you still serving food?

Gibt es noch etwas zu essen?
gheept es nawk et-vahs tsoo- es-sen

Was möchten Sie trinken?

What would you like to drink?

I'll have …, please.

Ich möchte … ish mush-tuh …

– a glass of red wine.

– **ein Glas Rotwein.**
eye-n glahs roht-vine

– a bottle of white wine.

– **eine Flasche Weißwein.**
eye-nuh flahsh-uh vice-vine

– a carafe of house wine.

– **eine Karaffe Hauswein.**
eye-nuh kah-<u>rah</u>-fuh house-vine

– a beer.

– **ein Bier.** eye-n beer

– a pitcher of water.

– **eine Karaffe Wasser.**
eye-nuh kah-<u>rah</u>-fuh vahs-suh

– some more bread.

– **noch etwas Brot.**
nawk et-vahs broht

– a *small* / *large* bottle of mineral water.

– **eine *kleine* / *große* Flasche Mineralwasser.** eihn-uh *kleye-nuh* / *gros-suh* flahsh-uh min-air-<u>ahl</u>-vahs-suh

– a cup of coffee.

– **eine Tasse Kaffee.**
eye-nuh tah-suh kaf-fay

94

info Especially in the wine-growing areas, restaurants usually have a separate wine list, which can be of impressive dimensions. The waiter or waitress will be happy to give you additional information on the wines and to help you make your choice.

Do you sell wine by the glass?	**Haben Sie auch offenen Wein?** hah-ben zee owk <u>awf</u>-en-nen vine
Was möchten Sie essen?	What would you like to eat?
What do you recommend?	**Was empfehlen Sie mir?** vahs emp-<u>fay</u>-len zee mere
What are the regional specialities here?	**Was sind die Spezialitäten aus dieser Region?** vahs zint dee shpets-ee-ahl-ih-<u>tay</u>-ten ows dee-zuh ray-ghee-<u>ohn</u>
Do you serve ...	**Haben Sie ...** hah-ben zee ...
– diabetic meals?	– **diabetische Kost?** dee-ah-<u>bay</u>-tish-uh kawst
– dietary meals?	– **Diätkost?** dee-<u>ate</u>-kawst
– vegetarian dishes?	– **vegetarische Gerichte?** vay-guh-<u>tah</u>-rish-uh guh-<u>rish</u>-tuh

95

Does it have … in it?
I'm not allowed to eat any.

Ist… in dem Gericht? Ich darf das nicht essen.   ist … in dame guh-<u>risht</u>? Ish dahf dahs nisht es-sen

Could I have … instead of …?

Könnte ich … statt … haben? kern-tuh ish … shtaht … hah-ben

Was nehmen Sie als Vorspeise / Nachtisch?

What would you like as *an appetizer* / *for dessert*?

I won't have *an appetizer* / *a dessert*, thank you

Danke, ich nehme *keine Vorspeise* / *keinen Nachtisch*.   dahn-kuh ish nay-muh *keye-nuh <u>faw</u>-shpy-zuh* / *keye-nen nahk-tish*

Wie möchten Sie Ihr Steak?

How would you like your steak?

Rare.

Blutig.   bloo-tik

Medium-rare.

Englisch.   ayn-glish

Medium.

Medium.   <u>may</u>-dee-oom

Well done.

Gut durchgebraten. goot <u>doorsh</u>-guh-brah-ten

Please bring me some more …

Bitte bringen Sie mir noch etwas… bit-tuh bring-en zee mere nawk et-vahs …

Complaints

That's not what I ordered. I wanted …

Das habe ich nicht bestellt. Ich wollte …   dahs hah-buh ish nisht buh-<u>shtelt</u> ish vol-tuh …

Eating and Drinking

Have you forgotten my …?	**Haben Sie mein … vergessen?** hah-ben zee mine … vair-<u>ghes</u>-sen
There's / There are no …	**Hier** *fehlt / fehlen* **noch …** here *faylt / fay-len* nawk
The food is *cold / too salty*.	**Das Essen ist** *kalt / versalzen*. dahs es-sen ist *kahlt / fair-<u>zahl</u>-tsen*
The meat isn't cooked through.	**Das Fleisch ist nicht lang genug gebraten.** dahs flysh ist nisht lahng guh-<u>nook</u> guh-<u>brah</u>-ten
Please take it back.	**Bitte nehmen Sie es zurück.** bit-tuh nay-men zee es tsoo-<u>rewk</u>

Paying

The bill, please.	**Die Rechnung bitte.** dee resh-noong bit-tuh
I'd like a receipt, please.	**Ich möchte bitte eine Quittung.** ish mush-tuh bit-tuh eye-nuh kvit-toong

info In Germany service is usually included in the bill, but you can tip the waiter or waitress by rounding up the bill or adding a few euros if the service was worth it.

We'd like to pay separately.	**Wir möchten getrennt bezahlen.** veer mush-ten guh-<u>trent</u> buh-<u>tsahl</u>-en
All together, please.	**Bitte alles zusammen.** bit-tuh ahl-les tsoo-<u>zahm</u>-men
I think there's been a mistake.	**Ich glaube, hier stimmt etwas nicht.** ish glauw-buh here shtimt et-vahs nisht

Please go through it with me.	**Bitte rechnen Sie es mir vor.** bit-tuh resh-nen zee es mere for
Hat es Ihnen geschmeckt?	Did you enjoy it?

▶ *Expressing Likes and Dislikes, page 21*

Please give my compliments to the chef.	**Sagen Sie dem Koch mein Kompliment!** zah-gen zee daym kawk mine kom-plee-<u>ment</u>

Having Lunch / Dinner Together

info It is common to say **Guten Appetit!** (Enjoy your meal!) before you start eating and to raise or clink glasses at the beginning or during the course of a meal.

Enjoy your meal!	**Guten Appetit!** goo-ten ah-puh-<u>teet</u>
Cheers!	**Zum Wohl!** tsoom vole
Schmeckt es Ihnen?	Are you enjoying your meal?
It's very nice, thank you.	**Danke, sehr gut.** dahn-kuh zair goot
Möchten Sie hiervon?	Would you like some of this?
Noch etwas …?	Would you like some more …?
Yes, please.	**Ja, gern.** yah gairn
No, thank you, I'm full.	**Danke, ich bin satt.** dahn-kuh ish bin zaht
What's that?	**Was ist das?** vahs ist dahs

Eating and Drinking

Could you pass me the …, please?	Würden Sie mir bitte … reichen?
	wew-den zee mere bit-tuh … rye-shen
I don't want to drink any alcohol.	Ich möchte keinen Alkohol trinken.
	ish mush-tuh keye-nen <u>ahl</u>-ko-hole trink-en
Do you mind if I smoke?	Stört es Sie, wenn ich rauche?
	shtert es zee ven ish rauwk-uh
Thank you very much for the invitation.	Danke für die Einladung.
	dahn-kuh fur dee <u>eye-n</u>-lah-doong
I'd like to pay for your meal.	Ich möchte Sie einladen.
	ish mush-tuh zee <u>eye-n</u>-lah den
It was excellent.	Es war ausgezeichnet.
	es vah ows-guh-<u>tsigh</u>-shnet

Eating and Drinking: Additional Words

appetizer	die Vorspeise dee <u>faw</u>-shpy-zuh
ashtray	der Aschenbecher
	dair <u>ahsh</u>-en-besh-uh
bar	die Kneipe dee kuh-<u>nigh</u>-puh
beef	das Rindfleisch dahs rint-flysh
bottle	die Flasche dee flahsh-uh
breakfast	das Frühstück dahs frew-shtewk
to have breakfast	frühstücken <u>frew</u>-shtewk-en
butter	die Butter dee boo-tuh
cake	der Kuchen dair koo-khen
chair	der Stuhl dair shtool
cocoa	der Kakao dair kah-<u>cow</u>
cold	kalt kahlt
complete meal	das Menü dahs men-<u>ew</u>
course	der Gang dair gahng
cover charge	das Gedeck dahs guh-<u>dek</u>

cream	die Sahne dee zah-nuh
cup	die Tasse dee tah-suh
diet	die Diät dee dee-<u>ate</u>
dinner	das Abendessen dahs <u>ah</u>-bent-es-sen
dressing	die Salatsoße dee zah-<u>laht</u>-zo-suh
drink	das Getränk dahs guh-<u>trenk</u>
to drink	trinken trink-en
to eat	essen es-sen
fatty	fett fatt
fish bone	die Gräte dee gray-tuh
food	das Essen dahs es-sen
fork	die Gabel dee gah-bel
fresh	frisch frish
fruit	das Obst dahs ohpst
to be full	satt sein zaht zeye-n
garlic	der Knoblauch dair kuh-<u>no</u>-blauwk
glass	das Glas dahs glahs
gravy	die Soße dee zo-suh
homemade	hausgemacht <u>house</u>-guh-mahkt
hot	heiß hice
hot (spicy)	scharf shahf
to be hungry	hungrig sein hoong-rish zeye-n
jam	die Marmelade dee mah-muh-<u>lah</u>-duh
ketchup	der Ketchup dair ketchup
knife	das Messer dahs mes-suh
lean	mager mah-guh
light food	die Schonkost dee shone-kawst
lunch	das Mittagessen dahs <u>mit</u>-tahk-es-sen
main course	das Hauptgericht
	dahs <u>howpt</u>-guh-risht
margarine	die Margarine dee mah-guh-<u>ree</u>-nuh
mayonnaise	die Mayonnaise dee mayo-<u>nay</u>-zuh
meal	das Gericht dahs guh-<u>risht</u>
meat	das Fleisch dahs flysh

(sparkling / non-sparkling) mineral water	das Mineralwasser (*mit / ohne* Kohlensäure) dahs min-air-<u>ahl</u>-vas-suh (*mit / oh-nuh* <u>kol</u>-en-soi-ruh)
mushrooms	Pilze <u>pil</u>-tsuh
mustard	der Senf dair zenf
napkin	die Serviette dee zair-vee-<u>et</u>-tuh
oil	das Öl dahs erl
to order	bestellen buh-<u>shtel</u>-en
pasta	Nudeln <u>noo</u>-deln
pastries	das Gebäck dahs guh-<u>bek</u>
to pay	bezahlen buh-<u>tzah</u>-len
to pay separately	getrennt bezahlen guh-<u>trent</u> buh-<u>tzah</u>-len
to pay together	zusammen bezahlen tsu-<u>zahm</u>-men buh-<u>tsah</u>-len
(ground) pepper	der Pfeffer dair <u>fef</u>-fuh
piece	das Stück dahs shtewk
pizza	die Pizza dee pizza
plate	der Teller dair <u>tel</u>-uh
portion	die Portion dee paw-tsee-<u>ohn</u>
potatoes	Kartoffeln kah-<u>tawf</u>-eln
raw	roh ro
restaurant	das Restaurant dahs rest-oh-<u>rahng</u>
rice	der Reis dair rice
roll	das Brötchen dahs <u>brert</u>-shen
salad	der Salat dair zah-<u>laht</u>
salt	das Salz dahs zahlts
sandwich	das belegte Brot dahs buh-<u>layk</u>-tuh broht
sauce	die Soße dee <u>zo</u>-suh
seasoned	gewürzt guh-<u>vewtst</u>
service	die Bedienung dee buh-<u>deen</u>-oong
side dish	die Beilage dee <u>by</u>-lah-guh
silverware	das Besteck dahs buh-<u>shtek</u>

soup	die Suppe dee zoop-uh
sour	sauer sour
specialty	die Spezialität dee shpets-ee-ahl-ee-<u>tayt</u>
spoon	der Löffel dair lerf-el
sugar	der Zucker dair tzook-uh
sweet	süß zews
sweetener	der Süßstoff dair zews-shtawf
table	der Tisch dair tish
to taste	schmecken shmek-en
tea	der Tee dair tay
to be thirsty	durstig sein doors-tish zeye-n
tip	das Trinkgeld dahs trink-ghelt
toothpick	der Zahnstocher dair <u>tsahn</u>-shtawk-uh
vegetables	das Gemüse dahs guh-<u>mew</u>-zuh
vinegar	der Essig dair <u>es</u>-sish
waiter	der Kellner dair kel-nuh
waitress	die Kellnerin dee <u>kel</u>-nuh-rin
water	das Wasser dahs vahs-suh
wine	der Wein dair vine
yogurt	der Joghurt dair yogurt

▶ *More Food Items, page 109*

Shopping

I'm just looking, thanks.
Danke, ich sehe mich nur um.

Do you have it in a different color?
Haben Sie das auch in einer anderen Farbe?

Paying

How much is that?	**Wie viel kostet das?** vee feel kaws-tet dahs
How much *is / are* …?	**Was *kostet / kosten* …?** vahs *kaws-tet / kaws-ten* …
That's too expensive.	**Das ist mir zu teuer.** dahs ist mere tsu toi-uh
Do you have anything cheaper?	**Haben Sie auch etwas Preiswerteres?** hah-ben zee owk et-vahs <u>price</u>-vair-tuh-res
Can you come down a little?	**Können Sie mir mit dem Preis etwas entgegenkommen?** kern-en zee mere mit daym price et-vahs ent-<u>gay</u>-ghen-kom-en
Do you have anything on sale?	**Haben Sie ein Sonderangebot?** hah-ben zee eye-n <u>zon</u>-duh-ahn-guh-boat
Can I pay with this credit card?	**Kann ich mit (dieser) Kreditkarte zahlen?** kahn ish mit (dee-zuh) kre-<u>deet</u>-kah-tuh tsah-len
I'd like a receipt, please.	**Ich hätte gern eine Quittung.** ish het-tuh gairn eye-nuh kvit-oong

General Requests

Where can I get …?	**Wo bekomme ich …?** vo buh-<u>kom</u>-uh ish …
Was wünschen Sie?	What would you like?

Kann ich Ihnen helfen?

Can I help you?

I'm just looking, thanks.

Danke, ich sehe mich nur um.
dahn-kuh ish say-uh mish noor oom

I'm being helped, thanks.

Ich werde schon bedient, danke.
ish vair-duh shone buh-<u>deent</u> dahn-kuh

I'd like …

Ich hätte gern …   ish het-tuh gairn …

I don't like that so much.

Das gefällt mir nicht so gut.   dahs guh-<u>felt</u> mere nisht zo goot

Could you show me …, please?

Zeigen Sie mir bitte …
tsigh-gen zee mere bit-tuh …

Is there anything else you could show me?

Können Sie mir noch etwas anderes zeigen?   kern-en zee mere nawk et-vahs <u>ahn</u>-duh-res tsigh-ghen

I'll have to think about it.

Ich muss mir das noch mal über-legen.   ish moos mere dahs nawk mahl ew-buh-<u>lay</u>-ghen

I like that. I'll take it.

Das gefällt mir. Ich nehme es.
dahs guh-<u>felt</u> mere ish nay-muh es

Darf es sonst noch etwas sein?	Anything else?
That's all, thanks.	**Danke, das ist alles.** dahn-kuh dahs ist ahl-les
Do you have a bag?	**Haben Sie eine Tüte?** hah-ben zee eye-nuh tew-tuh
Could you wrap it up for my trip, please?	**Können Sie es mir für die Reise verpacken?** kern-en zee es mere fur dee rise-uh fair-<u>pahk</u>-en
Could you wrap it up as a present, please?	**Können Sie es als Geschenk einpacken?** kern-en zee es ahls guh-<u>shenk</u> eye-<u>n</u>-pahk-en
Can you send that *to the US/UK* for me?	**Können Sie mir das *in die USA / nach Großbritannien* schicken?** kern-en zee meer dahs *in dee oo-ess-<u>ah</u> / nahk gross-brit-<u>tahn</u>-ee-en* shik-en
I'd like to *exchange / return* this.	**Ich möchte das *umtauschen / zurückgeben*.** ish mush-tuh dahs <u>oom</u>-tauw-shen / tsu-<u>rewk</u>-gay-ben

General Requests: Additional Words

(too) big	**(zu) groß** (tsoo) gross
bigger	**größer** grers-suh
to buy	**kaufen** cow-fen
check	**der Scheck** dair shek
to cost	**kosten** kawst-en
credit card	**die Kreditkarte** dee kre-<u>deet</u>-kah-tuh
end of season sales	**der Schlussverkauf** dair <u>shloos</u>-fair-cowf

(too) expensive	(zu) teuer (tsoo) toi-uh
money	das Geld dahs ghelt
receipt	die Quittung dee kvit-oong
to return	zurückgeben tsoo-<u>rewk</u>-gay-ben
sale	der Ausverkauf dair <u>ows</u>-fair-cowf
self-service	die Selbstbedienung
	dee <u>zelpst</u>-buh-deen-oong
to show	zeigen tsigh-ghen
window display	das Schaufenster
	dahs <u>shauw</u>-fen-stuh

Shops and Stores

antique shop	das Antiquitätengeschäft
	dahs ahn-tee-kvee-<u>tay</u>-ten-guh-sheft
bakery	die Bäckerei dee bek-air-<u>eye</u>
barber	der Friseur dair free-<u>zur</u>
bookstore	die Buchhandlung
	dee <u>book</u>-hahnt-loong
butcher's	die Fleischerei dee flysh-uh-<u>rye</u>
candy store	der Süßwarenladen
	dair <u>zews</u>-vah-ren-lah-den
delicatessen	das Feinkostgeschäft
	dahs <u>fine</u>-kawst-guh-sheft
department store	das Kaufhaus dahs cowf-house
dry cleaner's	die Reinigung dee <u>rye</u>-nih-goong
electronics store	die Elektrohandlung
	dee ay-<u>lek</u>-tro-hahnt-loong
fish store	das Fischgeschäft
	dahs <u>fish</u>-guh-sheft
florist	das Blumengeschäft
	dahs <u>bloo</u>-men-guh-sheft
fruit and vegetable store	das Obst- und Gemüsegeschäft
	dahs ohpst-unt-guh-<u>mees</u>-uh-guh-sheft

grocery store	das Lebensmittelgeschäft
	dahs <u>lay</u>-bens-mit-tel-guh-sheft
hairdresser	der Friseursalon dair free-<u>zur</u>-sah-long
hardware store	Haushaltswaren <u>house</u>-hahlts-vah-ren
jeweler's	der Juwelier dair you-vel-<u>leer</u>
kiosk	der Kiosk dair kee-awsk
laundromat	der Waschsalon dair <u>vash</u>-sah-long
leather goods store	das Lederwarengeschäft
	dahs <u>lay</u>-duh-vah-ren-guh-sheft
market	der Markt dair mahkt
music store	das Musikgeschäft
	dahs moo-<u>zeek</u>-guh-sheft
newsstand	der Zeitungsstand
	dair <u>tsigh</u>-toongs-shtahnt
optician	der Optiker dair <u>awp</u>-tee-kuh
pastry shop	die Konditorei dee cone-dee-taw-<u>rye</u>
perfume shop	die Parfümerie dee pah-fewm-uh-<u>ree</u>
pharmacy	die Apotheke dee ah-po-<u>tay</u>-kuh
photo shop	das Fotogeschäft
	dahs <u>foto</u>-guh-sheft
shoe repair shop	der Schuhmacher dair <u>shoe</u>-mah-kuh
shoe store	das Schuhgeschäft
	dahs <u>shoe</u>-guh-sheft
shopping center	das Einkaufszentrum
	dahs <u>eye-n</u>-cowfs-tsen-troom
souvenir shop	der Andenkenladen
	dair <u>ahn</u>-denk-en-lah-den
sporting goods store	das Sportgeschäft
	dahs <u>shport</u>-guh-sheft
stationery store	das Schreibwarengeschäft
	dahs <u>shryp</u>-vah-ren-guh-sheft
supermarket	der Supermarkt dair <u>zoo</u>-puh-mahkt
tobacconist	Tabakwaren <u>tah</u>-bahk-vah-ren
watch shop	der Uhrmacher dair <u>oor</u>-mah-kuh

info Stores in Germany are generally open Monday through Saturday from 8 or 9 AM to 8 PM. Some stores are closed during lunchtime, from 12 to 1 or 2 PM, except department stores or supermarkets. Almost all stores are closed on Sundays except in some airports and train stations.

Food

What's that?	**Was ist das?** vahs ist dahs
Please give me …	**Bitte geben Sie mir …** bit-tuh gay-ben zee mere …
– a hundred grams (3.5 Oz.) of …	– **100 Gramm …** hoon-dairt grahm …
– a kilo (2.2 lb) of …	– **1 Kilo …** eye-n kee-lo …
– a liter of …	– **1 Liter …** eye-nen lee-tuh …
– half a liter of …	– **1 halben Liter …** eye-nen hahl-ben lee-tuh …
– four slices of …	– **vier Scheiben …** feer shy-ben …
– a piece of …	– **ein Stück …** eye-n shtewk …

A little *less* / *more*, please.	Etwas *weniger* / *mehr* bitte.
	<u>et</u>-vahs *mair* / <u>vay</u>-nih-guh bit-tuh
Could I try some?	**Kann ich davon etwas probieren?**
	cahn ish dah-fun et-vahs-pro-<u>bee</u>-ren

Food: Additional Words

apple cider (alcoholic)	der Apfelwein dair <u>ahp</u>-fel-vine
apple juice	der Apfelsaft dair <u>ahp</u>-fel-zahft
apricot	die Aprikose dee ah-pree-<u>ko</u>-suh
artichoke	die Artischocke dee ah-tee-<u>sho</u>-kuh
asparagus	der Spargel dair <u>shpah</u>-ghel
avocado	die Avocado dee ah-vo-<u>cah</u>-do
baby food	die Babynahrung
	dee <u>baby</u>-nah-roong
balsamic vinegar	der Balsamessig <u>bahl</u>-zahm-<u>es</u>-sish
basil	das Basilikum dahs bah-<u>zee</u>-lih-koom
beer	das Bier dahs beer
bell pepper	die Paprikaschote
	dee <u>pah</u>-pree-kah-sho-tuh
boiled ham	der gekochte Schinken
	dair guh-<u>kawk</u>-tuh shink-en
bread	das Brot dahs broht
broccoli	der Brokkoli dair <u>braw</u>-ko-lee
butter	die Butter dee boo-tuh
cabbage	der Kohl dair coal
cake	der Kuchen dair koo-ken
canned foods	Konserven con-<u>zair</u>-ven
canned sardine	die Ölsardine dee <u>erl</u>-zah-deen-uh
carrot	die Möhre dee mair-uh
cereal	das Müsli dahs mewz-lee
cheese	der Käse dair kay-zuh
cherry	die Kirsche dee keersh-uh

110

chicken	das Hähnchen dahs hayn-shen
chicory	der Chicorée dair she-ko-ray
chili pepper	die Peperoni dee pep-pair-ohn-ee
chives	der Schnittlauch dair shnit-lauwk
chocolate	die Schokolade dee sho-ko-lah-duh
cocoa	der Kakao dair kah-cow
coffee	der Kaffee dair kah-fay
coffee creamer	die Kaffeesahne
	dee kah-fay-zah-nuh
cold cuts	der (Wurst)Aufschnitt
	dair voorst(owf-shnit)
cookie	der Keks dair cakes
corn	der Mais dair mice
cream	die Sahne dee zah-nuh
cucumber	die Gurke dee goor-kuh
cutlet	das Kotelett dahs kaw-teh-let
egg	das Ei dahs eye
eggplant	die Aubergine dee oh-bair-jeen-uh
fish	der Fisch dair fish
fruit	das Obst dahs ohpst
garlic	der Knoblauch dair kuh-no-blauwk
grape	die Weintraube dee vine-trauw-buh
green bean	die grüne Bohne
	dee grew-nuh bo-nuh
ground meat	das Hackfleisch dahs hahk-flysh
ham	der Schinken dair shink-en
herbal tea	der Kräutertee dair kroi-tuh-tay
herbs	Kräuter kroi-tuh
honey	der Honig dair ho-nik
ice cream	das Eis dahs ice
iceberg lettuce	der Eisbergsalat
	dair ice-berg-zah-laht
jam	die Marmelade
	dee mah-muh-lah-duh

juice	der Saft dair zahft
ketchup	der Ketchup dair ketchup
kiwi	die Kiwi dee kiwi
lamb	das Lammfleisch dahs <u>lahm</u>-flysh
leek	der Lauch dair lauwk
lemon	die Zitrone dee tsih-<u>tro</u>-nuh
lettuce	der Salat dair zah-<u>laht</u>
liver pâté	die Leberpastete dee <u>lay</u>-buh-pahs-tay-tuh
lowfat milk	die fettarme Milch dee <u>fet</u>-ahm-uh milsh
margarine	die Margarine dee mah-guh-<u>reen</u>-uh
marmalade	die Orangenmarmelade dee o-<u>rahn</u>-jen-mah-muh-lah-uh
meat	das Fleisch dahs flysh
melon	die Melone dee mel-<u>o</u>-nuh
milk	die Milch dee milsh
(sparkling / non- sparkling) mineral water	das Mineralwasser (*mit / ohne* Kohlensäure) dahs min-air-<u>ahl</u>-vas- suh (*mit / <u>oh</u>-nuh* <u>coal</u>-en-soi-ruh)
mushrooms	Pilze pil-tsuh
nectarine	die Nektarine dee nek-tah-<u>ree</u>-nuh
nut	die Nuss dee nooss
oil	das Öl dahs erl
olive oil	das Olivenöl dahs o-<u>lee</u>-ven-erl
olives	die Olive dee o-<u>lee</u>-vuh
onion	die Zwiebel dee <u>tsvee</u>-bel
orange juice	der Orangensaft dair o-<u>rahn</u>-jen-zahft
oregano	der Oregano dair o-ray-<u>gahn</u>-o
oyster	die Auster dee ows-ter
paprika (spice)	der Paprika dair <u>pah</u>-pree-kah
parsley	die Petersilie dee pay-tuh-<u>zeel</u>-yuh
peach	der Pfirsich dair feer-zish

peanut	die Erdnuss dee aird-nooss
pear	die Birne dee beer-nuh
pea	Erbse dee airp-suh
(ground) pepper	der Pfeffer dair fef-fuh
pepperoni	die Salami dee zah-<u>lah</u>-mee
pickle	die eingelegte Gurke
	dee <u>eye-n</u>-guh-laygt-uh goor-kuh
pineapple	die Ananas dee <u>ah</u>-nah-nahs
plum	die Pflaume dee flauw-muh
pork	das Schweinefleisch
	dahs <u>shvine</u>-nuh-flysh
potato	die Kartoffel dee kah-<u>tawf</u>-el
poultry	das Geflügel dahs guh-<u>flew</u>-gull
raspberry	die Himbeere dee <u>him</u>-bair-uh
red wine	der Rotwein dair roht-vine
rice	der Reis dair rice
roll	das Brötchen dahs brert-shen
rolled oats	Haferflocken <u>hah</u>-fuh-flaw-ken
rosemary	der Rosmarin dair <u>rose</u>-mah-rin
rye bread	das Roggenbrot
	dahs <u>raw</u>-ghen-broht
salt	das Salz dahs zahlts
sausage (small)	das Würstchen dahs weerst-shen
semolina	der Grieß dair grees
smoked ham	der rohe Schinken
	dair ro-uh shink-en
spice	das Gewürz dahs guh-<u>veerts</u>
spinach	der Spinat dair shpin-<u>aht</u>
strawberry	die Erdbeere dee <u>airt</u>-bair-uh
sugar	der Zucker dair tsook-kuh
sweetener	der Süßstoff dair zews-shtawf
tarragon	der Estragon dair <u>es</u>-trah-gohn
tea	der Tee dair tay
tea bag	der Teebeutel dair <u>tay</u>-boi-tel

thyme	der Thymian dair <u>tew</u>-mee-ahn
tomato	die Tomate dee to-<u>mah</u>-tuh
tuna	der Thunfisch dair toon-fish
veal	das Kalbfleisch dahs kahlp-flysh
vegetable	das Gemüse dahs guh-<u>mew</u>-zuh
vinegar	der Essig dair es-sish
watermelon	die Wassermelone
	dee <u>vas</u>-suh-mel-o-nuh
white bean	die weiße Bohne dee vice-uh bo-nuh
white bread	das Weißbrot dahs vice-broht
white wine	der Weißwein dair vice-vine
whole grain bread	das Vollkornbrot dahs <u>fol</u>-korn-broht
wine	der Wein dair vine
without preservatives	ohne Konservierungsstoffe
	oh-nuh con-zair-<u>veer</u>-oongs-shtawf-fuh
yogurt	der Joghurt dair yogurt
zucchini	Zucchini zoo-<u>kee</u>-nee

Souvenirs

I'd like …	Ich möchte … ish mush-tuh …
– a nice souvenir.	– ein hübsches Andenken.
	eye-n hewp-shes <u>ahn</u>-denk-en
– a present.	– ein Geschenk. eye-n guh-<u>shenk</u>
– something typical of the region.	– etwas Typisches aus dieser Gegend. et-vahs <u>tee</u>-pish-es ows dee-zuh gay-ghent
Is this handmade?	Ist das Handarbeit? ist dahs <u>hahnt</u>-ah-bite
Is this antique / genuine?	Ist das antik / echt? ist dahs ahn-<u>teek</u> / esht

114

Souvenirs: Additional Words

antique	die Antiquität dee ahn-tee-kvee-<u>tate</u>
arts and crafts	das Kunsthandwerk dahs <u>koonst</u>-hahnt-vairk
belt	der Gürtel dair gewr-tel
blanket	die Decke dee dek-uh
ceramics	die Keramik dee kair-<u>ahm</u>-ik
certificate	das Zertifikat dahs tsair-tee-fee-<u>kaht</u>
crockery	das Geschirr dahs guh-<u>sheer</u>
genuine	echt esht
glass	das Glas dahs glahs
handbag	die Handtasche dee <u>hahnt</u>-tah-shuh
handmade	handgefertigt <u>hahnt</u>-guh-fair-tikt
jewelry	der Schmuck dair shmook
jug	die Kanne dee kah-nuh
leather	das Leder dahs lay-duh
pottery	die Töpferware dee <u>terp</u>-fair-vah-ruh
tableware	das Geschirr dahs gu-sheer
teapot	die Teekanne dee tay-<u>kah</u>-nuh
teaset	das Teeservice dahs tee-zair-<u>vees</u>

Clothing

Buying Clothes

I'm looking for …	Ich suche … ish zoo-kuh
Welche Größe haben Sie?	What size are you?
I'm (US) size …	Ich habe (die amerikanische) Größe … ish hah-buh (dee ah-<u>mair</u>-ih-<u>kah</u>-nish-uh) grer-suh

info

	Dresses / Suits						Shirts			
American	8	10	12	14	16	18	15	16	17	18
British	10	12	14	16	18	20				
Continental	38	40	42	44	46	48	38	41	43	45

Do you have it in a size …?
Haben Sie das in Größe …?
hah-ben zee dahs in grer-suh

Do you have it in a different color?
Haben Sie das in einer anderen Farbe? hah-ben zee dahs in eye-nur <u>ahn</u>-duh-run fah-buh

► *Colors, page 117*

Could I try this on?
Kann ich das anprobieren?
kahn ish dahs <u>ahn</u>-pro-beer-en

Where is there a mirror?
Wo ist ein Spiegel?
vo ist eye-n spee-ghel

Where are the fitting rooms?
Wo sind die Umkleidekabinen?
vo sint dee <u>oom</u>-kligh-duh-kah-been-en

What fabric is this?
Welches Material ist das?
velsh-es mah-tair-ee-<u>ahl</u> ist dahs

It doesn't fit me.
Das passt mir nicht.
dahs pahst mere nisht

It's too *big / small*.
Das ist mir zu *groß / klein*.
dahs ist mere tsoo *gross / kline*

It fits nicely.
Das passt gut. dahs pahst goot

Laundry and Dry Cleaning

I'd like this dry-cleaned.	Ich möchte das reinigen lassen.
	ish mush-tuh dahs <u>rye</u>-nee-ghen lahs-sen
Could you remove this stain?	Können Sie diesen Fleck entfernen?
	kern-en zee dee-zen flek ent-<u>fair</u>-nen
When can I pick it up?	Wann kann ich es abholen?
	vahn kahn ish es <u>ahp</u>-ho-len

Fabrics and Materials

camel hair	Kamelhaar kah-<u>mayl</u>-hah
cashmere	Kaschmir kahsh-mere
cotton	Baumwolle <u>bauwm</u>-vol-luh
fleece	Fleece fleece
lambswool	Schafwolle <u>shahf</u>-vol-luh
leather	Leder lay-duh
linen	Leinen line-nen
man-made fiber	Synthetik zeen-<u>tay</u>-tik
microfiber	Mikrofaser <u>mee</u>-kro-fah-zuh
natural fiber	Naturfaser nah-<u>toor</u>-fah-zuh
pure new wool	reine Schurwolle
	rye-nuh <u>shoor</u>-vol-luh
silk	Seide zeye-duh
suede	Wildleder <u>vilt</u>-lay-duh
wool	Wolle vol-luh

Colors

beige	beige beige
black	schwarz shvahts
blue	blau blauw
brown	braun brown

burgundy	dunkelrot <u>doon</u>-kel-roht
colorful	bunt boont
golden	golden gawl-den
gray	grau grauw
green	grün grewn
hot pink	pink pink
light blue	hellblau hell-blauw
navy blue	dunkelblau <u>doon</u>-kel-blauw
pink	rosa ro-zah
purple	lila lee-lah
red	rot roht
silver	silbern zil-bairn
turquoise	türkis tewr-<u>kees</u>
white	weiß vice
yellow	gelb gelp

Clothing: Additional Words

anorak	der Anorak dair <u>ah</u>-no-rahk
bathing suit	der Badeanzug
	dair <u>bah</u>-duh-ahn-tsook
bathrobe	der Bademantel
	dair <u>bah</u>-duh-mahn-tel
beach hat	der Sonnenhut dair <u>zun</u>-nen-hoot
belt	der Gürtel dair <u>gewr</u>-tel
bikini	der Bikini dair bikini
blazer	der Blazer dair blazer
blouse	die Bluse dee bloo-zuh
bra	der BH dair bay-<u>hah</u>
briefs	der Slip dair slip
coat	der Mantel dair <u>mahn</u>-tel
dress	das Kleid dahs clyt
glove	der Handschuh dair <u>hahnt</u>-shoe
hat	der Hut dair hoot

hat, cap	die Mütze dee <u>mew</u>-tsuh
jacket	die Jacke dee <u>yah</u>-kuh
jeans	Jeans jeans
long	lang lahng
long sleeves	lange Ärmel <u>lahng</u>-uh <u>air</u>-mel
pajamas	der Schlafanzug
	dair <u>shlahf</u>-ahn-zook
panties	der Slip dair slip
pants	die Hose dee <u>ho</u>-zuh
pantyhose	die Strumpfhose
	dee <u>shtroomf</u>-ho-zuh
raincoat	der Regenmantel
	dair <u>ray</u>-gen-mahn-tel
scarf	das Halstuch dahs <u>hahls</u>-took
scarf	der Schal dair shahl
shirt	das Hemd dahs hempt
short	kurz koorts
short sleeves	kurze Ärmel <u>koor</u>-tsuh <u>air</u>-mel
shorts	Shorts shorts
skirt	der Rock dair rock
sock	die Socke dee zaw-kuh
sports jacket	der Sakko dair <u>zahk</u>-ko
stocking	der Strumpf dair stroompf
suit (men's)	der Anzug dair <u>ahn</u>-tsook
suit (women's)	das Kostüm dahs kaws-<u>tewm</u>
sweater	der Pullover dair pull-<u>o</u>-vair
swimming trunks	die Badehose dee <u>bah</u>-duh-ho-zuh
swim suit	der Badeanzug
	dair <u>bah</u>-duh-ahntsook
T-shirt	das T-Shirt dahs t-shirt
tie	die Krawatte dee kruh-<u>vaht</u>-tuh
undershirt	das Unterhemd dahs <u>oon</u>-tuh-hempt
underwear	die Unterwäsche
	dee <u>oon</u>-tuh-vesh-uh
vest	die Weste dee ves-tuh
wrinkle-free	bügelfrei <u>bew</u>-ghel-fry

In the Shoe Store

I'd like a pair of …

Ich möchte ein Paar …
ish mush-tuh eye-n pahr …

Welche Schuhgröße haben Sie?

What's your shoe size?

I wear size …

Ich habe Größe …
ish hah-buh grer-suh …

info

	Women's Shoes				Men's Shoes							
American	6	7	8	9	6	7	8	8½	9	9½	10	11
British	4½	5½	6½	7½								
Continental	37	38	39	40	38	39	40	41	42	43	44	44

The heels are too *high / low*.

Der Absatz ist zu *hoch / niedrig*.
dair ahp-zahts ist tsoo *hawk / nee-drik*

They're too *big / small*.

Sie sind zu *groß / klein*.
zee sint tsoo *gross / kline*

I'd like these shoes *reheeled / resoled*.

Bitte erneuern Sie die *Absätze / Sohlen*. but-uh air-<u>noi</u>-airn zee dee <u>ahp</u>-zets-uh / *zoh-len*

Shoe Store: Additional Words

boot   der Stiefel dair stee-fel
flip-flop   der Badeschuh dair <u>bah</u>-duh-shoe
high heels   Pumps pewmps
hiking boot   der Bergschuh dair bairk-shoe

insole	die Einlegsohle
	dee <u>eye-n</u>-layg-so-luh
leather	das Leder dahs lay-duh
leather sole	die Ledersohle dee <u>lay</u>-duh-zo-luh
rubber boot	der Gummistiefel
	dair <u>goom</u>-ee-shtee-fel
sandal	die Sandale dee zahn-<u>dah</u>-luh
shoe	der Schuh dair shoe
shoe polish	die Schuhcreme dee shoe-krem
shoelace	der Schnürsenkel
	dair <u>shnewr</u>-zenk-el
size	die Größe dee <u>grers</u>-suh
sneaker	der Turnschuh dair toorn-shoe
suede	das Wildleder dahs <u>vilt</u>-lay-duh
tight	eng ehng
walking shoe	der Wanderschuh
	dair <u>vahn</u>-duh-shoe

Jewelry and Watches

I need a new battery for my watch.	**Ich brauche eine neue Batterie für die Uhr.** ish brow-kuh eye-nuh noi-uh bah-tuh-<u>ree</u> fur dee oor
I'm looking for a nice *souvenir / present*.	**Ich suche ein hübsches *Andenken / Geschenk*.** ish zook-uh eye-n heep-shes <u>ahn</u>-denk-en / guh-<u>shenk</u>
Wie viel darf es denn kosten?	How much do you want to spend?
What's this made of?	**Woraus ist das?** vo-rauws ist dahs

Jewelry and Watches: Additional Words

alarm clock	**der Wecker** dair vek-kuh
bracelet	**das Armband** dahs ahm-bahnt
brooch	**die Brosche** dee braw-shuh
carat	**das Karat** dahs kah-<u>raht</u>
clip-on earring	**der Ohrklipps** dair or-klips
diamond	**der Diamant** dair dee-ah-<u>mahnt</u>
earring	**der Ohrring** dair or-ring
gold	**das Gold** dahs gawlt
gold-plated	**vergoldet** fair-<u>gawl</u>-det
jewelry	**der Schmuck** dair shmook
necklace	**die Kette** dee ket-tuh
pearl	**die Perle** dee pair-luh
pendant	**der Anhänger** dair <u>ahn</u>-heng-uh
platinum	**das Platin** dahs plah-teen
ring	**der Ring** dair ring
silver	**das Silber** dahs zil-buh
watch	**die Uhr** dee oor
watchband	**das Uhrarmband** dahs <u>oor</u>-ahm-bahnt

Health and Beauty

adhesive bandage	**das Pflaster** dahs flah-stuh
allergy-tested	**allergiegetestet** ahl-air-<u>ghee</u>-guh-test-et
baby powder	**der Babypuder** dair <u>bay</u> bee-poo-duh
barrette	**die Haarspange** dee <u>hah</u>-shpahng-uh
blush	**das Rouge** dahs rooj
body lotion	**die Körperlotion** <u>ker</u>-puh-lo-tsee-ohn
brush	**die Bürste** dee bewr-stuh
comb	**der Kamm** dair kahm
condom	**das Kondom** dahs kon-<u>dome</u>
cotton balls	**die Watte** dee vaht-tuh
cotton swabs	**das Wattestäbchen** dahs <u>waht</u>-tuh-shtayp-shen
dental floss	**die Zahnseide** dee <u>tsahn</u>-zeye-duh
deodorant	**das Deo** dahs <u>day</u>-oh
detergent	**das Waschmittel** dahs <u>vahsh</u>-mit-tel
eye shadow	**der Lidschatten** dair <u>leet</u>-shaht-ten
eyeliner (pencil)	**der Kajalstift** dair kah-<u>yahl</u>-shtift
face wash	**die Reinigungsmilch** dee <u>rye</u>-nee-goongs-milsh

123

fragrance-free	parfümfrei pah-_fewm_-fry
(elastic) hairband	das Haargummi dahs _hah_-goom-ee
hairclip	die Haarklammer dee _hah_-klah-muh
hairspray	das Haarspray dahs hah-spray
hand cream	die Handcreme dee hahnt-krem
lip balm	der Lippenpflegestift
	dair _lip_-pen-flay-guh-shtift
lipstick	der Lippenstift dair _lip_-pen-shtift
mascara	die Wimperntusche
	dee _vim_-pairn-too-shuh
mirror	der Spiegel dair shpee-gull
moisturizer	die Tagescreme dee _tah_-ghes-krem
mosquito repellent	der Mückenschutz
	dair _mewk_-en-shoots
mousse	der Schaumfestiger
	dair _shauwm_-fes-tih-guh
nail file	die Nagelfeile dee _nah_-ghel-fy-luh
nail polish	der Nagellack dair _nah_-ghel-lahk
nail polish remover	der Nagellackentferner
	dair _nah_-ghel-lahk-ent-fair-nuh
nail scissors	die Nagelschere
	dee _nah_-ghel-shair-uh
nailbrush	die Nagelbürste
	dee _nah_-ghel-bewr-stuh
night cream	die Nachtcreme die nahkt-krem
perfume	das Parfüm dahs pah-_fewm_
razor blade	die Rasierklinge
	dee rah-_zeer_-kling-uh
sanitary napkin	die Binde dee bin-duh
shampoo	das Shampoo dahs shahm-poo
shaving cream	der Rasierschaum
	dair rah-_zeer_-shauwm
shower gel	das Duschgel dahs doosh-gel
soap	die Seife dee zeye-fuh
styling gel	das Haargel dahs hah-gel

sun protection factor (SPF)	der Lichtschutzfaktor dair <u>lisht</u>-shoots-fahk-tor
sunscreen	die Sonnencreme dee <u>zun</u>-en-krem
suntan lotion	die Sonnenmilch dee <u>zun</u>-en-milsh
tampon	das Tampon dahs tahm-pon
tissue (paper)	das Papiertaschentuch dahs pah-<u>peer</u>-tash-en-tookh
toilet paper	das Toilettenpapier dahs toi-<u>let</u>-ten-pah-<u>peer</u>
toothbrush	die Zahnbürste dee <u>tsahn</u>-bewr-stuh
toothpaste	die Zahnpasta dee <u>tsahn</u>-pahs-tah
toothpick	der Zahnstocher dair <u>tsahn</u>-shtawk-uh
tweezers	die Pinzette dee pin-<u>tset</u>-tuh
washcloth	der Waschlappen dair <u>vahsh</u>-lahp-pen
wipes	feuchte Tücher <u>foish</u>-tuh <u>tewsh</u>-uh

Household Articles

aluminum foil	die Alufolie dee <u>ah</u>-loo-fol-yuh
bottle opener	der Flaschenöffner dair <u>flahsh</u>-en-erf-nuh
broom	der Besen dair bay-zen
bucket	der Eimer dair eye-muh
can opener	der Dosenöffner dair <u>do</u>-zen-erf-nuh
candle	die Kerze dee kair-tsuh
charcoal	die Grillkohle dee <u>grill</u>-ko-luh
cleaning product	das Reinigungsmittel dahs <u>rye</u>-nee-goongs-mit-tel
clothes pin	die Wäscheklammer dee <u>vesh</u>-uh-klahm-uh
cooler	die Kühltasche dee <u>kewl</u>-tah-shuh

125

corkscrew	der Korkenzieher
	dair <u>kaw</u>-ken-tsee-uh
cup	die Tasse dee tahs-suh
detergent	das Waschpulver
	dahs <u>vahsh</u>-pull-vuh
dishtowel	das Spültuch dahs spewl-tookh
dishwashing detergent	das Spülmittel dahs <u>spewl</u>-mit-tel
fork	die Gabel dee gah-bel
frying pan	die Pfanne dee fah-nuh
glass	das Glas dahs glahs
knife	das Messer dahs mes-suh
laundry line	die Wäscheleine dee <u>vesh</u>-uh-lie-nuh
light bulb	die Glühbirne dee <u>glee</u>-beer-nuh
lighter	das Feuerzeug dahs <u>foi</u>-uh-tsoik
napkin	die Serviette dee zair-vee-<u>et</u>-tuh
paper towel	die Küchenrolle
	dee <u>kewsh</u>-en-rol-luh
plastic cup	der Plastikbecher
	dair <u>plahs</u>-tik-besh-uh
plastic plate	der Plastikteller dair <u>plahs</u>-tik-tel-luh
plastic untensils	das Plastikbesteck
	dahs <u>plahs</u>-tik-buh-shtek
plastic wrap	die Frischhaltefolie
	dee <u>frish</u>-hahl-tuh-fol-yuh
plate	der Teller dair tel-luh
pocket knife	das Taschenmesser
	dahs <u>tah</u>-shen-mes-suh
safety pin	die Sicherheitsnadel
	dee <u>zish</u>-uh-hights-nah-del
saucepan	der Kochtopf dair kokh-tawpf
scissors	die Schere dee shay-ruh
sewing needle	die Nähnadel dee <u>nay</u>-nah-del
sewing thread	das Nähgarn dahs nay-gahn
spoon	der Löffel dair lerf-fel

stain remover	der Fleckentferner
	dair <u>flek</u>-ent-fair-nuh
thermos	die Thermosflasche
	dee <u>tair</u>-mohs-flah-shuh

Electrical Articles

adapter	der Adapter dair ah-<u>dahp</u>-tuh
alarm clock	der Wecker dair vek-kuh
battery	die Batterie dee bah-tuh-<u>ree</u>
extension cord	die Verlängerungsschnur
	dee fair-<u>leng</u>-air-oongs-shnoor
flashlight	die Taschenlampe
	dee <u>tah</u>-shen-lahm-puh
hairdryer	der Föhn dair fern
pocket calculator	der Taschenrechner
	dair <u>tahsh</u>-shen-resh-nair
razor	der Rasierapparat
	dair rah-<u>zeer</u>-ah-pah-raht

At the Optician

My glasses are broken.	Meine Brille ist kaputt.
	my-nuh bril-luh ist kah-<u>poot</u>
Can you repair this?	Können Sie das reparieren?
	kern-nen zee dahs ray-pah-<u>ree</u>-ren
I'd like some disposable lenses.	Ich hätte gern Eintageslinsen.
	ish het-tuh gairn <u>eye-n</u>-tah-ghes-lin-zen
I'm *near-sighted* / *far-sighted*.	Ich bin *kurzsichtig* / *weitsichtig*.
	ish bin <u>koorts</u>-zish-tish / <u>vide</u>-zish-tish

Wie viel Dioptrien haben Sie?	What's your prescription?
I've got … dioptres in the left eye and … dioptres in the right.	Ich habe links … Dioptrien und rechts … Dioptrien. ish hah-buh linx … dee-awp-<u>tree</u>-en oond reshts … dee-awp-<u>tree</u>-en
I've *lost* / *broken* a contact lens.	Ich habe eine Kontaktlinse *verloren* / *kaputt gemacht*. ish hah-buh eye-nuh kon-<u>tahkt</u>-lin-zuh fair-<u>lor</u>-en / kah-<u>poot</u>-guh-mahkt
I need some saline solution for *hard* / *soft* contact lenses.	Ich brauche Aufbewahrungslösung für *harte* / *weiche* Kontaktlinsen. ish brauwk-uh <u>owf</u>-buh-vah-roongs-ler-zoong fur *hah-tuh* / *vigh-shuh* kon<u>tahkt</u>-lin-zen
I need some cleaning solution for *hard* / *soft* contact lenses.	Ich brauche Reinigungslösung für *harte* / *weiche* Kontaktlinsen. ish brauwk-uh <u>rye</u>-nee-goongs-ler-zoong fur *hah-tuh* / *vigh-shuh* kon<u>tahkt</u>linzen

At the Photo Store

I'd like …	Ich hätte gern … ish het-tuh gairn …
– a memory card for this camera.	– eine Speicherkarte für diesen Apparat. eye-nuh <u>shpy</u>-shuh-kah-tuh fur dee-zen ah-pah-<u>raht</u>
– a film for this camera.	– einen Film für diesen Apparat. eye-nen film fur dee-zen ah-pah-<u>raht</u>
– a color film.	– einen Farbnegativfilm. eye-nen <u>fahp</u>-neg-ah-teef-film

– a ...-ASA film.

– a slide film.

– a 24 / 36-exposure film.

– some batteries for this camera.

I'd like to get this *memory card / film* developed.

A *glossy / matte* print of each negative, please.

When will the prints be ready?

Can you repair my camera?

It won't advance.

The *shutter release / flash* doesn't work.

I'd like to have some passport photos taken.

– einen Film mit ... ASA.
eye-nen film mit ... ah-sah

– einen Diafilm. eye-nen dee-ah-film

– einen Film mit *24 / 36* Aufnahmen.
eye-nen film mit *fear-oont-tsvahn-tsish / sex-oont-dry-sish* owf-nah-men

– Batterien für diesen Apparat.
bah-tuh-<u>ree</u>-en fur dee-zen ah-pah-<u>raht</u>

Ich möchte diese *Speicherkarte / diesen Film* entwickeln lassen. ish mush-tuh dee-zuh *shpy-shuh-kah-tuh / dee-zen film* ent-<u>vik</u>-eln lahs-sen

Die Abzüge bitte *glänzend / matt*.
dee <u>ahp</u>-zee-guh bit-tuh *glentz-ent / maht*.

Wann sind die Bilder fertig?
vahn sint dee bil-duh fair-tish

Können Sie meinen Fotoapparat reparieren? kern-en-zee my-nen <u>fo</u>-toh-ah-pah-raht ray-pah-<u>ree</u>-ren

Er transportiert nicht.
air trahns-por-<u>teert</u> nisht

Der Auslöser / Das Blitzlicht funktioniert nicht. *dair <u>ows</u>-lerzuh / dahs blits-lisht* foonk-tsee-oh-<u>neert</u> nisht

Ich möchte gern Passbilder machen lassen. ish mush-tuh gairn pahs-bil-duh mahk-en lahs-sen

Photo Store: Additional Words

black and white film	der Schwarz-Weiß-Film
	dair shvahts-<u>vice</u>-film
camcorder	der Camcorder dair camcorder
CD / DVD	die CD / DVD
	dee tsay <u>day</u> / day fauw <u>day</u>
digital camera	die Digitalkamera
	dee dee-ghee-<u>tahl</u>-kah-mair-ah
exposure meter	der Belichtungsmesser
	dair buh-<u>lish</u>-toongs-mes-suh
filter	der Filter dair fil-tuh
flash	der Blitz dair blits
lens	das Objektiv dahs ohp-yek-<u>teef</u>
negative	das Negativ dahs <u>neh</u>-gah-teef
photo	das Bild dahs bilt
self-timer	der Selbstauslöser
	dair <u>zelpst</u>-ows-ler-suh
SLR camera	die Spiegelreflexkamera dee
	shpee-gull-ray-<u>flex</u>-kah-mair-ah
(film) speed	die Empfindlichkeit
	dee emp-<u>fint</u>-lish-kite
telephoto lens	das Teleobjektiv
	dahs <u>tay</u>-luh-ohp-yek-teef
UV filter	der UV-Filter dair oo-<u>fauw</u>-fil-tuh
video camera	die Videokamera
	dee <u>video</u>-kah-mair-ah
video cassette	die Videokassette
	dee <u>video</u>-kahs-set-tuh
wide-angle lens	das Weitwinkelobjektiv
	dahs <u>vite</u>-vink-el-ohp-yek-teef
zoom lens	das Zoomobjektiv
	dahs <u>zoom</u>-ohp-yek-teef

At the Music Store

Do you have any CDs / cassettes by …?	Haben Sie CDs / Kassetten von …? hah-ben zee tsay-_days_ / kahs-_set_-ten fun
I'd like a CD of traditional German music.	Ich hätte gern eine CD mit traditioneller deutscher Musik. ish het-tuh gairn eye-nuh tsay-_day_ mit-trah-dih-tsee-o-_nel_-luh doitch-uh moo-_zeek_

Music: Additional Words

CD / DVD player	der CD / DVD-Spieler dair tsay-_day_ / day-fauw-_day_-shpee-luh
headphones	der Kopfhörer dair _kopf_-her-ruh
MP3 player	der MP3-Spieler dair em-pay-_dry_-shpee-luh
music	die Musik dee moo-_zeek_
portable	tragbar trahk-bah
radio	das Radio dahs _rah_-dee-oh
walkman	der Walkman dair walkman

Books and Stationery

I'd like …	Ich hätte gern … ish het-tuh gairn …
– an English newspaper.	– eine englische Zeitung. eye-nuh _ayng_-lish-uh tsigh-toong
– an English magazine.	– eine amerikanische Zeitschrift. eye-nuh ah-may-ree-_kah_-nish-uh _tsight_-shrift
– a map of the town.	– einen Stadtplan. eye-nen shtaht-plahn

Do you have any English books?	Haben Sie englischsprachige Bücher? hah-ben zee <u>ayng</u>-lish-shprahk-ih-guh bewsh-uh

Books and Stationery: Additional Words

ballpoint pen	der Kugelschreiber dair <u>koo</u>-gull-shry-buh
cookbook	das Kochbuch dahs <u>kawk</u>-bookh
detective novel	der Krimi dair <u>krih</u>-mee
dictionary	das Wörterbuch dahs <u>ver</u>-tuh-bookh
envelope	der Briefumschlag dair <u>breef</u>-oom-shlahk
eraser	der Radiergummi dair rah-<u>deer</u>-goo-mee
felt tip	der Filzstift dair <u>filts</u>-shtift
glue	der Klebstoff dair <u>klayp</u>-shtawf
hiking map	die Wanderkarte dee <u>vahn</u>-duh-kah-tuh
magazine	die Illustrierte dee il-loo-<u>streer</u>-tuh

map of cycling routes	die Radtourenkarte
	dee <u>raht</u>-tou-ren-kah-tuh
novel	der Roman dair ro-<u>mahn</u>
paper	das Papier dahs pah-<u>peer</u>
pencil	der Bleistift dair bligh-shtift
pencil sharpener	der Spitzer dair shpits-uh
playing cards	die Spielkarten dee <u>shpeel</u>-kah-tuh
postcard	die Ansichtskarte
	dee <u>ahn</u>-zishts-kah-tuh
printer cartridge	die Druckerpatrone
	dee <u>drook</u>-uh-pah-troh-nuh
road map	die Straßenkarte
	dee <u>shtrahs</u>-sen-kah-tuh
tape	das Klebeband dahs <u>klay</u>-buh-bahnt
travel guide	der Reiseführer dair <u>rise</u>-uh-fee-ruh
writing pad	der Schreibblock dair shryb-blawk
writing paper	das Briefpapier
	dahs <u>breef</u>-pah-pee-uh

At the Tobacco Shop

A pack of cigarettes *with* / *without* filters, please.	Eine Schachtel Zigaretten *mit* / *ohne* Filter, bitte. eye-nuh shahk-tel tsee-gah-<u>ret</u>-ten *mit* / *oh-nuh* fil-tuh bit-tuh
A *pack* / *carton* of ..., please.	Eine *Schachtel* / *Stange* ..., bitte. eye-nuh *shahk-tel* / *shtahng-uh* ... bit-tuh
Are these cigarettes *strong* / *mild*?	Sind diese Zigaretten *stark* / *leicht*? zint dee-zuh tsee-gah-<u>ret</u>-ten *shtahk* / *lighsht*

133

A pouch of *pipe /
cigarette tobacco*,
please.

Ein Päckchen *Pfeifentabak /
Zigarettentabak*, bitte.   eye-n pek-
shen _fife_-en-tah-bahk / tsee-gah-_ret_-ten-
tah-bahk bit-tuh

Could I have a *lighter /
book of matches*,
please?

Ein Feuerzeug / Streichhölzer, bitte.
eye-n _foi_-uh-zoik / _shtrysh_-herl-zuh bit-
tuh

Tobacco: Additional Words

cigarillo
cigar
pipe
pipe cleaner

das Zigarillo   dahs tsee-gah-_ree_-loh
die Zigarre   dee tsee-_gah_-ruh
die Pfeife   dee fife-uh
der Pfeifenreiniger
  dair _fife_-en-rye-nee-guh

Sports and Leisure

I'd like to rent a bicycle.
Ich möchte ein Fahrrad ausleihen.

Could you adjust the saddle for me?
Können Sie mir die Sattelhöhe einstellen?

Activities

Beach and Pool

How do we get to the beach?	**Wo geht es zum Strand?** vo gate es tsoom shtrahnt
Is swimming permitted here?	**Darf man hier baden?** dahf mahn here bah-den
Are there (strong) currents around here?	**Gibt es hier (starke) Strömungen?** gheept es here (shtah-kuh) <u>shtrer</u>-mo-ong-en
When is *low / high* tide?	**Wann ist *Ebbe / Flut*?** vahn ist <u>eb</u>-buh / floot
Are there jellyfish around here?	**Gibt es hier Quallen?** gheept es here kvahl-len
I'd like to rent …	**Ich möchte … ausleihen.** ish mush-tuh … <u>ows</u>-lye-en
– a deckchair.	– **einen Liegestuhl** eye-nen <u>lee</u>-guh-shtool
– an umbrella.	– **einen Sonnenschirm** eye-nen <u>zun</u>-en-sheerm
– a boat.	– **ein Boot** eye-n boat
I'd like to take a *diving / windsurfing* course.	**Ich möchte einen *Tauchkurs / Windsurfkurs* machen.** ish mush-tuh eye-nen *tauwk-koors / <u>vint</u>-surf-koors* mahk-en
Can I go out on a fishing boat?	**Kann ich mit einem Fischerboot mitfahren?** kahn ish mit eye-nem <u>fish</u>-uh-boat <u>mit</u>-fah-ren

———— Sports and Leisure ————

How much is it per *hour / day*?

Wie viel kostet es pro *Stunde / Tag*? vee feel kaws-tet es pro *shtoon-duh / tahk*

Would you mind watching my things for a moment, please?

Würden Sie bitte kurz auf meine Sachen aufpassen? wewr-den zee bit-tuh koorts owf my-nuh zakh-en <u>owf</u>-pas-sen

Is there an *indoor / outdoor* pool here?

Gibt es hier ein *Hallenbad / Freibad*? gheept es here eye-n <u>hah</u>-len-baht / fry-baht

What change do I need for the *lockers / hair dryers*?

Welche Münzen brauche ich für *das Schließfach / den Haartrockner*? velsh-uh mewnts-en browk-uh ish fur *dahs shleess-fahk / dane <u>hah</u>-trok-ner*

I'd like to rent / buy ...

Ich möchte ... *ausleihen / kaufen*. ish mush-tuh ... *ows-lye-en / cow-fen*

– a swimming cap.

– eine Badekappe eye-nuh <u>bah</u>-duh-kahp-puh

– swimming goggles.

– eine Schwimmbrille eye-nuh <u>shwim</u>-bril-luh

– a towel.

– ein Handtuch eye-n <u>hahnt</u>-tookh

Where's the *pool attendant / first-aid station*?

Wo ist *der Bademeister / die Erste-Hilfe-Station*? vo ist dair <u>bah</u>-duh-mice-tuh / dee airs-tuh-<u>hil</u>-fuh-shtah-tsee-ohn

137

Beach and Pool: Additional Words

air mattress	die Luftmatratze
	dee <u>looft</u>-mah-trah-tsuh
arm float	der Schwimmflügel
	dair <u>shwim</u>-flew-gull
beach	der Strand dair shtrahnt
beach ball	der Wasserball dair <u>vahs</u>-suh-bahl
beach chair	der Liegestuhl dair <u>lee</u>-guh-shtool
boat rentals	der Bootsverleih dair <u>boats</u>-fair-lye
changing room	die Umkleidekabine
	dee <u>oom</u>-kligh-duh-kah-bee-nuh
to dive	tauchen tauwk-en
diving board	das Sprungbrett dahs shproong-bret
diving equipment	die Taucherausrüstung
	dee <u>tauwk</u>-uh-ows-rews-toong
diving mask	die Taucherbrille
	dee <u>tauwk</u>-uh-bril-luh
diving suit	der Taucheranzug
	dair <u>tauwk</u>-uh-ahn-tsook

flipper	die Schwimmflosse
	dee <u>shwim</u>-flaws-sen
to fish	fischen fish-en
high tide	die Flut dee floot
lake	der See dair zay
life preserver	der Rettungsring
	dair <u>ret</u>-toongs-ring
low tide	die Ebbe dee eb-buh
moped	der Motorscooter
	dair <u>mo</u>-tor-scoo-tuh
motorboat	das Motorboot dahs mo-<u>taw</u>-boat
non-swimmers	Nichtschwimmer <u>nisht</u>-shwim-muh
nude beach	der FKK-Strand
	dair ef-kah-<u>kah</u>-shtrahnt
ocean	das Meer dahs mair
pedal boat	das Tretboot dahs trayt-boat
playing field	die Spielwiese dee <u>shpeel</u>-vee-zuh
(rubber) raft	das Schlauchboot
	dahs shlauwk-boat
row boat	das Ruderboot dahs <u>roo</u>-duh-boat
to sail	segeln zay-gheln
sail boat	das Segelboot dahs <u>zay</u>-gull-boat
sand	der Sand dair zahnt
sandy beach	der Sandstrand dair <u>zahnt-shtrahnt</u>
shade	der Schatten dair shaht-ten
shell	die Muschel dee moosh-el
shower	die Dusche dee doo-shuh
snorkel	der Schnorchel dair shnaw-shel
storm warning	die Sturmwarnung
	dee <u>shtoorm</u>-wah-noong
sun	die Sonne dee zun-nuh
sunglasses	die Sonnenbrille
	dee <u>zun</u>-nen-bril-luh
sunscreen	die Sonnencreme
	dee <u>zun</u>-nen-krem

surfboard	das Surfbrett dahs surf-bret
to swim	schwimmen shwim-men
water	das Wasser dahs vahs-suh
water ski	der Wasserski dair _vas_-suh-shee
wave	die Welle dee vel-luh
wave pool	das Wellenbad
	dahs _vel_-len-baht

Games

Do you mind if I join in?	Darf ich mitspielen? dahf ish _mit_-spee-len
We'd like to rent a squash court for (half) an hour.	Wir hätten gern einen Squashcourt für eine (halbe) Stunde. veer het-ten gairn eye-nuh squash-court fur eye-nuh hahl-buh shtoon-duh
We'd like to rent a *tennis / badminton* court for an hour.	Wir hätten gern einen *Tennisplatz / Badmintonplatz* für eine Stunde. veer het-ten gairn eye-nen *tennis-plahts / badminton-plahts* fur eye-nuh shtoon-duh
Where can you *go bowling / play pool* here?	Wo kann man hier *Bowling / Billard* spielen? vo kahn mahn here *bowling / bil-yaht* spee-len
I'd like to rent …	Ich möchte … ausleihen. ish mush-tuh … _ows_-lye-en
Where can I get tickets for …?	Wo bekommt man Karten für …? vo buh-_komt_ mahn kah-ten fur

Games: Additional Words

badminton	das Badminton dahs badminton
badminton racket	der Federballschläger dair <u>fay</u>-duh-bahl-shlay-guh
ball	der Ball dair bahl
basketball	der Basketball dair <u>bahs</u>-ket-bahl
to bowl	kegeln <u>kay</u>-gheln
bowling alley	die Kegelbahn dee <u>kay</u>-gull-bahn
double	Doppel dawp-pel
game	das Spiel dahs shpeel
goal	das Tor dahs tor
goalkeeper	der Torwart dair tor-vaht
golf	das Golf dahs golf
golf ball	der Golfball dair golf-bahl
golf club	der Golfschläger dair <u>golf</u>-shlay-guh
golf course	der Golfplatz dair golf-plahts
to lose	verlieren fair-<u>lee</u>-ren
miniature golf course	der Minigolfplatz dair minigolf-plahts
to play	spielen shpeel-en
referee	der Schiedsrichter dair <u>sheets</u>-rish-tuh

soccer ball	der Fußball dair <u>foos</u>-bahl
soccer field	der Fußballplatz
	dair <u>foos</u>-bahl-plahts
soccer game	das Fußballspiel
	dahs <u>foos</u>-bahl-shpeel
squash	das Squash dahs squash
squash ball	der Squashball dair squash-bahl
squash racket	der Squashschläger
	dair <u>squash</u>-shlay-guh
table tennis	das Tischtennis dahs tish-tennis
team	die Mannschaft dee mahn-shahft
tennis	das Tennis dahs tennis
tennis ball	der Tennisball dair tennis-bahl
tennis racket	der Tennisschläger
	dair <u>tennis</u>-shlay-guh
(a) tie	unentschieden <u>oon</u>-ent-shee-den
umpire	der Schiedsrichter
	dair <u>sheets</u>-rish-tuh •
volleyball	der Volleyball dair <u>volley</u>-bahl
to win	gewinnen guh-<u>vin</u>-en

Indoor Activities

Do you have any *playing cards* / *board games*?	Haben Sie *Spielkarten* / *Gesellschaftsspiele*? hah-ben zee <u>shpeel</u>-kah-ten / guh-<u>zel</u>-shahfts-shpeel-uh
Do you play chess?	Spielen Sie Schach? shpeel-en zee shahk
Could you lend us a chess game?	Können Sie uns ein Schachspiel ausleihen? kern-en zee oons eye-n shahk-shpeell <u>ows</u>-lye-en

Is there a sauna / gym here? | **Gibt es hier *eine Sauna* / *ein Fitnessstudio*?** gheept es here eye-nuh sow-nah / eye-n *fit*-ness-shtoo-dee-o

Do you offer *aerobics* / *exercise classes* as well? | **Bieten Sie auch *Aerobicstunden* / *Gymnastikstunden* an?** bee-ten zee owk *ae*robic-stoon-den / ghim-*nahs*-tik-shtoon-den ahn

Hiking

I'd like to *go to* / *climb* … | **Ich möchte *nach* / *auf den* …** ish mush-tuh *nahk* / *owf dane* …

About how long will it take? | **Wie lange dauert es ungefähr?** vee lahng-uh dow-airt es oon-guh-fair

Is the trail *well marked* / *safe for walking*? | **Ist der Weg *gut markiert* / *gesichert*?** ist dair vayk *goot mah-keert* / *guh-zish-airt*

Can I go in these shoes? | **Kann ich in diesen Schuhen gehen?** kahn ish in dee-zen shoe-en gay-en

Are there guided walks? | **Gibt es geführte Touren?** gheept es guh-*fur*-tuh tour-en

Is this the right way to …? | **Sind wir hier auf dem richtigen Weg nach …?** zint veer here owf dame *rish*-tee-ghen vayk nahk

How far is it to …? | **Wie weit ist es noch bis …?** vee vite ist es nawk biss

Hiking: Additional Words

aerial tramway	die Seilbahn dee zile-bahn
climbing boot	der Bergschuh dair bairk-shoe
crampon	das Steigeisen dahs <u>shtike</u>-eye-zen
food	der Proviant dair pro-vee-<u>ahnt</u>
hiking trail	der Wanderweg dair <u>vahn</u>-duh-vayk
jogging	das Jogging dahs jogging
mountain	der Berg dair bairk
mountain climbing	das Bergsteigen dahs <u>bairg</u>-shtigh-gen
mountain guide	der Bergführer dair <u>bairg</u>-fur-uh
mountain rescue service	die Bergwacht dee bairg-vahkt
path	der Weg dair vayk
ravine	die Schlucht dee shlookht
rope	das Seil dahs zile
shelter	die Schutzhütte dee shoots-hew-tuh
summit	der Gipfel dair ghip-fel
to climb	klettern klet-tairn
to hike	wandern vahn-dairn
to jog	joggen joggen
walkers' map	die Wanderkarte dee <u>vahn</u>-duh-kah-tuh
walking shoe	der Wanderschuh dair <u>vahn</u>-duh-shoe
walking stick	der Wanderstock dair <u>vahn</u>-duh-shtok

Bicycling

I'd like to rent a bicycle / mountain bike.	Ich möchte ein *Fahrrad / Mountainbike* mieten. ish mush-tuh eye-n *fah-raht / mountainbike* mee-ten
Do you have a bicycle with a backpedal brake?	Haben Sie auch ein Fahrrad mit Rücktritt? hah-ben zee owk eye-n fah-raht mit rewk-trit
I'd like to rent it for …	Ich möchte es für … mieten. ish mush-tuh es fur … mee-ten
– one day.	– einen Tag eye-nen tahk
– two days.	– zwei Tage tsvigh <u>tah</u>-guh
– a week.	– eine Woche eye-nuh vawk-uh
Could you adjust the saddle for me?	Können Sie mir die Sattelhöhe einstellen? ker-nen zee mere dee zah-tel-her-uh <u>eye-n</u>-shtel-en
Please give me a helmet as well.	Bitte geben Sie mir auch einen Fahrradhelm. bit-tuh gay-ben zee mere owkh eye-nen <u>fah</u>-raht-helm
Do you have a cycling map?	Haben Sie eine Radtourenkarte? hah-ben zee eye-nuh <u>raht</u>-touren-kah-tuh

Bicycling: Additional Words

back light	das Rücklicht dahs <u>rewk</u>-lisht
bicycle repair kit	das Fahrradflickzeug dahs <u>fah</u>-raht-flik-tsoik
bike basket	der Fahrradkorb dair <u>fah</u>-raht-kawp
child seat	der Kindersitz dair <u>kin</u>-duh-zits
child's bicycle	das Kinderfahrrad dahs <u>kin</u>-duh-fah-raht

145

cycling path	der Radweg dair <u>raht</u>-vayk
front light	das Vorderlicht dahs <u>faw</u>-duh-lisht
generator	der Dynamo dair <u>dee</u>-nah-mo
hand brake	die Handbremse
	dee <u>hahnt</u>-brem-zuh
inner tube	der Schlauch dair shlauwk
light	das Licht dahs lisht
pump	die Luftpumpe dee <u>looft</u>-poom-puh
saddle	der Sattel dair zah-tel
saddlebag	die Satteltasche die <u>zah</u>-tel-tahsh-uh
tire	der Reifen dair rye-fen
tire pressure	der Reifendruck dair <u>rye</u>-fen-drook
valve	das Ventil dahs ven-<u>teel</u>

Adventure Sports

ballooning	das Ballonfliegen
	dahs bah-<u>long</u>-flee-ghen
canoe	das Kanu dahs <u>kah</u>-noo
free climbing	das Freeclimbing dahs freeclimbing
glider	das Segelflugzeug
	dahs <u>zay</u>-gull-flook-tsoik
gliding	das Segelfliegen
	dahs <u>zay</u>-gull-flee-gen
hang-gliding	das Drachenfliegen
	dahs <u>drahk</u>-en-flee-gen
kayak	das Kajak dahs kah-yahk
paragliding	das Gleitschirmfliegen dahs
	gl-eye-t-sheerm-flee-gen
regatta	die Regatta dee ray-<u>gaht</u>-tuh
river rafting	das Rafting dahs rahfting
row boat	das Ruderboot dahs <u>roo</u>-duh-boat
skydiving	das Fallschirmspringen
	dahs <u>fahl</u>-sheerm-shpring-en

thermal current	die Thermik dee tair-mik
to ride (horseback)	reiten rye-ten
to sail	segeln zay-gheln

Winter Sports

I'd like a lift pass for …	Ich möchte einen Skipass für … ish mush-tuh eye-nen she-pahss fur …
– one day.	– einen Tag. eye-nen tahk
– two days.	– zwei Tage. tsvigh tah-ghuh
– one week.	– eine Woche. eye-nuh vaw-kuh
Sie brauchen ein Passbild.	You need a passport photo.
I'd like to take ski lessons.	Ich möchte einen Skikurs machen. ish mush-tuh eye-nen she-koors mahken
I'm a *beginner / an intermediate* skier.	Ich bin *Anfänger / ein mittelmäßiger* Fahrer. ish bin <u>ahn</u>-feng-uh / eye-n <u>mit</u>-tel-mace-ih-guh fah-ruh

147

I'd like to rent …	Ich möchte … ausleihen.
	ish mush-tuh … <u>ows</u>-lye-en …
– cross-country skis.	– Langlaufski <u>lahng</u>-lauwf-shee
– a snow board.	– ein Snowboard eye-n snow board
– skates size …	– Schlittschuhe Größe …
	<u>shlit</u>-shoe-uh grers-suh …
– a sled.	– einen Schlitten eye-nen shlit-ten

Winter Sports: Additional Words

avalanche	die Lawine dee lah-<u>vee</u>-nuh
binding	die Bindung dee bin-doong
curling	das Eisstockschießen
	dahs <u>ice</u>-shtawk-shee-ssen
drag lift	der Schlepplift dair shlep-lift
pole	der Skistock dair shee-shtok
ski mask	die Skibrille dee shee-bril-uh
skiing instructor	der Skilehrer dair shee-lair-uh
skiing wax	das Skiwachs dahs shee-vahx
to go sledding	rodeln rod-eln
trail	die Loipe dee loi-puh

Beauty

At the Salon

I'd like an appointment for ….	Ich hätte gern einen Termin für …
	ish het-tuh gairn eye-nen tair-<u>meen</u> fur
Was wird bei Ihnen gemacht?	What are you having done?

I'd like …

Ich möchte … ish mush-tuh …

– a haircut.

– mir die Haare schneiden lassen.
meer dee hah-ruh shnigh-den lahs-sen

– a perm.

– eine Dauerwelle.
eye-nuh <u>dow</u>-uh-vel-luh

– some highlights.

– Strähnchen. shtrayn-shen

– my hair colored.

– eine Tönung. eye-nuh turn-oong

Wash, cut and blow-dry, please.

Waschen, schneiden und föhnen, bitte. vahsh-en shny-den oont fer-nen bit-tuh

Just a trim, please.

Bitte nur schneiden.
bit-tuh noor shny-den

Wie hätten Sie's denn gern?

How would you like it?

Not too short, please.

Nicht zu kurz, bitte.
nisht tsoo koorts bit-tuh

A bit shorter, please.

Etwas kürzer, bitte.
et-vahs kewrts-uh bit-tuh

Could you take some off …, please?

Könnten Sie … etwas wegnehmen?
kern-ten zee … et-vahs <u>vayk</u>-nay-men

– in the back

– hinten hint-en

– in the front

– vorne faw-nuh

– at the sides

– an den Seiten ahn dane sigh-ten

– on top

– oben oh-ben

The part on the *left* / *right*, please.

Den Scheitel bitte *links* / *rechts*.
dane <u>shy</u>-tel bit-tuh *linx* / *reshts*

Thanks, that's fine.

Vielen Dank, so ist es gut.
feel-en dahnk zo ist es goot

149

At the Salon: Additional Words

bangs	der Pony dair pon-nee
beard	der Bart dair bahrt
black	schwarz shvahts
blond	blond blont
brown	braun brown
curls	Locken law-ken
dandruff	Schuppen shoop-en
to dye	färben fair-ben
gel	das Gel dahs gel
gray	grau grauw
hairspray	das Haarspray das hah-spray
hairstyle	die Frisur dee free-<u>zoor</u>
mousse	der Schaumfestiger
	dair <u>shauwm</u>-festi-guh
rinse	die Spülung dee shpew-loong
shampoo	das Shampoo dahs shahm-poo
to shave	rasieren rah-<u>zee</u>-ren

Beauty Treatments

I'd like a facial, please.	Ich hätte gern eine Gesichts-behandlung. ish het-tuh gairn eye-nuh guh-<u>zikts</u>-buh-hahnt-loong
I have …	Ich habe … ish hah-buh …
– normal skin.	– normale Haut. naw-<u>mah</u>-luh howt
– oily skin.	– fettige Haut <u>fet</u>-ti-guh howt
– dry skin.	– trockene Haut. <u>trok</u>-en-uh howt
– combination skin.	– Mischhaut. mish-howt
– sensitive skin.	– empfindliche Haut. emp-<u>fint</u>-lish-uh howt

150

Please use only *fragrance-free* / *hypoallergenic* products.	Bitte verwenden Sie nur *parfümfreie* / *allergiegetestete* Produkte. bit-tuh fair-ven-den-zee noor *pah-feem-fry-uh* / *ahl-air-<u>ghee</u>-ghuh-tes-tet-uh* pro-<u>dook</u>-tuh
Do you also do *facial toning* / *lymphatic drainage*?	Machen Sie auch *Gesichts-massagen* / *Lymphdrainagen*? mahk-en zee owk guh-<u>ziks</u>-mah-sah-jen / <u>limpf</u>-dray-nah-jen
Could you tweeze my eyebrows?	Könnten Sie mir die Augenbrauen zupfen? kern-ten zee mere dee <u>ow</u>-ghen-brow-en tsoop-fen
I'd like to have my *eyelashes* / *eyebrows* dyed.	Ich möchte mir die *Wimpern* / *Augenbrauen* färben lassen. ish mush-tuh mere dee *vimp-airn* / <u>ow</u>-gen-brow-en fair-ben lahs-sen
A *manicure* / *pedicure*, please.	Bitte eine *Maniküre* / *Pediküre*. bit-tuh eye-nuh *mahn-ee-<u>kew</u>-ruh* / *pay-dee-<u>kew</u>-ruh*

Beauty Treatments: Additional Words

cleansing	die Reinigung dee <u>rye</u>-nee-goong
face	das Gesicht dahs guh-<u>sisht</u>
mask	die Maske dee mahs-kuh
moisturizing mask	die Feuchtigkeitsmaske dee <u>foish</u>-tish-kites-mas-kuh
neck	der Hals dair hahls
peeling	das Peeling dahs peeling

Well-Being

acupuncture | die Akupunktur
dee ah-koo-poonk-<u>tour</u>

massage | die Massage dee mah-<u>sah</u>-juh

meditation | die Meditation
dee may-dee-tah-tsee-<u>ohn</u>

mud mask | der Fango dair <u>fahn</u>-go

purification | die Entschlackung
dee ent-<u>shlahk</u>-oong

reflexology massage | die Fußreflexzonenmassage dee
<u>foos</u>-reh-flex-tson-en-mah-sah-juh

sauna | die Sauna dee <u>sow</u>-nah

tanning salon | das Solarium dahs zo-<u>lah</u>-ree-um

yoga | das Yoga dahs <u>yo</u>-ghah

Things to Do

I'd like a map of the town, please.
Ich möchte einen Stadtplan.

I'd like to visit …
Ich möchte … besichtigen.

Sightseeing

info Tourist information offices are often located in the center of town. Look for signs with Fremdenverkehrsamt or Verkehrsbüro.

Tourist Information

Where's the tourist information office?	Wo ist die Touristeninformation? vo ist dee tour-<u>is</u>-ten-in-for-mah-tsee-ohn
I'd like …	Ich möchte … ish mush-tuh …
– a map of the town	– einen Stadtplan. eye-nen shtaht-plahn
– a subway map	– einen U-Bahn-Plan. eye-nen <u>oo</u>-bahn-plahn
– an events guide	– einen Veranstaltungskalender. eye-nen fair-<u>ahn</u>-shtahl-toongs-kah-len-duh
I'd like to visit …	Ich möchte … besichtigen. ish mush-tuh … buh-<u>zish</u>-tee-gen
Are there *sightseeing tours of the town* / *guided walks around the town*?	Gibt es *Stadtrundfahrten* / *Stadtführungen*? gheept es <u>shtaht</u>-roont-fah-ten / <u>shtaht</u>-fur-oong-en
How much is the *sightseeing tour* / *guided walk*?	Was kostet die *Rundfahrt* / *Führung*? vahs kaws-tet dee *roont-faht* / *fur-roong*
How long does the *sightseeing tour* / *guided walk* take?	Wie lange dauert die *Rundfahrt* / *Führung*? vee lahng-uh dow-airt dee *roont-faht* / *fur-oong*

A ticket / Two tickets for the sightseeing tour, please.	Bitte *eine Karte / zwei Karten* für die Stadtrundfahrt. bit-tuh *eye-nuh kah-tuh / tsvigh kah-ten* fur dee <u>shaht</u>-roont-faht
One ticket / Two tickets for tomorrow's excursion to ..., please.	Bitte für den Ausflug morgen nach ... *einen Platz / zwei Plätze*. bit-tuh fur dane ows-flook maw-gen nahk ... *eye-nen plahts / tsvigh pleh-tsuh*
When / Where do we meet?	*Wann / Wo* treffen wir uns? *vahn / vo* tref-fen veer oons
Do we also visit ...?	Besichtigen wir auch ...? buh-<u>zish</u>-tee-ghen veer owk
When do we get back?	Wann kommen wir zurück? vahn kom-en veer tsoo-<u>rewk</u>

Accommodations, page 25; Asking for Directions, page 38; Public Transportation, page 55

Excursions and Sights

When is ... open?
Wann ist ... geöffnet?
vahn ist ... ghuh-<u>erf</u>-net

What's the admission charge?
Wie hoch ist der Eintritt?
vee hawk ist dair eye-n-trit

How much is the guided tour?
Wie viel kostet die Führung?
vee feel kaws-tet dee <u>fur-oong</u>

Are there guided tours in English, too?
Gibt es auch Führungen auf Englisch? gheept es owk <u>fur</u>-oong-en owf ayng-lish

Are there discounts for ...
Gibt es eine Ermäßigung für ...
gheept es eye-nuh air-<u>macy</u>-goong fur ...

– families?
– children?
– senior citizens?
– students?

– **Familien?** fahm-<u>eel</u>-yen
– **Kinder?** <u>kin-duh</u>
– **Senioren?** sen-<u>yor</u>-en
– **Studenten?** shtoo-<u>dent</u>-en

When does the guided tour start?
Wann beginnt die Führung?
vahn buh-<u>ghint</u> dee fur-oong

Two adults and two children, please.
Zwei Erwachsene, zwei Kinder, bitte. tsvigh air-<u>vahx</u>-en-uh tsvigh kin-duh bit-tuh

Are we allowed to take photographs?
Darf man fotografieren?
dahf mahn foto-grah-<u>fee</u>-ren

Do you have a *brochure/guide*?
Haben Sie einen Katalog/Führer?
hah-ben zee eye-nen *Kaht-ah-lohk/fur-uh*

Excursions and Sights: Additional Words

abbey	die Abtei dee ahp-<u>tye</u>
aqueduct	das Aquädukt dahs ahk-kveh-<u>dookt</u>
art	die Kunst dee koonst
art collection	die Gemäldesammlung
	dee guh-<u>mail</u>-duh-zahm-loong
artist	der Künstler dair kewnst-luh
baroque	der Barock dair bah-<u>rawk</u>
bell tower	der Glockenturm
	dair <u>glaw</u>-ken-toorm
botanical garden	der botanische Garten
	dair bo-<u>tahn</u>-ish-uh gah-ten
brewery	die Brauerei dee brow-uh-<u>rye</u>
bridge	die Brücke dee brewk-uh
building	das Gebäude dahs guh-<u>boi</u>-duh
bust	die Büste dee bews-tuh
carving	die Schnitzerei dee shnits-uh-<u>rye</u>
castle	die Burg dee boork
cathedral	der Dom dair dome
Catholic	katholisch kah-<u>toe</u>.lish
cave	die Höhle dee herl-uh
ceiling	die Decke dee dek-uh
cemetery	der Friedhof dair freet-hohf
ceramic	die Keramik dee keh-<u>rah</u>-mik
chapel	die Kapelle dee kah-<u>pel</u>-uh
choir	der Chor dair core
church	die Kirche dee keer-shuh
church tower	der Kirchturm dair keersh-toorm
classical; ancient	antik ahn-<u>teek</u>
cloisters	der Kreuzgang dair kroits-ghahng
closed	geschlossen guh-<u>shlaws</u>-sen
collection	die Sammlung dee zahm-loong
copy	die Kopie dee kaw-<u>pee</u>

157

dome	die Kuppel dee koop-pel
drawing	die Zeichnung dee tsigh-shnoong
excavation	die Ausgrabung dee <u>ows</u>-grah-boong
exhibition	die Ausstellung dee <u>ows</u>-shtel-oong
facade	die Fassade dee fahs-<u>sah</u>-duh
flea market	der Flohmarkt dair flo-mahkt
folk museum	das Volkskundemuseum
	dahs <u>folks</u>-koon-duh-moo-zay-oom
forest	der Wald dair vahlt
fortress	die Festung dee fes-toong
fountain	der Brunnen dair broon-nen
fresco	das Fresko dahs fres-ko
gallery	die Galerie dee ghahl-ah-<u>ree</u>
gate	das Tor dahs tor
grave	das Grab dahs grahp
hall	der Saal dair zahl
harbor	der Hafen dair hah-fen
indoor market	die Markthalle dee <u>mahkt</u>-hahl-luh
inscription	die Inschrift dee in-shrift
island	die Insel dee in-zel
Jewish	jüdisch yew-dish
king	der König dair ker-nik
lake	der See dair zay
landscape	die Landschaft dee lahnt-shahft
library	die Bibliothek dee bib-lee-o-<u>take</u>
marble	der Marmor dair mah-mor
market	der Markt dair mahkt
mausoleum	das Mausoleum
	dahs mauw-zo-<u>lay</u>-oom
memorial	die Gedenkstätte
	dee guh-<u>denk</u>-shteh-tuh
mill	die Mühle dee mew-luh
model	das Modell dahs mo-<u>del</u>
modern	modern mo-<u>dairn</u>

monastery	das Kloster dahs klohs- tuh
monument	das Denkmal dahs denk-mahl
mosaic	das Mosaik dahs mo-zah-<u>eek</u>
mountains	das Gebirge dahs guh-<u>beer</u>-guh
museum	das Museum dahs moo-<u>zay</u>-oom
nature preserve	das Naturschutzgebiet
	dahs nah-<u>toor</u>-shoots-guh-beet
obelisk	der Obelisk dair o-buh-<u>lisk</u>
observatory	die Sternwarte dee shtairn-wah-tuh
old part of town	die Altstadt dee ahlt-shtaht
open	geöffnet guh-<u>erf</u>-net
opera house	das Opernhaus dahs <u>o</u>-pairn-house
organ	die Orgel dee aw-gull
original	das Original dahs or-ee-ghi-<u>nahl</u>
painter	der Maler dair mah-luh
painting	das Gemälde dahs guh-<u>mail</u>-duh
palace	der Palast dair pah-<u>lahst</u>
park	der Park dair pahk
pedestrian zone	die Fußgängerzone
	dee <u>foos</u>-gheng-uh-tsoh-nuh
peninsula	die Halbinsel dee <u>hahlp</u>-in-zel
pillar	die Säule dee zoi-luh
planetarium	das Planetarium
	dahs plah-nuh-<u>tah</u>-ree-oom
portrait	das Porträt dahs paw-<u>tray</u>
poster	das Plakat dahs plah-<u>kaht</u>
pottery	die Töpferei dee terp-fuh-<u>rye</u>
queen	die Königin dee <u>ker</u>-nee-ghen
relief	das Relief dahs rel-<u>yef</u>
remains	Überreste <u>ew</u>-buh-res-tuh
restored	restauriert res-tauw-<u>reert</u>
river	der Fluss dair floos
ruin	die Ruine dee roo-<u>ee</u>-nuh
sculptor	der Bildhauer dair <u>bilt</u>-how-uh

159

sculpture	die Skulptur dee skoolp-<u>toor</u>
square	der Platz dair plats
stadium	das Stadion dahs <u>shtah</u>-dee-on
statue	die Statue dee <u>shtah</u>-too-uh
style	der Stil dair shteel
synagogue	die Synagoge dee zin-ah-<u>go</u>-guh
temple	der Tempel dair temple
theater	das Theater dahs tay-<u>ah</u>-tuh
tour boat	das Ausflugsboot dahs <u>ows</u>-flooks-boat
tourist guide	der Fremdenführer dair <u>frem</u>-den-fur-uh
tower	der Turm dair toorm
town center	die Innenstadt dee <u>in</u>-nen-shtaht
town gate	das Stadttor dahs shtaht-tor
town hall	das Rathaus dahs raht-house
vault	das Gewölbe dahs guh-<u>verl</u>-buh
wall	die Mauer dee mauw-uh
window	das Fenster dahs fens-tuh
zoo	der Zoo dair tsoh

Cultural Events

What's on *this / next* week?	Welche Veranstaltungen finden *diese / nächste* Woche statt? velsh-uh fair-<u>ahn</u>-shtahl-toong-en fin-den *dee-zuh / nayx-tuh* vaw-kuh shtaht
Do you have a program of events?	Haben Sie einen Veranstaltungs-kalender? hah-ben zee eye-nen fair-<u>ahn</u>-shtahl-toongs-kah-len-duh
What's on tonight?	Was wird heute Abend gespielt? vahs veert hoi-tuh ah-bent ghe-<u>shpeelt</u>

Where can I get tickets?

Wo bekommt man Karten?
vo buh-<u>komt</u> mahn kah-ten

When does … start?

Wann beginnt … vahn buh-<u>gheent</u>

– the performance

– **die Vorstellung?**
dee <u>faw</u>-shtel-oong

– the concert

– **das Konzert?** dahs kon-<u>tsairt</u>

– the film

– **der Film?** dair film

What time does the performance end?

Wann ist die Vorstellung zu Ende?
vahn ist dee <u>vaw</u>-shtel-oong tsoo <u>en</u>-duh?

Can I reserve tickets?

Kann man Karten reservieren lassen? kahn mahn kah-ten ray-zair-<u>veer</u>-en lahs-sen

I reserved tickets under the name of …

Ich hatte Karten vorbestellt auf den Namen … ish haht-uh kah-ten <u>faw</u>-buh-shtelt owf dane nah-men …

Do you have any tickets for today?

Haben Sie noch Karten für heute?
hah-ben zee nawk kah-ten fur hoi-tuh

How much are the tickets?

Wie viel kosten die Karten?
vee feel kaws-ten dee kah-ten

One ticket / Two tickets for …, please.

Bitte *eine Karte / zwei Karten* für … bit-tuh *eye-nuh kah-tuh / tsvigh kah-ten* fur …

– today

– **heute.** hoi-tuh

– tonight

– **heute Abend.** hoi-tuh ah-bent

– tomorrow

– **morgen.** maw-gen

– the … o'clock performance.

– **die Vorstellung um … Uhr.**
dee <u>vaw</u>-shtel-oong oom … oor

– the … o'clock movie.

– **den Film um … Uhr.**
dane film oom … oor

Are there discounts for ...	Gibt es eine Ermäßigung für ... gheept es eye-nuh air-<u>macy</u>-goong fur ...
– children?	– Kinder? kin-duh
– senior citizens?	– Senioren? sen-<u>yor</u>-en
– students?	– Studenten? shtoo-<u>den</u>-ten
I'd like to rent a pair of opera glasses.	Ich möchte ein Opernglas ausleihen. ish mush-tuh eye-n <u>o</u>-pairn-glahs <u>ows</u>-lie-en

info Local papers and, in bigger cities, weekly entertainment guides tell you what's on. In large cities like Munich, Hamburg and Berlin you'll even find publications in English.

At the Box Office

Abendkasse	box office
Ausverkauft	sold out
Erster Rang	front mezzanine
Galerie	balcony
Links	left
Loge	box
Mitte	center
Parkett	orchestra (seating)
Platz	seat
Rechts	right
Reihe	row
Stehplatz	standing room ticket
Vorverkauf	advance booking
Zweiter Rang	rear mezzanine

Cultural Events: Additional Words

actor	der Schauspieler
	dair <u>shauw</u>-shpee-luh
actress	die Schauspielerin
	dee <u>shauw</u>-spee-luh-rin
ballet	das Ballett dahs bah-<u>lett</u>
cabaret	das Kabarett dahs kah-bah-<u>rett</u>
choir	der Chor dair kore
circus	der Zirkus dair <u>tsir</u>-koos
coatroom	die Garderobe dee gah-duh-<u>ro</u>-buh
conductor	der Dirigent dair dee-ree-<u>ghent</u>
director	der Regisseur dair reh-jee-<u>ser</u>
festival	das Festspiel dahs fest-shpeel
intermission	die Pause dee pow-zuh
movie theater	das Kino dahs kee-no
music	die Musik dee moo-<u>zeck</u>
musical	das Musical dahs musical
open-air theater	die Freilichtbühne
	dee <u>fry</u>-lisht-bew-nuh
opening night	die Premiere dee prem-<u>yair</u>-uh
opera	die Oper dee oh-pair
operetta	die Operette dee oh-pair-<u>et</u>-tuh
orchestra	das Orchester dahs aw-<u>kest</u>-tuh
original version	die Originalfassung
	dee aw-ree-ghee-<u>nahl</u>-fah-soong
play	das Theaterstück
	dahs tay-<u>ah</u>-tuh-shtewk
pop concert	das Popkonzert dahs <u>pop</u>-kon-tsairt
program	das Programmheft
	dahs proh-<u>grahm</u>-heft
seat	der Platz dair plats
subtitle	der Untertitel dair <u>oon</u>-tair-tee-tel
theater	das Theater dahs tay-<u>ah</u>-tuh
variety show	das Varieté dahs vah-ree-ay-<u>tay</u>

163

Nightlife

What's there to do here in the evening?	Was kann man hier abends unternehmen? wahs kahn mahn here ah-bens oon-tuh-<u>nay</u>-men
Is it for *younger / older* people?	Ist dort mehr *jüngeres / älteres* Publikum? ist dawt mair *<u>yewng</u>-air-es / <u>el</u>-tair-es* <u>poo</u>-blee-koom
Is evening attire required?	Trägt man dort Abendgarderobe? traygt mahn dawt <u>ah</u>-bent-gah-duh-ro-buh
Is this seat taken?	Ist hier schon besetzt? ist here shone buh-<u>zetst</u>
What would you like to drink?	Was *möchten Sie / möchtest du* trinken? wahs *mush-ten zee / mush-test doo* trink-en
Would you like to dance?	Tanzen Sie mit mir? tahn-tsen zee mit mere
You dance very well.	Sie tanzen sehr gut. zee tahn-tsen zair goot

▶ Asking Someone Out, page 19

Nightlife: Additional Words

bar	die Bar dee bah
bar (counter)	die Theke dee tay-kuh
casino	das Spielkasino dahs <u>shpeel</u>-kah-zeen-o
cocktail	der Cocktail dair cocktail
drink	der Drink dair drink
loud	laut lout

164

Money,
Mail and
Police

I'd like to cash some traveler's checks.
Ich möchte Reiseschecks einlösen.

Where's the nearest post office?
Wo ist das nächste Postamt?

Money Matters

info The currency in Germany and Austria is the Euro, devided into 100 cents (**Cent**), the currency in Switzerland is the Swiss franc, **Schweizer Franken**, devided into 100 **Rappen** Most banks provide exchange services. Cash can also be obtained from ATMs with credit cards. Instructions are often in English.

Excuse me, where's there a bank around here?	**Entschuldigung, wo ist hier eine Bank?** ent-<u>shool</u>-dee-ghoong vo ist here eye-nuh bahnk
Where can I exchange some money?	**Wo kann ich Geld wechseln?** vo kahn ish ghelt vex-eln
I'd like to change … *dollars / pounds*.	**Ich möchte …** *Dollar / Pfund* **umtauschen.** ish mush-tuh … *dol-ahr / pfoond* <u>oom</u>-tauwsh-en
I'd like to cash some travelers checks.	**Ich möchte Reisechecks einlösen.** ish mush-tuh <u>rise</u>-uh-sheks eye-n-ler-zen
Ihren Pass, bitte.	Your passport, please.
Unterschreiben Sie bitte hier.	Sign here, please.
Wie möchten Sie das Geld haben?	How would you like it?
In small bills, please.	**In kleinen Scheinen, bitte.** in kline-nen shy-nen bit-tuh
Please give me some change as well.	**Geben Sie mir bitte auch etwas Kleingeld.** gay-ben zee mere bit-tuh owk et-vahs kline-ghelt

► *Numbers, see inside front cover*

Money Matters: Additional Words

amount	der Betrag dair buh-<u>trahk</u>
automatic teller machine (ATM)	der Geldautomat dair <u>ghelt</u>-ow-to-maht
card number	die Kartennummer dee <u>kah</u>-ten-noom-muh
cash transfer	die Banküberweisung dee <u>bahnk</u>-ew-buh-vize-oong
coin	die Münze dee mewnt-suh
counter	der Schalter dair shahl-tuh
credit card	die Kreditkarte dee kreh-<u>deet</u>-kah-tuh
currency	die Währung dee vair-oong
currency exchange	die Wechselstube dee <u>vex</u>-el-shtoo-buh
exchange rate	der Kurs dair koors
PIN	die Geheimzahl dee guh-<u>hime</u>-tsahl
savings bank	die Sparkasse dee <u>shpah</u>-kahs-suh
signature	die Unterschrift dee <u>oon</u>-tuh-shrift
transfer	die Überweisung dee ew-buh-<u>vize</u>-oong

Post Office

Where's the nearest *post office / mailbox*?	Wo ist *das nächste Postamt / der nächste Briefkasten*? vo ist *dahs nayx-tuh post-ahmt / dair nayx-tuh <u>brief</u>-kahs-ten*
How much is a *letter / postcard* to …	Was kostet *ein Brief / eine Karte* nach … vahs kaws-tet *eye-n brief / eye-nuh kah-tuh* nahk

Three ...-cent stamps, please.	Drei Briefmarken zu ... Cent, bitte. dry brief-mah-ken tsoo ... tsent bit-tuh
I'd like to send this letter ..., please.	Diesen Brief ... bitte. dee-zen brief ... bit-tuh
– by airmail	– per Luftpost pair looft-post
– special delivery	– per Express pair ex-press
– by regular mail	– per Seepost pair zeh-post
I'd like to send this package.	Ich möchte dieses Paket aufgeben. ish mush-tuh dee-zes pah-kate owf-gay-ben

Post Office: Additional Words

address	die Adresse dee ah-dress-uh
addressee	der Empfänger dair emp-feng-uh
declaration of value	die Wertangabe dee vairt-ahn-gah-buh
express letter	der Eilbrief dair eye-l-brief
insured package	das Wertpaket dahs vairt-pah-kate
package	das Paket dahs pah-kate
postcard	die Ansichtskarte dee ahn-zishts-kah-tuh
to send	schicken shik-en
sender	der Absender dair ahp-zen-duh
small package	das Päckchen dahs pek-shen
stamp	die Briefmarke dee brief-mah-kuh
zip code	die Postleitzahl dee post-light-tsahl

Police

info	To get the Polizei in an emergency, call 110 in Germany, 133 in Austria and 117 in Switzerland.

Where's the nearest police station?	**Wo ist das nächste Polizeirevier?** vo ist dahs nayx-tuh po-leet-<u>sigh</u>-ruh-veer

I'd like to report …
Ich möchte … anzeigen. ish mush-tuh … <u>ahn</u>-tsigh-ghen

a theft.
– einen Diebstahl eye-nen deep-shtahl

– a mugging.
– einen Überfall eye-nen <u>ew</u>-buh-fahl

– a rape.
– eine Vergewaltigung eye-nuh fair-guh-<u>vahl</u>-tee-goong

▶ *Accidents, page 51*

My … has been stolen.
Man hat mir … gestohlen. mahn haht mere … guh-<u>shtoh</u>-len

I've lost …
Ich habe … verloren. ish hah-buh … fair-<u>loh</u>-ren

My car's been broken into.
Mein Auto ist aufgebrochen worden. mine <u>ow</u>-to ist <u>owf</u>-guh-brawk-en vor-den

I've been *cheated / beaten up.*
Ich bin *betrogen / zusammengeschlagen* worden. ish bin buh-<u>tro</u>-gen / tsoo-<u>zahm</u>-men-guh-shlah-gen vor-den

I need a report for insurance purposes.	Ich brauche eine Bescheinigung für meine Versicherung. ish brow-khuh eye-nuh beh-<u>shine</u>-ih-goong fur my-nuh fair-<u>zik</u>-uh-roong
I'd like to speak to my *lawyer* / *consulate*.	Ich möchte mit meinem *Anwalt* / *Konsulat* sprechen. ish mush-tuh mit my-nem *ahn-vahlt* / *kon-zoo-<u>laht</u>* shpre-shen
I'm innocent.	Ich bin unschuldig. ish bin <u>oon</u>-shool-dik
Ihren Ausweis, bitte.	Your identification, please.
Wenden Sie sich bitte an Ihr Konsulat.	Please contact your consulate.

Police: Additional Words

accident	der Unfall dair oon-fahl
to arrest	verhaften vair-<u>hahf</u>-ten
handbag	die Handtasche dee <u>hahnt</u>-tah-shuh
lost and found	das Fundbüro dahs <u>foont</u>-bew-<u>ro</u>
to molest	belästigen buh-<u>les</u>-tee-ghen
narcotics	das Rauschgift dahs rauwsh-gift
pickpocket	der Taschendieb dair <u>tah</u>-shen-deep
policeman	der Polizist dair po-lee-<u>tsist</u>
policewoman	die Polizistin dee po-lee-<u>tsis</u>-tin
radio	das Radio dahs rah-dee-o
thief	der Dieb dair deep
wallet	das Portemonnaie dahs pawt-mo-<u>nay</u>
witness	der Zeuge dair tsoi-guh

Health

I need this medicine.
Ich brauche dieses Medikament.

Please call a doctor.
Bitte rufen Sie einen Arzt.

Pharmacy

Where's the nearest pharmacy?	**Wo ist die nächste Apotheke?** vo ist dee nayx-tuh ah-po-<u>tay</u>-kuh
Do you have anything for …?	**Haben Sie etwas gegen …?** hah-ben zee et-wahs gay-ghen

► *Illnesses and Complaints, page 182*

I need this medicine.	**Ich brauche dieses Medikament.** ish brow-kuh dee-zes med-ee-kah-<u>ment</u>
A small pack will do.	**Eine kleine Packung genügt.** eye-nuh kline-nuh pah-koong guh-<u>newgt</u>
Dieses Medikament ist rezeptpflichtig.	You need a prescription for this medicine.
Das haben wir leider nicht da.	I'm afraid we don't have that.
When can I pick it up?	**Wann kann ich es abholen?** vahn cahn ish es <u>ahp</u>-hol-en
How should I take it?	**Wie muss ich es einnehmen?** vee moos ish es <u>eye-n</u>-nay-men

Medication Information

ingredients	Zusammensetzung
active ingredient	Wirkstoff
applications	Anwendungsgebiete
contraindications	Gegenanzeigen
dosage instructions	Dosierungsanleitung

infants	Säuglinge
children (*over/under* … years)	Kinder (*ab / bis zu* … Jahren)
pregnant women	schwangere Frauen
adults	Erwachsene
three times a day	dreimal täglich
one tablet / one caplet	eine Tablette / eine Kapsel
ten drops	zehn Tropfen
one teaspoon	ein Teelöffel
to be taken as directed	nach Anweisung des Arztes

directions	Einnahme

dissolve on the tongue	im Munde zergehen lassen
before / after meals	*vor / nach* dem Essen
on an empty stomach	auf nüchternen Magen
to be swallowed whole, unchewed	unzerkaut einnehmen

application	Anwendung

external	äußerlich
rectal	rektal
internal	innerlich
oral	oral

side effects	Nebenwirkungen

may cause drowsiness	kann zu Müdigkeit führen
you are advised not to drive	kann zu Beeinträchtigungen im Straßenverkehr führen

Medicine and Medications

adhesive bandage	das Pflaster dahs flahs-tuh
after sunburn lotion	die Salbe gegen Sonnenbrand dee zahl-buh gay-ghen <u>zon</u>-nen-brahnt
anti-itch cream	die Salbe gegen Juckreiz dee zahl-buh gay-gen <u>yook-rights</u>
antibiotic	das Antibiotikum dahs ahn-tee-bee-<u>o</u>-tee-koom
antiseptic	das Desinfektionsmittel dahs des-in-fek-tsee-<u>ohns</u>-mit-tel
antiseptic ointment	die Wundsalbe dee <u>voont</u>-zahl-buh
birth control pill	die Antibabypille dee ahn-tee-<u>bay</u>-bee-pil-luh
condom	das Kondom dahs con-<u>dome</u>
cough medicine	der Hustensaft dair <u>hoo</u>-sten-zahft
drops	Tropfen trop-fen
ear drops	Ohrentropfen <u>o</u>-ren-trop-fen
elastic bandage	die Elastikbinde dee ay-<u>lahs</u>-teek-bin-duh
eye drops	Augentropfen <u>ow</u>-ghen-trop-fen
first-aid kit	das Verbandszeug dahs vair-<u>bahnts</u>-tsoik
gauze bandage	die Mullbinde dee <u>mool</u>-bin-duh
headache pill	die Kopfschmerztablette dee <u>kopf</u>-shmairts-tah-blet-tuh
homeopathic	homöopathisch ho-meh-o-<u>pah</u>-tish
indigestion tablet	die Magentablette dee <u>mah</u>-ghen-tah-blet-tuh
injection	die Spritze dee shprits-uh
insulin	das Insulin dahs in-soo-<u>leen</u>
iodine	das Jod dahs yoht
laxative	das Abführmittel dahs <u>ahp</u>-fur-mit-tel
nose drops	Nasentropfen <u>nah</u>-zen-trop-fen

174

ointment	die Salbe dee zahl-buh
ointment for mosquito bites	die Salbe gegen Mückenstiche dee zahl-buh gay-gen <u>mewk</u>-en-shtish-uh
painkiller	das Schmerzmittel dahs <u>shmairts</u>-mit-tel
powder	das Pulver dahs pool-vuh
prescription	das Rezept dahs ray-<u>tsept</u>
sleeping pill	die Schlaftablette dee <u>shlahf</u>-tah-blet-ten
something for …	etwas gegen … et-vahs gay-ghen …
suppository	das Zäpfchen dahs tsepf-shen
tablet	die Tablette dee tah-blet-tuh
thermometer	das Fieberthermometer dahs <u>fee</u>-buh-tair-mo-may-tuh
throat drop	die Halsschmerztablette die <u>hahls</u>-shmairts-tah-blet-tuh
tranquilizer	das Beruhigungsmittel dahs buh-<u>roo-ee</u>-goongs-mit-tel

info In a medical emergency, call for an ambulance: In Germany and Austria dial 112, in Austria and in Switzerland 144 (most areas).

Looking for a Doctor

Can you recommend a *doctor / dentist*?	Können Sie mir einen praktischen *Arzt / Zahnarzt* empfehlen? kern-en zee mere eye-nen <u>prahk</u>-tish-en *ahtst / tsahn-ahtst* emp-<u>fay</u>-len
Does *he / she* speak English?	Spricht *er / sie* Englisch? shprisht *air / zee* ayng-lish

Where's *his / her* office?	**Wo ist *seine / ihre* Praxis?** vo ist *zeye-nuh / ee-ruh* prahk-sis
Can *he / she* come here?	**Kann *er / sie* herkommen?** kahn *air / zee* <u>hair</u>-kom-en
Please call *an ambulance / a doctor!*	**Rufen Sie bitte einen *Kranken-wagen / Arzt!*** roo-fen zee bit-tuh eye-nen <u>*krahn*</u>-*ken-vah-ghen / ahtst*
My husband / wife is sick.	***Mein Mann / Meine Frau* ist krank.** *mine mahn / my-nuh frow* ist krahnk

Physicians

dentist	**der Zahnarzt** dair tsahn-ahtst
dermatologist	**der Hautarzt** dair howt-ahtst
doctor	**der Arzt** dair ahtst
ear, nose and throat doctor	**der Hals-Nasen-Ohren-Arzt** dair hahls-nah-zen-<u>o-ren</u>-ahtst
eye specialist	**der Augenarzt** dair <u>ow</u>-gen-ahtst
female doctor	**die Ärztin** dee airts-tin
female gynecologist	**die Frauenärztin** dee <u>frow</u>-en-airts-tin
homeopathic doctor	**der Heilpraktiker** dair <u>highl</u>-prahk-tee-kuh
internist	**der Internist** dair in-tair-<u>nist</u>
orthopedist	**der Orthopäde** dair or-to-<u>pay</u>-duh
pediatrician	**der Kinderarzt** dair <u>kin</u>-duh-ahtst
urologist	**der Urologe** dair oor-o-<u>lo</u>-guh
veterinarian	**der Tierarzt** dair teer-ahtst

▶ *At the Dentist's, page 187*

At the Doctor's Office

I have a (bad) cold.	**Ich bin (stark) erkältet.** ish bin (shtahk) air-<u>kel</u>-tet
I don't feel well.	**Ich fühle mich nicht wohl.** ish fewl-uh mish nisht vohl
I'm dizzy.	**Mir ist schwindelig.** mere ist <u>shvin</u>-duh-lish
I have …	**Ich habe …** ish hah-buh …
– a headache	– **Kopfschmerzen** <u>kopf</u>-shmairts-en
– a sore throat	– **Halsschmerzen** <u>hahls</u>-shmairts-en
– a (very high) temperature.	– **(hohes) Fieber.** (ho-es) fee-buh
– the flu.	– **eine Grippe.** eye-nuh grip-puh
– diarrhea.	– **Durchfall.** doorsh-fahl
My … *hurts / hurt*.	**Mir tut / tun … weh.** mere *toot / toon* … vay

▶ *Body Parts and Organs, page 180*

It hurts here.	**Hier habe ich Schmerzen.** here hah-buh ish shmairts-en

I've vomited (several times).	Ich habe mich (mehrmals) übergeben. ish hah-buh mish (mair-mahls) ew-buh-<u>gay</u>-ben
I've got an upset stomach.	Ich habe mir den Magen verdorben. ish hah-buh mere dane mah-gen fair-<u>daw</u>-ben
I was unconscious.	Ich war ohnmächtig. ish vahr <u>ohn</u>-mesh-tish
I can't move (my) ….	Ich kann … nicht bewegen. ish kahn … nisht buh-<u>vay</u>-ghen
I've hurt myself.	Ich habe mich verletzt. ish hah-buh mish fair-<u>letst</u>
I fell.	Ich bin gestürzt. ish bin guh-<u>shtewrtst</u>
I've been *stung* / *bitten* by ….	Ich bin von … *gestochen* / *gebissen* worden. ish bin fun … guh-<u>shtawk</u>-en / guh-<u>bis</u>-sen vaw-den
I'm allergic to penicillin.	Ich bin allergisch gegen Penizillin. ish bin ah-<u>lair</u>-ghish gay-ghen pen-ee-tsee-<u>leen</u>
I've got *high* / *low* blood pressure.	Ich habe *hohen* / *niedrigen* Blutdruck. ish hah-buh *ho-en* / *<u>nee</u>-dree-ghen* bloot-drook
I've got a pacemaker.	Ich habe einen Herzschrittmacher. ish hah-buh eye-nen <u>hairts</u>-shrit-mahk-uh
I'm (… months) pregnant.	Ich bin (im … Monat) schwanger. ish bin (im … mo-naht) shvahng-uh
I'm diabetic.	Ich bin Diabetiker. ish bin dee-ah-<u>bay</u>-tee-kuh

Wo haben Sie Schmerzen?	Where does it hurt?
Tut es hier weh?	Does that hurt?
Öffnen Sie den Mund.	Open your mouth.
Bitte machen Sie den Oberkörper frei.	Undress to the waist, please.
Wir müssen Sie röntgen.	We'll have to X-ray you.
Atmen Sie tief ein. Atem anhalten.	Take a deep breath. Hold your breath.
Wie lange haben Sie diese Beschwerden schon?	How long have you had this problem?
Ich brauche eine Blutprobe / Urinprobe.	I'll need a blood / urine sample.
Sie müssen operiert werden.	You'll have to have an operation.
Es ist nichts Ernstes.	It's nothing serious.
Kommen Sie *morgen* / *in … Tagen* wieder.	Come back *tomorrow* / *in … days*.
Can you give me a doctor's note?	**Können Sie mir ein Attest ausstellen?** kern-en zee mere eye-n ah-<u>test</u> ows-shtel-len
Do I have to come back?	**Muss ich noch einmal kommen?** moos ish nawk eye-n-mal kom-en
Please give me a receipt for my medical insurance.	**Geben Sie mir bitte eine Quittung für meine Versicherung.** gay-ben zee mere eye-nuh kvit-toong fur my-nuh fair-<u>zish</u>-air-oong

Body Parts and Organs

abdomen	der Bauch dair bowk
ankle	der Knöchel dair kuh-<u>neh</u>-shel
appendix	der Blinddarm dair blint-dahm
arm	der Arm dair ahm
back	der Rücken dair rewk-ken
bladder	die Blase dee blah-zuh
blood	das Blut dahs bloot
body	der Körper dair ker-puh
bone	der Knochen dair kuh-<u>naw</u>-ken
bottom	das Gesäß dahs guh-<u>zess</u>
brain	das Gehirn dahs guh-<u>heern</u>
bronchial tubes	Bronchien <u>brawn</u>-shee-en
calf	die Wade dee vah-duh
cartilage	der Knorpel dair kuh-<u>naw</u>-pel
chest	die Brust dee broost
collarbone	das Schlüsselbein dahs <u>shlews</u>-sel-bine
disc	die Bandscheibe dee <u>bahnt</u>-shigh-buh
ear	das Ohr dahs aw-uh
eye	das Auge dahs ow-guh
face	das Gesicht dahs guh-<u>zisht</u>
finger	der Finger dair fing-uh
foot	der Fuß dair foos
forehead	die Stirn dee shteern
frontal sinus	die Stirnhöhle dee <u>steern</u>-her-luh
gall bladder	die Galle dee gahl-luh
genital	das Geschlechtsorgan dahs guh-<u>shleshts</u>-aw-gahn
hand	die Hand dee hahnt
head	der Kopf dair kopf
heart	das Herz dahs heirts

heel	die Ferse dee fair-zuh
hip	die Hüfte dee hewf-tuh
intestine	der Darm dair dahm
joint	das Gelenk dahs guh-<u>lenk</u>
kidney	die Niere dee nee-ruh
knee	das Knie dahs kuh-<u>nee</u>
kneecap	die Kniescheibe dee kuh-<u>nee</u>-shigh-buh
leg	das Bein dahs bine
liver	die Leber dee lay-buh
lung	die Lunge dee loong-uh
mouth	der Mund dair moont
mucus membrane	die Schleimhaut dee shlime-howt
muscle	der Muskel dair moos-kel
neck	der Hals dair hahls
neck	der Nacken dair nahk-en
nerve	der Nerv dair nairf
nose	die Nase dee nah-zuh
pelvis	das Becken dahs bek-en
rib	die Rippe dee rip-puh
shinbone	das Schienbein dahs sheen-bine
shoulder	die Schulter dee shool-tuh
sinus	die Nebenhöhle dee <u>nay</u>-ben-her-luh
skin	die Haut dee howt
spine	die Wirbelsäule dee <u>veer</u>-bel-zoi-luh
stomach	der Magen dair mah-ghen
tendon	die Sehne dee zay-nuh
throat	der Hals dair hahls
thyroid gland	die Schilddrüse dee <u>shilt</u>-drew-zuh
toe	die Zehe dee tsay-uh
tongue	die Zunge dee tsoong-uh
tonsils	Mandeln mahn-deln
tooth	der Zahn dair tsahn
vertebrae	der Wirbel dair veer-bel

Illnesses and Complaints

abscess	der Abszess dair ahps-<u>tsess</u>
AIDS	das Aids dahs aids
allergy	die Allergie dee ah-lair-<u>ghee</u>
appendicitis	die Blinddarmentzündung
	dee <u>blint</u>-dahm-ent-zewn-doong
asthma	das Asthma dahs ahst-mah
bite	der Biss dair biss, der Stich dair shtish
blister	die Blase dee blah-zuh
blood pressure	der Blutdruck dair bloot-drook
blood poisoning	die Blutvergiftung
	dee <u>bloot</u>-fair-ghif-toong
breathing problems	Atembeschwerden
	<u>ah</u>-tem-buh-shvair-den
broken	gebrochen guh-<u>braw</u>-khen
bronchitis	die Bronchitis dee bron-<u>shee</u>-tis
bruise	die Prellung dee <u>prel</u>-loong
burn	die Verbrennung
	dee fair-<u>bren</u>-noong
bypass	der Bypass dair by-pahs
cancer	der Krebs dair krayps
cardiac infarction	der Herzinfarkt dair <u>heirts</u>-in-fahkt
chicken pox	Windpocken <u>vint</u>-paw-ken
chills	der Schüttelfrost dair <u>shew</u>-tel-frost
circulatory problems	Kreislaufstörungen
	<u>krighs</u>-lauf-shter-oong-en
cold	die Erkältung dee air-<u>kel</u>-toong
cold (nasal)	der Schnupfen dair shnoop-fen
colic	die Kolik dee ko-lik
concussion	die Gehirnerschütterung
	dee guh-<u>heern</u>-air-shew-tair-oong
conjunctivitis	die Bindehautentzündung
	dee <u>bin</u>-duh-howt-ent-zewn-doong

constipation	die Verstopfung
	dee fair-shtop-foong
cough	der Husten dair hoos-ten
cramp	der Krampf dair krahmpf
cyst	die Zyste dee tsis-tuh
cystitis	die Blasenentzündung
	dee blah-zen-ent-zewnd-doong
diabetes	die Diabetes dee dee-ah-bay-tes
diarrhea	der Durchfall dair doorsh-fahl
disease	die Krankheit dee krahnk-hight
dislocated	verrenkt fair-renkt
dizziness	der Schwindel dair shvin-del
fever	das Fieber dahs fee-buh
flu	die Grippe dee grip-puh
food poisoning	die Lebensmittelvergiftung
	dee lay-bens-mit-tel-fair-ghif-toong
fungal infection	die Pilzinfektion
	dee pilts-in-fek-tsee-ohn
gallstones	Gallensteine gahl-len-shtigh-nuh
German measles	Röteln rer-teln
hay fever	der Heuschnupfen
	dair hoi-shnoop-fen
heart	das Herz dahs heirts
heart attack	der Herzanfall dair heirts-ahn-fahl
heart problem	der Herzfehler dair heirts-fay-luh
heartburn	das Sodbrennen dahs zoht-bren-nen
hemorrhage	die Blutung dee bloo-toong
hemorrhoids	Hämorrhoiden hem-aw-ree-den
hernia	der Leistenbruch dair lice-ten-brookh
herpes	der Herpes dair hair-pes
high blood pressure	der hohe Blutdruck
	dair ho-uh bloot-drook
infection	die Infektion dee in-fek-tsee-ohn
infectious	ansteckend ahn-shtek-ent

inflammation	die Entzündung
	dee ent-<u>zewn</u>-doong
inflammation of the middle ear	die Mittelohrentzündung
	dee <u>mit</u>-tel-aw-ent-zewn-doong
injury	die Verletzung dee fair-<u>lets</u>-oong
kidney stones	Nierensteine <u>nearen</u>-shtigh-nuh
low blood pressure	der niedrige Blutdruck dair nee-drih-guh bloot-drook
lower back pain	der Hexenschuss dair <u>hex</u>-en-shoos
malaria	die Malaria dee mah-<u>lah</u>-ree-ah
measles	Masern mah-zairn
meningitis	die Hirnhautentzündung
	dee <u>hirn</u>-howt-ent-zewn-doong
migraine	die Migräne dee mee-<u>gray</u>-nuh
motion sickness	die Reisekrankheit
	dee <u>rise</u>-uh-krahnk-hight
mumps	der Mumps dair mumps
nausea	die Übelkeit dee <u>ew</u>-bel-kite
neuralgia	die Neuralgie dee noi-rahl-<u>ghee</u>
nose bleed	das Nasenbluten
	dahs <u>nah</u>-zen-bloo-ten
pacemaker	der Herzschrittmacher
	dair <u>heirts</u>-shrit-mahk-uh
period	die Menstruation
	dee men-stroo-ah-tsee-<u>ohn</u>
pneumonia	die Lungenentzündung
	dee <u>loong</u>-en-ent-zewn-doong
polio	die Kinderlähmung
	dee <u>kin</u>-duh-lay-moong
pulled ligament	die Bänderzerrung
	dee <u>ben</u>-duh-tsair-oong
pulled muscle	die Muskelzerrung
	dee <u>moos</u>-kel-tsair-oong
pulled tendon	die Sehnenzerrung
	dee <u>zay</u>-nen-tsair-oong

184

rash	der Ausschlag dair <u>ows</u>-shlahk
rheumatism	das Rheuma dahs <u>roi</u>-mah
salmonella poisoning	die Salmonellenvergiftung
	dee zahl-mo-<u>nel</u>-en-fair-ghif-toong
scarlet fever	der Scharlach dair <u>shah</u>-lahk
sciatica	der Ischias dair <u>ish</u>-ee-ahs
sexually transmitted	die Geschlechtskrankheit
disease (STD)	dee guh-<u>shlekts</u>-krahnk-hight
shock	der Schock dair shock
sore	das Geschwür dahs guh-<u>shvewr</u>
sprained	verstaucht fair-<u>shtowkt</u>
sting	der Stich dair shtish
stomach ache	der Magenschmerz
	dair <u>mah</u>-ghen-shmairts
stomach ulcer	das Magengeschwür
	dahs <u>mah</u>-gen-guh-shvewr
stroke	der Schlaganfall dair <u>shlahk</u>-ahn-fahl
sunburn	der Sonnenbrand
	dair <u>zon</u>-nen-brahnt
sunstroke	der Sonnenstich dair <u>zon</u>-nen-shtish
swelling	die Schwellung dee <u>shvel</u>-loong
tetanus	der Tetanus dair <u>teh</u>-tah-noos
tick bite	der Zeckenbiss dair <u>tsek</u>-en-biss
tonsillitis	die Madelentzündung
	dee <u>mahn</u>-del-ent-zewn-doong
torn ligament	der Bänderriss dair <u>ben</u>-duh-riss
tumor	der Tumor dair <u>too</u>-mor
ulcer	das Geschwür dahs guh-<u>shvewr</u>
vomiting	das Erbrechen dahs air-<u>bresh</u>-en
whooping cough	der Keuchhusten dair <u>koish</u>-hoos-ten
wound	die Wunde dee voon-duh

At the Hospital

I'd like to speak to a doctor.

Ich möchte mit einem Arzt sprechen. ish mush-tuh mit eye-nem ahtst shpre-shen

I'd rather have the operation in the US.

Ich möchte mich lieber in den USA operieren lassen. ish mush-tuh mish lee-buh in dane oo-es-_ah_ op-pair-_ree_-ren lahs-sen

Please let my family know.

Bitte benachrichtigen Sie meine Familie. bit-tuh buh-_nakh_-rish-tee-ghen zee my-nuh fah-_meel_-yuh

Could you help me, please?

Könnten Sie mir bitte helfen? kern-ten zee mere bit-tuh hel-fen

Could you give me a _painkiller / sleeping pill_?

Geben Sie mir etwas _gegen die Schmerzen / zum Einschlafen_. gay-ben zee mere et-vahs _gay-ghen dee shmairts-en / tsoom eye-n-shlah-fen_

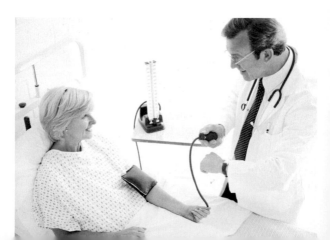

At the Dentist's

This tooth hurts.	**Dieser Zahn hier tut weh.** dee-zuh tsahn here toot vay
This tooth is broken.	**Der Zahn ist abgebrochen.** dair tsahn ist <u>aph</u>-guh-brawk-en
I've lost *a filling* / *a crown*.	**Ich habe eine *Füllung* / *Krone* verloren.** ish hah-buh eye-nuh *fewl-loong* / *kroh-nuh* fair-<u>loh</u>-ren
Could you do a temporary job on the tooth?	**Können Sie den Zahn provisorisch behandeln?** kern-en zee dane tsahn pro-vee-<u>zoh</u>-rish buh-<u>hahn</u>-deln
Give me an injection, please.	**Geben Sie mir bitte eine Spritze.** gay-ben zee mere bit-tuh eye-nuh shprits-uh
I'd rather not have an injection, please.	**Geben Sie mir bitte keine Spritze.** gay-ben zee mere bit-tuh kigh-nuh shprits-uh
Can you repair these dentures?	**Können Sie diese Prothese reparieren?** kern-en zee dee-zuh pro- <u>tay</u>-zuh ray-pah-<u>reer</u>-en
Sie brauchen ...	You need ...
– eine Brücke.	– a bridge.
– eine Füllung.	– a filling.
– eine Krone.	– a crown.
Ich muss den Zahn ziehen.	I'll have to take the tooth out.
Bitte zwei Stunden nichts essen.	Don't eat anything for two hours.

At the Dentist's: Additional Words

amalgam filling	die Amalgamfüllung
	dee ah-mahl-<u>gahm</u>-fewl-loong
brace	die Zahnspange
	dee <u>zahn</u>-shpahng-uh
cavity	die Karies dee <u>kah</u>-ree-es
composite filling	die Kunststofffüllung
	dee <u>koonst</u>-stawf-fewl-loong
denture	das Gebiss dahs guh-<u>biss</u>
gold filling	das Goldinlay dahs <u>gawlt</u>-in-lay
gum infection	die Zahnfleischentzündung
	dee <u>tsahn</u>-flysh-ent-zewn-doong
gum	das Zahnfleisch dahs tsahn-flysh
impression	der Abdruck dair ahp-drook
inlay	das Inlay dahs inlay
jaw	der Kiefer dair kee-fuh
nerve	der Nerv dair nairf
periodontal disease	die Parodontose
	dee pah-rah-dawn-<u>toe</u>-zuh
porcelain filling	die Porzellanfüllung
	dee paw-tsel-<u>lahn</u>-fewl-loong
root	die Wurzel dee voor-tsel
root canal	die Wurzelbehandlung
	dee <u>voor</u>-tsel-buh-hahnt-loong
tartar	der Zahnstein dair tsahn-shtein
temporary filling	das Provisorium
	dahs pro-vee-<u>zo</u>-ree-um
tooth	der Zahn dair tsahn
wisdom tooth	der Weisheitszahn
	dair <u>vice</u>-hights-tsahn

Time
and the
Calendar

What time is it?
Wie spät ist es?

It's 12:30.
Es ist halb eins.

The official time system uses the 24-hour clock. In ordinary conversation, time is often expressed as shown below, sometimes with the addition of **morgens** (in the morning), **nachmittags** (in the afternoon), **abends** (in the evening) or **nachts** (at night).

Time of the Day

What time is it?	**Wie spät ist es?** vee shpayt ist es
It's one o'clock.	**Es ist ein Uhr.** es ist eye-n oor
It's two o'clock.	**Es ist zwei Uhr.** es ist tsvigh oor
It's twelve o'clock.	**Es ist 12 Uhr.** es ist tsvelf oor
It's five after four.	**Es ist 5 (Minuten) nach 4.** es ist fewnf (min-oo-ten) nahk feer
It's a quarter after five.	**Es ist Viertel nach 5.** es ist feer-tel nahk fewnf
It's 6:30.	**Es ist halb 7.** es ist hahlp zee-ben
It's twenty-five to four.	**Es ist 15 Uhr 35.** es ist fewnf-tsane oor finf-oont-<u>dry</u>-sish
It's a quarter to nine.	**Es ist Viertel vor 9.** es ist feer-tel for noin
It's ten to eight.	**Es ist 10 (Minuten) vor 8.** es ist tsane (min-oo-ten) for ahkt
At what time?	**Um wie viel Uhr?** oom vee feel oor
At ten o'clock.	**Um 10 Uhr.** oom tsane oor
Until eleven (o'clock).	**Bis 11 (Uhr).** bis elf (oor)

190

———Time and the Calendar———

From eight till nine.	**Von 8 bis 9 Uhr.**
	fon ahkt bis noin oor
Between ten and twelve.	**Zwischen 10 und 12 Uhr.**
	tsvish-en tsane oont tsvelf oor
In half an hour.	**In einer halben Stunde.**
	in eye-nuh hahl-ben shtoon-duh
It's (too) late.	**Es ist (zu) spät.** es ist (tsoo) shpayt
It's too early.	**Es ist noch zu früh.**
	es ist nawk tsoo frew

➤ *Numbers, see inside front cover*

Time: Additional Words

a month ago	**vor einem Monat**
	faw eye-nem mo-naht
afternoon	**der Nachmittag** dair <u>nahk</u>-mit-tahk
at	**um** oom
at around noon	**mittags** mit-tahks
at night	**nachts** nahkts
day	**der Tag** dair tahk
early	**früh** frew
evening	**der Abend** dair ah-bent
for	**seit** zight
half an hour	**die halbe Stunde**
	dee hahl-buh shtoon-duh
hour	**die Stunde** dee shtoon-duh
in the afternoon	**am Nachmittag** ahm <u>nahk</u>-mit-tahk
in the evening	**abends** ah-bens
in the morning	**morgens** maw-ghens
in two weeks	**in 14 Tagen** in feer-zane tah-gen
late	**spät** shpayt
later	**später** shpay-tuh

191

minute	die Minute dee min-oo-tuh
month	der Monat dair mo-naht
morning	der Vormittag dair <u>faw</u>-mit-tahk
next year	nächstes Jahr nayx-tes yah
night	die Nacht die nahkt
now	jetzt yetst
quarter of an hour	die Viertelstunde
	dee feer-tel-<u>shtoon</u>-duh
recently	vor kurzem faw koorts-em
second	die Sekunde dee zeh-<u>koon</u>-duh
since	seit zight
sometimes	manchmal mahnsh-mahl
soon	bald bahlt
the day after tomorrow	übermorgen <u>ew</u>-buh-maw-ghen
the day before yesterday	vorgestern <u>faw</u>-ghes-tairn
this afternoon	heute Nachmittag
	hoi-tuh <u>nahk</u>-mit-tahk
this morning	heute Morgen hoi-tuh maw-ghen
time	die Zeit dee tsight
today	heute hoi-tuh
tomorrow	morgen maw-ghen
tonight	heute Abend hoi-tuh ah-bent
until	bis bis
week	die Woche dee vaw-kuh
year	das Jahr dahs yah
yesterday	gestern ghes-tairn

Seasons

spring	der Frühling dair frew-ling
summer	der Sommer dair zaw-muh
fall	der Herbst dair hairpst
winter	der Winter dair winter

Date

What's today's date?	**Den Wievielten haben wir heute?** dane <u>vee</u>-feel-ten hah-ben veer hoi-tuh
Today's July 2nd.	**Heute ist der 2. Juli.** hoi-tuh ist dair tsvigh-tuh you-lee
On the 4th of *this* / *next* month.	**Am 4. *dieses* / *nächsten* Monats.** ahm feer-ten *dee-zes* / *nayx-ten* mo-nahts
Until March 10th.	**Bis zum 10. März.** bis tsoom tsayn-ten mairts
We're leaving on August 20th.	**Wir reisen am 20. August ab.** veer rise-en ahm tsvahn-tsik-sten ow-<u>goost</u> ahp

Days of the Week

Monday	**Montag** moan-tahk
Tuesday	**Dienstag** deens-tahk
Wednesday	**Mittwoch** mit-vawk
Thursday	**Donnerstag** <u>dawn</u>-airs-tahk
Friday	**Freitag** fry-tahk
Saturday	**Samstag** zahms-tahk
Sunday	**Sonntag** zun-tahk

Months

January	**Januar** <u>yan</u>-oo-ahr
February	**Februar** <u>fay</u>-broo-ahr
March	**März** mairts
April	**April** ah-<u>pril</u>

May	Mai my
June	Juni you-nee
July	Juli you-lee
August	August ow-_goost_
September	September sep_tem_ber
October	Oktober oc_tob_er
November	November no_vem_ber
December	Dezember day-_tsem_-ber

Holidays

All Saints' Day	Allerheiligen ahl-lair-_high_-lee-ghen
Ascension	Himmelfahrt _him_-mel-faht
Assumption	Mariä Himmelfahrt mah-_ree_-ah _him_-mel-faht
Christmas	Weihnachten _vy_-nahk-ten
Christmas Day	Weihnachtstag airs-tuh _vy_-nahkts-tahk
Christmas Eve	Heiligabend high-lik-_ah_-bent
Corpus Christi	Fronleichnam frohn-_lye_-shnahm
Easter	Ostern oh-stairn
Easter Monday	Ostermontag oh-stair-_mohn_-tahk
Good Friday	Karfreitag kah-_fry_-tahk
Labor Day (May 1st)	Tag der Arbeit tahk dair ah-bite
Mardi gras	Fasching, Karneval, Fassnacht fah-shing, _kah_-nuh-vahl, fahs-nahkt
National Unity Day (October 3rd)	Tag der Deutschen Einheit tahk dair doi-tschen eye-n-hite
New Year's Day	Neujahr noi-yah
New Year's Eve	Silvester zil-_ves_-tuh
Pentecost	Pfingsten fing-sten

Weather
and
Environment

What nice weather we're having today!
Was für ein schönes Wetter heute!

What's the weather forecast?
Was sagt der Wetterbericht?

Weather

What *nice / terrible*
weather we're having
today!

Was für ein *schönes / schlechtes*
Wetter heute! vahs fur eye-n *sh-
ern-es / shlesh-tes* vet-tuh hoi-tuh

What's the weather
going to be like *today /
tomorrow*?

Wie wird das Wetter *heute / morgen*? vee veert dahs vet-tuh
hoi-tuh / maw-ghen

What's the weather
forecast?

Was sagt der Wetterbericht?
vahs zahkt dair vet-tuh-buh-risht

It's / It's going to be …

Es *ist / wird* … es *ist / veert* …

– nice.
– bad.
– warm.
– hot.
– cold.
– humid.

– schön. shern
– schlecht. shlesht
– warm. vahm
– heiß. hice
– kalt. kahlt
– schwül. shwewl

It's going to *rain / be
stormy*.

Es wird *Regen / ein Gewitter*
geben. es veert *ray-ghen / eye-n
guh-<u>vit</u>-tuh gay-ben*

The sun's shining.

Die Sonne scheint.
dee zon-nuh shine-t

It's pretty windy.

Es ist ziemlich windig.
es ist <u>tseem</u>-lish vin-dik

It's raining.

Es regnet. es rayg-net

It's snowing.

Es schneit. es shnight

What's the
temperature?

Wie viel Grad haben wir?
vee feel graht hah-ben veer

——— Weather and Environment ———

It's … degrees
(centigrade).

Es sind … Grad (Celsius).
es sint … graht (<u>tsel</u>-see-oos)

▶ *Numbers, see inside front cover*

Weather: Additional Words

air	die Luft dee looft
barometric pressur	der Luftdruck dair looft-drook
black ice	das Glatteis dahs glaht-ice
bright	heiter high-tuh
clear	klar klahr
climate	das Klima dahs klee-mah
cloud	die Wolke dee vol-kuh
cloudy	bewölkt buh-<u>vulkt</u>
cool	kühl kewl
damp	feucht foisht
dawn	die Dämmerung dee <u>dem</u>-mair-oong
degree	der Grad dair graht
drizzle	der Nieselregen dair <u>nee</u>-zel-ray-ghen
dry	trocken <u>trawk</u>-en
dusk	die Dämmerung dee <u>dem</u>-mair-oong
fog	der Nebel dair nay-bel
frost	der Frost dair frawst
hail	der Hagel dair hah-ghel
hazy	diesig <u>dee</u>-zik
heat	die Hitze dee hit-tsuh
heatwave	die Hitzewelle dee <u>hit</u>-tsuh-vel-luh
lightning	der Blitz dair blits
moon	der Mond dair mohnt

197

precipitation	der Niederschlag
	dair <u>nee</u>-duh-shlahk
rainy	regnerisch <u>rake</u>-nair-ish
shower	der Regenschauer
	dair <u>ray</u>-ghen-show-uh
snow	der Schnee dair shnay
star	der Stern dair stairn
storm	der Sturm dair shtoorm
stormy	stürmisch shtewr-mish
sun	die Sonne dee zon-nuh
sunny	sonnig zon-nik
sunrise	der Sonnenaufgang
	dair <u>zon</u>-nen-owf-gahng
sunset	der Sonnenuntergang
	dair <u>zon</u>-nen-oont-uh-gahng
temperature	die Temperatur
	dee tem-peh-rah-<u>toor</u>
thunder	der Donner dair dawn-nuh
thunderstorm	das Unwetter dahs <u>oon</u>-vet-tuh
variable	wechselhaft <u>vex</u>-el-hahft
wet	nass nahss
wind	der Wind dair vint

Environment

It's very loud here.	**Hier ist es sehr laut.** here ist es zair loud
Could you please shut off that noise?	**Können Sie diesen Lärm abstellen?** kern-en zee dee-zen lairm <u>ahp</u>-shtel-en
It smells bad here.	**Hier riecht es unangenehm.** here reesht es <u>oon</u>-ahn-guh-name
Where's that smell coming from?	**Woher kommt dieser Geruch?** vo-her komt dee-zuh guh-<u>rook</u>
Can you drink the water?	**Ist das Wasser trinkbar?** ist dahs vahs-suh trink-bah
The *water / air* is polluted.	*Das Wasser / Die Luft* ist **verschmutzt.** *dahs vahs-suh / dee looft* ist fair-<u>shmootst</u>
Is that dangerous?	**Ist das gefährlich?** ist dahs guh-<u>fair</u>-lish

Environment: Additional Words

air pollution	**die Luftverschmutzung** dee <u>looft</u>-fair-shmoots-oong
avalanche	**die Lawine** dee lah-<u>veen</u>-uh
danger of avalanches	**die Lawinengefahr** dee lah-<u>veen</u>-en-guh-fah
dust	**der Staub** dair shtauwp
earthquake	**das Erdbeben** dahs <u>airt</u>-bay-ben
environmental pollution	**die Umweltverschmutzung** dee <u>oom</u>-velt-fair-shmoots-oong

exhaust fume	das Abgas dahs ahp-gahs
flood	die Überschwemmung
	dee ew-buh-<u>shvem</u>-moong
forest fire	der Waldbrand dair vahlt-brahnt
landslide	der Erdrutsch dair airt-rootch
polluted	verschmutzt fair-<u>shmootst</u>
smog	der Smog dair smog
water quality	die Wasserqualität
	dee <u>vahs</u>-suh-kvah-lee-tate

Grammar

Grammar

Regular Verbs and Their Tenses

The past is often expressed by using to have **haben** + past participle. The future is formed with **werden** + infinitive.

Infinitive: **kaufen** to buy **arbeiten** to work
Past Participle: **gekauft** bought **gearbeitet** worked

	Present	Past	Future
ich I	kaufe	habe gekauft	werde kaufen
du you *inform.*	kaufst	hast gekauft	wirst kaufen
Sie you *form.*	kaufen	haben gekauft	werden kaufen
er/sie/es he/she/it	kauft	hat gekauft	wird kaufen
wir we	kaufen	haben gekauft	werden kaufen
ihr you *pl. inform.*	kauft	habt gekauft	werdet kaufen
Sie you *pl. form.*	kaufen	haben gekauft	werden kaufen
sie they	kaufen	haben gekauft	werden kaufen

Irregular verbs have to be memorized. Verbs that indicate movement are conjugated with to be **sein**, e.g. to go **gehen**:

	Present	Past	Future
ich I	gehe	bin gegangen	werde gehen
du you *inform.*	gehst	bist gegangen	wirst gehen
Sie you *form.*	gehen	sind gegangen	werden gehen
er/sie/es he/she/it	geht	ist gegangen	wird gehen
wir we	gehen	sind gegangen	werden gehen
ihr you *pl. inform.*	geht	seid gegangen	werdet gehen
Sie you *pl. form.*	gehen	sind gegangen	werden gehen
sie they	gehen	sind gegangen	werden gehen

To express future, usually the present tense is used together with a time adverb I'll work <u>tomorrow</u>. **Ich arbeite <u>morgen</u>**.

Nouns and Articles

All nouns are written with a capital letter. Their indefinite articles indicate their gender: der (masculine = *m*), die (feminine = *f*), das (neuter = *n*). In the plural (die) the genders don't matter.

Singular	Plural
<u>der</u> Mann the man	<u>die</u> Männer the men
<u>die</u> Frau the woman	<u>die</u> Frauen the women
<u>das</u> Kind the child	<u>die</u> Kinder the children

The indefinite article also indicates the gender of the noun: ein (*m,n*), eine (*f*). There is no article in the plural.

Examples: <u>ein</u> Zug a train   Züge trains
<u>eine</u> Karte a map   Karten maps

Possessives also relate to the gender of the noun that follows:

Nominative	Accusative	Dative
(*m,n/f*)	(*n/f/m*)	(*m,n/f*)
mein/e my	mein/e/en my	meinem/er my
dein/e your *inform.*	dein/e/en your	deinem/er your
Ihr/e your *form.*	Ihr/e/en your	Ihrem/er your
sein/e his	sein/e/en his	seinem/er his
ihr/e her	ihr/e/en her	ihrem/er her
sein/e its	sein/e/en its	seinem/er its
unser/e our	unser/e/en our	unserem/er our
ihr/e your *pl. inform.*	euer/re/ren your	eurem/er your
Ihr/e you *pl. form.*	Ihr/e/en your	Ihrem/er your
ihr/e their	ihr/e/en their	ihrem/er their

Examples: Wo ist <u>meine</u> Fahrkarte? Where is my ticket?
<u>Ihr</u> Taxi ist hier. Your taxi is here.
Hier ist <u>euer</u> Pass. Here is your passport.

Word Order

The conjugated verb comes after the subject and before the object. When a sentence doesn't begin with a subject, the word order changes.

Examples: **Er ist in Berlin.**   He is in Berlin.
            Heute ist er in Berlin.   Today he is in Berlin.
            Wir sind in Berlin gewesen.   We were in Berlin.

Questions are formed by reversing the order of subject and verb.

Examples: **Haben Sie Bücher?**
            Do you have books?
            Wie ist das Wetter?
            How is the weather?
            Seid ihr in Köln gewesen?
            Have you been to Cologne?

Negations

Negative sentences are formed by adding nicht (not) to that part of the sentence which is to be negated.

Examples: **Wir rauchen nicht.** We don't smoke.
            Der Bus fährt nicht ab. The bus doesn't leave.
            Warum schreibst du nicht? Why don't you write?

If a noun is used, the negation is made by adding kein. Its ending is defined by the noun's gender.

Examples: **Ich trinke kein Bier.**
            I don't drink beer.
            Wir haben keine Einzelzimmer.
            We don't have any single rooms.
            Gibt es keinen Zimmerservice?
            Is there no room service?

Grammar

Imperatives (Command Form)

du you *sing. inform.*	Geh! Go!	Sei still! Be quiet!
ihr you *pl. inform.*	Geht! Go!	Seid still! Be quiet!
Sie you *sing./pl. form.*	Gehen Sie! Go!	Seien Sie still! Be quiet!
wir we	Gehen wir! Let's go!	

Examples: Hört mal alle zu!
　　　　　 Listen everybody!
　　　　　 Seid nicht so laut!
　　　　　 Don't be so noisy!

Pronouns

Pronouns serve as substitutes and relate to the gender.

Nominative	Accusative	Dative
ich I	mich me	mir me
du you *inform.*	dich you	dir you
Sie you *form.*	Sie you	Ihnen you
er he	ihn him	ihm him
sie she	sie her	ihr her
es it	es it	ihm him
wir we	uns us	uns us
ihr you *pl. inform.*	euch you	euch you
Sie you *pl. form.*	Sie you	Ihnen you
sie they	sie them	ihnen them

Examples: Ich sehe sie.
　　　　　 I see them.
　　　　　 Hören Sie mich?
　　　　　 Do you hear me?

205

Adjectives

Adjectives describe nouns. Their endings depend on the case.

Examples: **Wir haben ein altes Auto.**
We have an old car.
Wo ist mein neuer Koffer?
Where is my new suitcase?
Gute Arbeit, Richard!
Good work, Richard!

Comparisons and Superlatives

Most German adjectives add **–er** for their comparative and **–(e)st** for their superlative. The following list contains only a small selection to illustrate formation and irregularities

Adjective	Comparative	Superlative
klein small, little	kleiner smaller	am kleinsten the smallest
billig cheap	billiger cheaper	am billigsten the cheapest
neu new	neuer newer	am neusten the newest
schlecht bad	schlechter worse	am schlechtesten the worst
groß big, large	größer bigger	am größten the biggest
alt old	älter older	am ältesten the oldest
lang long	länger longer	am längsten the longest
kurz short	kürzer shorter	am kürzesten the shortest
gut good	besser better	am besten the best
teuer expensive	teurer more expensive	am teuersten the most expensive

Examples: **Diese Postkarten sind billiger.**
These postcards are cheaper.
Wo ist der beste Buchladen?
Where is the best bookstore?

Adverbs and Adverbial Expressions

In German, adverbs are usually identical with adjectives. They describe verbs but, unlike adjectives, their endings don't change.

Examples: **Linda fährt sehr langsam.**
Linda drives very slowly.
Robert ist sehr nett.
Robert is very nice.
Sie sprechen gut Deutsch.
You speak German well.

Some common adverbial time expressions:

zur Zeit presently
bald soon
immer noch still
nicht mehr not anymore

Conversion Charts

The following conversion charts contain the most commonly used measures.

1 Gramm (g)	= 1000 milligrams	= 0.035 oz.
1 Pfund (Pfd)	= 500 grams	= 1.1 lb
1 Kilogramm (kg)	= 1000 grams	= 2.2 lb
1 Liter (l)	= 1000 milliliters	= 1.06 U.S / 0.88 Brit. quarts
		= 2.11 /1.8 US /Brit. pints
		= 34 /35 US /Brit. fluid oz.
1 Zentimeter (cm)	= 100 millimeter	= 0.4 inch
1 Meter (m)	= 100 centimeters	= 39.37 inches/3.28 ft.
1 Kilometer (km)	= 1000 meters	= 0.62 mile
1 Quadratmeter (qm)	= 10.8 square feet	
1 Hektar (qm)	= 10000 sq meters	= 2.5 acres
1 Quadratkilometer (qkm)	= 247 acres	

Not sure whether to put on a bathing suit or a winter coat? Here is a comparison of Fahrenheit and and Celsius / Centigrade degrees.

-40°C – -40°F	-1° C – 30° F	20° C – 68° F
-30°C – -22°F	0° C – 32° F	25° C – 77° F
-20°C – -4° F	5° C – 41° F	30° C – 86° F
-10°C – 14° F	10° C – 50° F	35° C – 95° F
-5° C – 23° F	15° C – 59° F	

When You Know	Multiply By	To Find
ounces	28.3	grams
pounds	0.45	kilograms
inches	2.54	centimeters
feet	0.3	meters
miles	1.61	kilometers
square inches	6.45	sq. centimeters
square feet	0.09	sq. meters
square miles	2.59	sq. kilometers
pints (US/Brit)	0.47 / 0.56	liters
gallons (US/Brit)	3.8 / 4.5	liters

Travel Dictionary
English – German

m masculine
f feminine
n neuter
pl plural

A

a little wenig vay-nish
a month ago vor einem Monat *m* faw eye-nem mo-naht
abbey Abtei *f* ahp-<u>tie</u>
abdomen Bauch *m* bowk
abscess Abszess *m* ahps-<u>tsess</u>
accident Unfall *m* oon-fahl
accident report Unfallprotokoll *n* <u>oon</u>-fahl-pro-toe-kawl
act Akt *m* ahkt
active ingredient Wirkstoff *m* vee-uh-k-shtof
actor Schauspieler *m* <u>shauw</u>-shpee-luh
actress Schauspielerin *f* <u>shauw</u>-spee-luh-rin
acupuncture Akupunktur *f* ah-koo-poonk-<u>tour</u>
adapter Adapter *m* ah-<u>dahp</u>-tuh
address Adresse *f* ah-<u>dress</u>-uh
addressee Empfänger *m* emp-<u>feng</u>-uh
adhesive bandage Pflaster *n* flah-stuh
adults Erwachsene *m/f pl* air-<u>vahx</u>-en-uh
advance booking Vorverkauf *m* <u>for</u>-fair-cowf

aerial tramway Seilbahn *f* zeye-l-bahn
after hinter <u>hin</u>-tuh
after sunburn lotion Salbe *f* gegen Sonnenbrand zahl-buh gay-ghen <u>zon</u>-nen-brahnt
afternoon Nachmittag *m* <u>nahk</u>-mit-tahk
age Epoche *f* eh-<u>paw</u>-kuh
AIDS Aids aids
air Luft *f* looft
air conditioning Klimaanlage *f* <u>klee</u>-muh-ahn-lah-guh
air filter Luftfilter *m* looft-filter
air mattress Luftmatratze *f* <u>looft</u>-mah-trah-tsuh
air pollution Luftverschmutzung *f* <u>looft</u>-fair-shmoots-oong
airport Flughafen *m* <u>flook</u> hah-fen
airport shuttle bus Flughafenbus *m* <u>flook</u>-hah-fen-boos
airport tax Flughafengebühr *f* <u>flook</u>-hah-fen-guh-bewr
alarm clock Wecker *m* vek-kuh
alcohol-free beer alkoholfreies Bier *n* ahl-ko-<u>hole</u>-fry-es beer
All Saints' Day Allerheiligen *n* ahl-lair-<u>high</u>-lih-ghen
allergy Allergie *f* ah-lair-<u>ghee</u>
allergy-tested allergie-getestet ahl-air-<u>ghee</u>-guh-test-et
almond Mandel *f* mahn-del
alone allein uh-line
altar Altar *m* ahl-tah

alternator Lichtmaschine *f*
lisht-mah-shee-nuh
aluminum foil Alufolie *f*
ah-loo-fol-yuh
amalgam filling
Amalgamfüllung *f* ah-
mahl-gahm-fewl-loong
amount Betrag *m* buh-
trahk
anchovy Sardelle *f* zah-del-
luh
ankle Knöchel *m* kuh-neh-
shel
anorak Anorak *m* ah-no-
rahk
anti-itch cream Salbe *f*
gegen Juckreiz zahl-buh
gay-ghen yook-rights
antibiotic Antibiotikum *n*
ahn-tee-bee-o-tee-koom
antifreeze Frostschutzmittel
n frawst-shoots-mit-tel
antique Antiquität *f* ahn-
tee-kvih-tate
antique shop
Antiquitätengeschäft *n*
ahn-tee-kvee-tay-ten-guh-
sheft
antiseptic
Desinfektionsmittel *n*
des-in-fek-tsee-ohns-mit-tel
antiseptic ointment
Wundsalbe *f* voont-zahl-
buh
apartment Appartement *n*
ah-part-ment
appendicitis
Blinddarmentzündung *f*
blint-dahm-ent-zewnd-doong
appetizer Vorspeise *f*
faw-shpy-zuh
apple Apfel *m* ahp-fel
apple cider (alcoholic)
Apfelwein *m* ahp-fel-vine
apple juice Apfelsaft *m*
ahp-fel-zahft

210

apple pie Apfelkuchen *m*
ahp-fel-kook-en
apple schnapps Apfelkorn
m ahp-fel-cawn
application Anwendung *f*
ahn-ven-doong
apricot Aprikose *f*
ah-pree-ko-suh
April April *m* ah-pril
aqueduct Aquädukt *n*
ahk-kveh-dookt
architect Architekt *m*
ahk-ee-tekt
area Gegend *f* gay-ghent
arm Arm *m* ahm
arm floats Schwimmflügel
m shwim-flew-gull
armchair Sessel *m* zes-sel
to arrest verhaften
fair-hahf-ten
arrival Ankunft *f*
ahn-koonft
to arrive ankommen
ahn-kom-en
art Kunst *f* koonst
art collection
Gemäldesammlung *f*
guh-mail-duh-zahm-loong
artichoke Artischocke *f*
ah-tee-sho-kuh
artist Künstler *m*
kewnst-luh
arts and crafts
Kunsthandwerk *f*
koonst-hahnt-vairk
Ascension Himmelfahrt *f*
him-mel-faht
ashtray Aschenbecher *m*
ahsh-en-besh-uh
asparagus Spargel *m*
shpah-ghel
Assumption Mariä
Himmelfahrt *f* mah-ree-ah
him-mel-faht
asthma Asthma *n* ahst-mah
at um oom

at around noon mittags
mit-tahks
at night nachts nahkts
au gratin überbacken
ew-buh-<u>bahk</u>-en
August August *m*
ow-<u>goost</u>
authorized repairs garage
Vertragswerkstatt *f*
fair-<u>trahgs</u>-vairk-shtaht
**automatic teller machine
(ATM)** Geldautomat *m*
<u>ghelt</u>-ow-to-maht
avalanche Lawine *f*
lah-<u>vee</u>-nuh
avocado Avocado *f*
ah-vo-<u>cah</u>-do
axle Achse *f* ahx-uh

B

baby bottle Babyfläschchen
n <u>bay</u>-bee-flesh-shen
baby food Babynahrung *f*
<u>baby</u>-nah-roong
baby powder Babypuder *m*
<u>bay</u>-bee-poo-duh
back Rücken *m*
rewk-ken
back light Rücklicht *n*
rewk-lisht
backpack Rucksack *m*
rook-zahk
back(wards) zurück
tsoo-<u>rewk</u>
bacon Speck *m* shpek
badminton Federball *m*
<u>ay</u>-duh-bahl
badminton racket
Federballschläger *m*
<u>fay</u>-duh-bahl-shlay-guh
bag Tasche *f* tah-shuh
baggage claim
Gepäckausgabe *f* guh-
<u>pek</u>-ows-gah-buh

baggage storage
Gepäckaufbewahrung *f*
guh-<u>pek</u>-owf-buh-vah-roong
baked gebacken guh-<u>bahk</u>-
en
bakery Bäckerei *f* bek-air-
<u>eye</u>
balcony Galerie *f* gahl-uh-
<u>ree</u>
ball Ball *m* bahl
ballet Ballett *n* bah-<u>lett</u>
ballooning Ballonfliegen *n*
bah-<u>long</u>-flee-ghen
ballpoint pen
Kugelschreiber *m* <u>koo</u>-
gull-shry-buh
balsamic vinegar
Balsamessig *m*
<u>bahl</u>-zahm-es-sish
banana Banane *f* bah-<u>nah</u>-
nuh
band Musikkapelle *f* moo-
<u>zeek</u>-kah-pel-luh
bangs Pony *m* pon-nee
bar Kneipe *f* kuh-<u>nigh</u>-puh
bar (counter) Theke *f* tay-
kuh
barbecued gegrillt
guh-<u>grilt</u>
barber Friseur *m* free-<u>zoor</u>
barometric pressure
Luftdruck *m* <u>looft</u>-drook
baroque Barock *m* bah-
<u>rawk</u>
barrette Haarspange *f*
hah-shpahng-uh
basil Basilikum *n*
bah-<u>zee</u>-lih-koom
basketball Basketball *m*
<u>bahs</u>-ket-bahl
bass Seebarsch *m* say-
bahrsh
bathing suit Badeanzug *m*
<u>bah</u>-duh-ahn-tsook
bathrobe Bademantel *m*
<u>bah</u>-duh-mahn-tel

bathtub Badewanne f
bah-duh-vahn-nuh
battery Batterie f baht-tuh-
ree
to be called; my name is
heißen; ich heiße high-sen
ish high-suh
to be from kommen aus
kom-en auws
to be full satt sein zaht
zeye-n
to be hungry hungrig sein
hoong-rish zeye-n
to be thirsty durstig sein
dours-tish zeye-n
beach Strand m shtrahnt
beach ball Wasserball m
vahs-suh-bahl
beach chair Strandkorb m
shtrahnt-kawp
beach hat Sonnenhut m
zun-nen-hoot
beach volleyball Beach-
Volleyball m
beach-volley-bahl
bean Bohne f bo-nuh
beard Bart m bahrt
bed Bett n bet
bed linen Bettwäsche f
bet-vesh-uh
bedspread Bettdecke f
bet-dek-uh
beef Rindfleisch n rint-flysh
beef roast Sauerbraten m
sour-brah-ten
beer Bier n beer
beets rote Bete f
ro-tuh bay-tuh
before vor for
before meals vor dem Essen
faw dame es-sen
behind hinter hin-tuh
beige beige beige
bell Glocke f glaw-kuh
bell pepper Paprikaschote f
pah-pree-kah-sho-tuh

bell tower Glockenturm m
glaw-ken-toorm
belt Gürtel m gewr-tel
bend Kurve f koor-vuh
beside neben nay-ben
beverage Getränk n guh-
trenk-uh
bicycle Fahrrad n fah-raht
big groß grohs
bigger größer grers-suh
bike basket Fahrradkorb m
fah-raht-kawp
bikini Bikini m bikini
bill Rechnung f
resh-noong
binding Bindung f bin-
doong
birth control pill
Antibabypille f ahn-tee-
bay-bee-pil-luh
bite Biss m biss
bite (sting) Stich m
shtish
black schwarz shvahts
black and white film
Schwarz-Weiß-Film m
shvahts-vice-film
black currant schwarze
Johannisbeere f shvahts-
uh yo-hahn-is-bair-eh
black ice Glatteis n glaht-
ice
blackberry Brombeere f
brom-bair-uh
bladder Blase f blah-zuh
blanket Decke f dek-uh
blazer Blazer m blazer
blind blind blint
blister Blase f blah-zuh
blond blond blont
blood Blut n bloot
blood poisoning
Blutvergiftung f bloot-fair-
ghif-toong
blouse Bluse f bloo-zuh
to blow-dry fönen fer-nen

212

blue blau blauw
blue cheese
 Blauschimmelkäse m
 blauw-shim-el-kay-zuh
blush Rouge n rooj
boarding pass Bordkarte f
 bawt-kah-tuh
boat rentals Bootsverleih m
 boats-fair-lie
body Körper m ker-puh
body lotion Körperlotion f
 ker-puh-lo-tsee-ohn
boiled gekocht guh-kawkt
boiled ham gekochter
 Schinken m guh-kawk-tuh
 shink-en
bone Knochen m kuh-naw-
 ken
bookstore Buchhandlung f
 book-hahnt-loong
boots Stiefel m stee-fel
border Grenze f gren-tsuh
botanical garden
 Botanischer Garten m bo-
 tahn-ish-uh gah-ten
bottle Flasche f flahsh-uh
bottle opener
 Flaschenöffner m flahsh-
 en-erf-nuh
bottle warmer
 Fläschchenwärmer m
 flesh-shen-vair-muh
bottom Gesäß n guh-zess
bouillon Fleischbrühe f
 flysh-bree-uh
boutique Boutique f boo-
 teek
to bowl kegeln kay-gheln
bowling alley Kegelbahn f
 kay-gull-bahn
box Loge f loh-juh
box office Theater /
 Kinokasse f
 tay-ah-tuh / kee-no-kahs-suh
boy Junge m yoong-uh

boyfriend, partner Freund
 m froint
bra BH m bay-hah
bracelet Armband n
 ahm-bahnt
braces Zahnspange f
 zahn-shpahng-uh
brain Gehirn n guh-heern
braised geschmort
 guh-shmawt
brake Bremse f
 brem-zuh
brake fluid Bremsflüssigkeit
 f brems-flew-sish-kite
brake light Bremslicht n
 brems-lisht
brandy Weinbrand m
 vine-brahnt
Brazil nut Paranuss f pah-
 rah-nooss
bread Brot n broht
breaded paniert
 pahn-eert
breakfast Frühstück n
 frew-shtewk
breakfast buffet
 Frühstücksbüfett n
 frew-stiks-bew-fay
breakfast room
 Frühstücksraum m
 frew-stiks-rauwm
breathing problems
 Atembeschwerden pl
 ah-tem-buh-shvair-den
brewery Brauerei f
 brow-uh-rye
bridge Brücke f brewk-uh
briefs Slip m slip
bright heiter high-tuh
broccoli Brokkoli m
 braw-ko-lee
brochure Prospekt m
 pro-spekt
broken kaputt kah-put
bronchitis Bronchitis f
 brun-shee-tis

brooch Brosche *f*
braw-shuh
broom Besen *m* bay-zen
brother Bruder *m*
broo-duh
brothers and sisters
Geschwister *pl*
guh-<u>shvis</u>-tuh
brown braun brown
bruise Prellung *f*
prel-loong
brush Bürste *f* bewr-stuh
brussels sprouts Rosenkohl
m <u>ro</u>-zen-coal
bucket Eimer *m* eye-muh
building Gebäude *n*
guh-<u>boi</u>-duh
bulb Glühbirne *f*
<u>glew</u>-beer-nuh
bumper Stoßstange *f*
<u>shtos</u>-stahng-uh
bungalow Bungalow *m*
<u>boon</u>-gah-lo
bungee jumping Bungee-
Springen *n*
<u>bungee</u>-shpring-en
bunk bed Etagenbett *n*
eh-<u>tah</u>-jen-bet
burger Frikadelle *f* frik-ah-
<u>del</u>-luh
burgundy wine Burgunder
m boor-<u>goon</u>-duh
burgundy dunkelrot
<u>doon</u>-kel-roht
burn Verbrennung *f*
fair-<u>bren</u>-noong
bus station Busbahnhof *m*
<u>boos</u>-bahn-hoaf
bus stop Bushaltestelle *f*
boos-<u>hahl</u>-tuh-shtel-uh
bust Büste *f* bews-tuh
butcher's Fleischerei *f*
flysh-uh-<u>rye</u>
butter Butter *f* boo-tuh
to buy kaufen cow-fen
bypass Bypass *m* by-pahs

214

C

cabaret Kabarett *f*
kah-bah-<u>rett</u>
cabbage Kohl *m* coal
cable Kabel *n* kah-bel
cake Kuchen *m* koo-khen
calf Wade *f* vah-duh
camcorder Camcorder *m*
cahm-caw-duh
camelhair Kamelhaar *n*
kah-<u>mayl</u>-hah
camera Fotoapparat *m* <u>fo</u>-
to-ahp-ah-raht
to camp zelten tselt-en
camping Camping *n* camping
campsite Campingplatz *m*
<u>cam</u>-ping-plats
can opener Dosenöffner *m*
<u>do</u>-zen-erf-nuh
cancer Krebs *m* krayps
candle Kerze *f* kair-tseh
candy Süßigkeit *f*
<u>zews</u>-sish-kite
canned food Konserve *f*
kon-<u>zair</u>-vuh
canoe Kanu *n* <u>kah</u>-noo
capital Hauptstadt *f*
howpt-shtaht
cappuccino Cappuccino *m*
cah-pu-<u>tshee</u>-no
captain Kapitän *m*
kah-pee-<u>tane</u>
car (train) Waggon *m*
vah-<u>gong</u>
car Auto *n* ow-toe
car ferry Autofähre *f* <u>ow</u>-
toe-fair-uh
car key Autoschlüssel *m*
<u>ow</u>-toe-shlews-sel
car radio Autoradio *n* <u>ow</u>-
to-rah-dee-o
car seat Kindersitz *m*
<u>kin</u>-duh-zits
carat Karat *n* kah-<u>raht</u>

carburetor Vergaser *m*
fair-<u>gah</u>-zuh
card number
Kartennummer *f* <u>kah</u>-ten-
noom-muh
cardiac infarction
Herzinfarkt *m* <u>heirts</u>-in-
fahkt
carp Karpfen *m* kahp-fen
carrot Möhre *f* mer-eh
carry-on Handgepäck *n*
<u>hahnt</u>-guh-pek
cartilage Knorpel *m*
kuh-<u>naw</u>-pel
carving Schnitzerei *f* shnits-
uh-<u>rye</u>
cash register Kasse *f* kahs-
suh
cash transfer
Banküberweisung *f*
<u>bahnk</u>-ew-buh-vize-oong
cashmere Kaschmir *m*
kahsh-meer
casino Spielkasino *n*
<u>shpeel</u>-kah-zeen-o
cassette Kassette *f*
kahs-<u>set</u>-tuh
castle Burg *f* boork
catalytic converter
Katalysator *m* kah-tah-lee-
<u>zah</u>-tor
cathedral Dom *m* dome
Catholic katholisch kah-<u>toe</u>-
lish
cauliflower Blumenkohl *m*
<u>bloom</u>-en-coal
cave Höhle *f* herl-uh
cavity Karies *f* <u>kah</u>-ree-es
CD/DVD CD/DVD *n* tsay
<u>day</u>/day fauw day
CD/DVD player CD/DVD-
Spieler *m* tsay-<u>day</u>/day-
fauw-<u>day</u>-shpee-luh
cell phone Handy *n* handy
ceiling Decke *f* dek-uh
celery Sellerie *m* <u>zel</u>-uh-ree

Celtic keltisch kel-tish
cemetery Friedhof *m*
freet-hohf
center Mitte *f* mit-tuh
century Jahrhundert *n* jah-
<u>hoon</u>-dairt
ceramic Keramik *f* keh-<u>rah</u>-
mik
cereal Müsli *n* mews-lee
certificate Zertifikat *n* tsair-
tih-fih-<u>kaht</u>
chair Stuhl *m* shtool
chair lift Sessellift *m* <u>zes</u>-
sel-lift
champagne Champagner *m*
shahm-<u>pahn</u>-yuh
changing room
Umkleidekabine *f* <u>oom</u>-
kligh-duh-kah-bee-nuh
changing table
Wickelkommode *f* <u>vik</u>-el-
kom-o-duh
chapel Kapelle *f* kah-<u>pel</u>-uh
charcoal Grillkohle *f*
<u>grill</u>-ko-luh
charcoal tablet
Kohletablette *f* <u>ko</u>-leh-tah-
blet-tuh
cheap billig <u>bil</u>-lig
check Scheck *m* shek
to check in aufgeben
<u>owf</u>-gay-ben
check-in Anmeldung *f* <u>ahn</u>-
mel-doong
check-in desk Schalter *m*
shahl-tuh
cheese Käse *m* kay-zuh
cheese omelet Käseomelett
n <u>kay</u>-zuh-um-let
cheese platter Käseplatte *f*
<u>kay</u>-zuh-plah-tuh
cheesecake Käsekuchen *m*
<u>kay</u>-zuh-kook-en
chemical toilet Chemieklo *n*
shay-<u>mee</u>-klo
cherry Kirsche *f* keer-sheh

215

chest Brust *f* broost
chestnut Esskastanie *f* ess-kah-stahn-yeh
chicken Huhn *n*, Hähnchen *n* hoon hayn-shen
chicken pox Windpocken *pl* vint-paw-ken
chickpea Kichererbse *f* kish-uh-airp-suh
chicory Chicorée *m* she-ko-ray
child Kind *n* kint
child safety belt Kindersicherheitsgurt *m* kin-duh-zik-uh-hites-goort
child seat Kindersitz *m* kin-duh-zits
children Kinder *pl* kin-duh
children's portion Kinderteller *m* kin-duh-tel-uh
child's bicycle Kinderfahrrad *n* kin-duh-fah-raht
chili pepper Peperoni *f* pep-pair-ohn-ee
chills Schüttelfrost *m* shih-tel-frost
chimes Glockenspiel *n* gla-wk-en-shpeel
chives Schnittlauch *m* shnit-lauwk
chocolate Schokolade *f* sho-ko-lah-duh
choir Chor *m* core
Christmas Weihnachten *n* vhy-nahk-ten
Christmas Day Weihnachtstag *m* airs-tuh vhy-nahkts-tahk
Christmas Eve Heiligabend *m* high-lish-ah-bent
church Kirche *f* keer-shuh
church service Gottesdienst *m* gawt-tes-deenst
church tower Kirchturm *m* keersh-toorm

cigarillo Zigarillo *n* tsee-gah-ree-loh
cigar Zigarre *f* tsee-gah-ruh
circulatory problems Kreislaufstörung *f* krighs-lowf-shter-oong
circus Zirkus *m* tseer-koos
city center Stadtzentrum *n* shtaht-tsen-troom
clam Venusmuschel *f* vay-noos-moosh-el
class Klasse *f* clahs-suh
classical; ancient antik ahn-teek
clean sauber sow-buh
cleaning product Reinigungsmittel *n* rye-nee-goongs-mit-tel
cleansing Reinigung *f* rye-nee-goong
clear klar klahr
climate Klima *n* klee-mah
to climb klettern klet-tairn
climbing boot Bergschuh *m* bairk-shoe
clip-on earring Ohrklipp *m* or-klip
cloisters Kreuzgang *m* kro-its-gahng
closed geschlossen guh-shlaws-sen
cloth Wischlappen *m* vish-lahp-pen
clothes pin Wäscheklammer *f* vesh-uh-klahm-air
cloud Wolke *f* vol-kuh
cloudy bewölkt buh-vulkt
clutch Kupplung *f* koop-loong
coast Küste *f* kee-stuh
coat Mantel *m* mahn-tel
coat of arms Wappen *n* vahp-pen
coatroom Garderobe *f* gah-duh-ro-buh
cocktail Cocktail *m* cocktail

216

cocoa Kakao *m* kah-<u>cow</u>
coconut Kokosnuss *f*
<u>ko</u>-koss-noos
cod Kabeljau *m* <u>kah</u>-bel-
yow
coffee Kaffee *m* kah-fay
coffee creamer Kaffeesahne
f <u>kah</u>-fay-zah-nuh
coffee-maker
Kaffeemaschine *f* <u>kah</u>-fay-
muh-shee-nuh
coin Münze *f* mewnt-suh
cold kalt kahlt
cold (sickness) Erkältung *f*
air-<u>kel</u>-toong
cold cuts Wurstaufschnitt *m*
<u>voorst</u>-owf-shnit
coleslaw Krautsalat *m*
<u>kraut</u>-zah-laht
colic Kolik *f* ko-lik
collapsible wheelchair
Faltrollstuhl *m* <u>fahlt</u>-roll-
shtool
collarbone Schlüsselbein *n*
<u>shlews</u>-sel-bine
collection Sammlung *f*
zahm-loong
colorful bunt boont
coloring book Malbuch *n*
mahl-bookh
comb Kamm *m* kahm
to come back wiederkom-
men <u>vee</u>-duh-kom-en
companion Begleitperson *f*
buh-<u>gleye</u>-t-pair-zone
compartment Abteil *n* ahp-
<u>tile</u>
complaint Beanstandung *f*
bay-<u>ahn</u>-shtahn-doong
complete meal Menü *n*
men-<u>ew</u>
composer Komponist *m*
kom-po-<u>nist</u>
composite filling
Kunststofffüllung *f*
<u>koonst</u>-stawf-fewl-loong

computer computer *m*
com-<u>puter</u>
concussion
Gehirnerschütterung *f*
guh-<u>heern</u>-air-shih-tair-oong
condom Kondom *n* kon-
<u>dome</u>
conductor (train) Schaffner
m shahf-nuh
conductor (orchestra)
Dirigent *m* dee-rih-<u>ghent</u>
conjunctivitis
Bindehautentzündung *f*
<u>bin</u>-duh-howt-ent-zewn-
doong
connecting flight
Anschlussflug *m* <u>ahn</u>-
shlooss-flook
connection Anschluss *m*
ahn-shlooss
consommé klare Brühe *f*
klah-ruh brew-uh
constipation Verstopfung *f*
fair-<u>shtup</u>-foong
contraindication
Gegenanzeige *f* <u>gay</u>-ghen-
ahn-tsigh-guh
convent Kloster *n* klohs-tuh
cookbook Kochbuch *n*
kawk-bukh
cookie Plätzchen *n* plaits-
shen
cool kühl kewl
coolant Kühlwasser *n*
<u>kewl</u>-vahs-suh
cooler Kühltasche *f*
<u>kewl</u>-tah-shuh
copy Kopie *f* kaw-<u>pee</u>
corkscrew Korkenzieher *m*
<u>kaw</u>-ken-tsee-uh
corn Mais *m* mice
corn on the cob Maiskolben
m <u>mice</u>-kol-ben
Corpus Christi
Fronleichnam *m* frohn-<u>lye</u>-
shnahm

to cost kosten kawst-en
costume jewelry
  Modeschmuck *m* <u>mo</u>-duh-shmook
cot (for a child) Kinderbett
  n <u>kin</u>-duh-bet
cotton Baumwolle *f* <u>bau-wm</u>-vol-luh
cotton balls Watte *f* vaht-tuh
cotton swab Wattestäbchen
  n <u>waht</u>-tuh-shtayp-shen
cough Husten *m* hoos-ten
cough medicine Hustensaft
  m <u>hoo</u>-sten-zahft
counter Schalter *m* shahl-tuh
counterfeit money
  Falschgeld *n* fahlsh-ghelt
country Land *n* lahnt
country road Landstraße *f*
  <u>lahnt</u>-strahs-suh
course Gang *m* gahng
court Hof *m* hohf
cover Gedeck *n* guh-<u>dek</u>
crab Krebs *m* krayps
cramp Krampf *m* krahmpf
crampon Steigeisen *n* <u>shti-ke</u>-eye-zen
cranberry Preiselbeere *f*
  <u>pry</u>-zel-bair-uh
crash Zusammenstoß *m*
  tsoo-<u>zah</u>-men-shtos
crayfish Languste *f* Lahn-<u>goose</u>-tuh
crayon Buntstift *m*
  boont-shtift
cream Sahne *f* zah-nuh
cream (whipped)
  Schlagsahne *f* <u>shlahk</u>-zah-nuh
cream cheese Frischkäse *m*
  frish-<u>kay</u>-zuh
credit card Kreditkarte *f*
  kreh-<u>deet</u>-kah-tuh

crockery, tableware
  Geschirr *n* guh-<u>sheer</u>
cross Kreuz *n* kroits
cross-country skiing
  Langlauf *m* lahng-lauwf
crown jewels Kronjuwelen
  pl krohn-you-vail-en
crudités Rohkost *f* ro-kawst
cruise Kreuzfahrt *f* kroits-faht
crutch Krücke *f* krew-kuh
crème caramel
  Karamellcreme *f* kah-rah-<u>mel</u>-krem
cucumber Gurke *f* goor-kuh
cup Tasse *f* tah-suh
curling Eisstockschießen *n*
  <u>ice</u>-shtawk-she-sen
curl Locke *f* law-kuh
currant Johannisbeere *f* yo-<u>hahn</u>-is-bair-uh
currency Währung *f* vair-oong
currency exchange
  Wechselstube *f*
  <u>vex</u>-el-shtoo-buh
curve Kurve *f* koor-vuh
custard Vanillesoße *f* van-<u>nil</u>-yuh-zos-suh
customs Zoll *m* tsol
customs declaration
  Zollerklärung *f* <u>tsol</u>-air-clair-oong
cutlet Kotelett *n* <u>kaw</u>-t-let
cycling path Radweg *m*
  raht-vayk
cyst Zyste *f* tsis-tuh
cystitis Blasenentzündung *f*
  <u>blah</u>-zen-ent-zewnd-doong

D

damp feucht foisht
dancer Tänzer *m,* **Tänzerin**
  f, ten-tsair, ten-tsai-rin

dandruff Schuppen *pl*
shoop-en
daughter Tochter *f* tokh-
tuh
dawn Dämmerung *f* <u>dem</u>-
mair-oong
day Tag *m* tahk
the day after tomorrow
übermorgen <u>ew</u>-buh-
maw-ghen
the day before yesterday
vorgestern <u>faw</u>-ghes-tairn
deaf taub tauwp
December Dezember *m*
day-<u>tsem</u>-ber
deck Deck *n* deck
deckchair Liegestuhl *m* <u>lee</u>-
guh-shtool
declaration of value
Wertangabe *f* <u>vairt</u>-ahn-
gah-buh
deep-fried frittiert
free-<u>teert</u>
degrees Grad *m* graht
delay Verspätung *f* fair-
<u>shpeh</u>-toong
delete löschen lersh-en
delicatessen
Feinkostgeschäft *n* <u>fine</u>-
kawst-guh-sheft
delighted erfreut air-<u>froit</u>
dental floss Zahnseide *f*
<u>tsahn</u>-zeye-duh
dentist Zahnarzt *m* tsahn-
ahtst
dentures *pl* Gebiss *n* guh-
<u>biss</u>
deodorant Deo *n* day-oh
department store Kaufhaus
n cowf-house
departure (plane) Abflug *m*
ahp-flook
departure Abfahrt *f* ahp-
faht
deposit Anzahlung *f* <u>ahn</u>-
tsahl-oong

deposit Kaution *f*
cow-tsee-<u>ohn</u>
dermatologist Hautarzt *m*
howt-ahtst
dessert Nachtisch *m* nahk-
tish
dessert wine Dessertwein
m des-<u>sair</u>-vine
detective novel Krimi *m*
kree-mee
detergent Waschmittel *n*
<u>vahsh</u>-mit-tel
diabetes Diabetes *f* dee-ah-
<u>bay</u>-tes
diamond Diamant *m* dee-
ah-<u>mahnt</u>
diarrhea Durchfall *m*
doorsh-fahl
dictionary Wörterbuch *n*
ver-tuh-bookh
diet Diät *f* dee-<u>ate</u>
digital camera
Digitalkamera *f* dee-ghee-
<u>tahl</u>-kah-mair-ah
dining car Speisewagen *m*
<u>shpy</u>-zuh-vah-ghen
dining room Speisesaal *m*
<u>shpy</u>-zuh-zahl
dinner Abendessen *n* <u>ah</u>-
bent-es-sen
direction Richtung *f* rish-
toong
directions Einnahme *f* eye-
n-nahm-uh
director Regisseur *m*
reh-jih-ser
dirty schmutzig shmoo-tsish
disc Bandscheibe *f* <u>bahnt</u>-
shigh-buh
discount Ermäßigung *f* air-
<u>macy</u>-goong
disease Krankheit *f* krahnk-
hight
dishes Geschirr *n* guh-<u>sheer</u>
dishtowel Spültuch *n* spe-
wl-tookh

dishwashing detergent
Spülmittel *n* spewl-mit-tel
dislocated verrenkt fair-renkt
to dive tauchen tauwk-en
diving board Sprungbrett *n*
shproong-bret
diving equipment
Taucherausrüstung *f* tau-wk-uh-ows-rews-toong
diving mask Taucherbrille *f*
tauwk-uh-bril-luh
diving suit Taucheranzug *m*
tauwk-uh-ahn-tsook
dizziness Schwindel *m*
shvin-del
to do the laundry waschen
vahsh-en
dock Anlegestelle *f* ahn-lay-guh-shtel-uh
doctor Arzt *m* ahtst
documents Papiere *pl* pah-pee-ruh
dome Kuppel *f* koop-pel
dormitory Schlafsaal *m*
shlahf-zahl
dosage instructions
Dosierungsanleitung *f*
doh-zeer-oongs-ahn-ligh-toong
double doppel dawp-pel
double bed Doppelbett *n*
dop-pel-bet
doughnut Krapfen *m*
krahp-fen
down the steps die Treppe
f hinunter dee trep-puh hin-oon-tuh
draft Entwurf *m* ent-voorf
drag lift Schlepplift *m*
shlep-lift
drain Abfluss *m* ahp-floos
draught beer Bier *n* vom
Fass beer fum fahss
drawing Zeichnung *f* tsigh-shnoong

dress Kleid *n* kleye-t
dressing Salatsoße *f* zah-laht-zo-suh
drink Drink *m* drink
to drink trinken trink-en
drinking water Trinkwasser
n trink-vas-suh
to drive fahren fah-ren
driver Fahrer *m* fah-ruh
driver's license
Führerschein *m* fur-uh-shine
drizzle Nieselregen *m* nee-zel-ray-ghen
drop Tropfen *m* trop-fen
dry trocken trawk-en
dry cleaner's Reinigung *f*
rye-nih-goong
dryer Wäschetrockner *m*
vehsh-uh-truk-nuh
dubbed synchronisiert zink-ro-nih-zeert
duck Ente *f* en-tuh
duffle bag Seesack *m*
zay-zahk
dumpling Knödel *m*
kuh-ner-del
dusk Dämmerung *f* dem-mair-oong
dust Staub *m* shtauwp
to dye färben fair-ben

E

ear Ohr *n* aw
ear drops Ohrentropfen *pl*
o-ren-trop-fen
ear, nose and throat doctor
Hals-Nasen-Ohren-Arzt *m*
hahls-nah-zen-o-ren-ahtst
early früh frew
earring Ohrring *m* or-ring
earthquake Erdbeben *n*
airt-bay-ben
Easter Ostern *n* oh-stairn

Easter Monday
Ostermontag *m* oh-stair-<u>mohn</u>-tahk
to eat essen es-sen
eel Aal *m* ahl
egg Ei *n* eye
eggplant Aubergine *f* oh-bair-<u>jeen</u>-uh
elastic bandage
Elastikbinde *f* ay-<u>lahs</u>-teek-bin-duh
electronics store
Elektrohandlung *f* ay-<u>lek</u>-tro-hahnt-loong
elevator Aufzug *m* owf-tsook
emergency brake
Handbremse *f* <u>hahnt</u>-brem-zuh
emergency exit
Notausgang *m* <u>noht</u>-auws-gahng
engaged verlobt fair-<u>lohpt</u>
engine Motor *m* mo-tor
engine oil Motoröl *n* <u>mo</u>-tor-erl
envelope Briefumschlag *m* <u>breef</u>-oom-shlahk
environmental pollution
Umweltverschmutzung *f* <u>oom</u>-velt-fair-shmoots-oong
eraser Radiergummi *m* räh-<u>deer</u>-goo-mee
espresso Espresso *m* es-<u>press</u>-o
essential oil Aromaöl *n* ah-<u>ro</u>-mah-erl
evening Abend *m* ah-bent
excavation Ausgrabung *f* <u>ows</u>-grah-boong
excess baggage
Übergepäck *n* <u>ew</u>-buh-guh-pek
exchange rate Kurs *m* ko-orss

exhaust Auspuff *m* ows-poof
exhaust fume Abgas *n* ahp-gahs
exhibition Ausstellung *f* <u>ows</u>-shtel-oong
exit Ausgang *m* ows-gahng
expensive teuer toi-uh
express letter Eilbrief *m* eye-l-brief
expressway Autobahn *f* <u>ow</u>-toe-bahn
extension cord
Verlängerungsschnur *f* fair-<u>leng</u>-air-oongs-shnoor
external äußerlich <u>oi</u>-sair-lish
extra week
Verlängerungswoche *f* fair-<u>leng</u>-air-oongs-vaw-kuh
eye Auge ow-guh
eye drop Augentropfen *m* <u>ow</u>-ghen-trawp-fen
eye shadow Lidschatten *m* <u>leet</u>-shaht-ten
eye specialist Augenarzt *m* <u>ow</u>-ghen-ahtst
eyeliner Kajalstift *m* <u>kah</u>-yahl-shtift

F

facade Fassade *f* fahs-<u>sah</u>-duh
face Gesicht *n* guh-<u>zikt</u>
face wash Reinigungsmilch *f* <u>rye</u>-nee-goongs-milsh
fall Herbst *m* hairpst
flashlight Taschenlampe *f* <u>tah</u>-shen-lahm-puh
fan Ventilator *m* ventee-<u>lah</u>-tor
fanbelt Keilriemen *m* <u>kyle</u>-ree-men
fare Fahrpreis *m* fah-price

221

father Vater *m* fah-tuh
fatty fett fett
faucet Wasserhahn *m* vahs-suh-hahn
feature film Spielfilm *m* speel-film
February Februar *m* fay-broo-ahr
felt tip Filzstift *m* filts-shtift
fender Kotflügel *m* coat-flew-gull
fennel Fenchel *m* fen-shel
festival Festspiel *n* fest-shpeel
feta Schafskäse *m* shahfs-kay-zuh
fever Fieber *n* fee-buh
fiancé Verlobter *m* fair-lohp-tur
fiancée Verlobte *f* fair-lohp-tuh
fig Feige *f* fye-ghe
filet Filet *n* fee-lay
film Film *m* film
to film filmen fil-men
filter Filter *m* fil-tuh
finger Finger *m* fing-uh
finish Lack *m* lahk
fire extinguisher Feuerlöscher *m* foi-uh-lersh-uh
fireplace Kamin *m* kah-meen
firewood Kaminholz *n* kah-meen-holts
first-aid kit Verbandskasten *m* fair-bahnts-kahs-ten
fish Fisch *m* fish
to fish fischen fish-en
fish bone Gräte *f* gray-tuh
fish store Fischgeschäft *n* fish-guh-sheft
flambé flambiert flahm-beert
flash Blitz *m* blits

flea market Flohmarkt *m* flo-mahkt
fleece Fleece *n* fleece
flight Flug *m* flook
flight attendant (male) Steward *m* stoo-art
flight attendant (female) Stewardess *f* stoo-ar-dess
flip-flop Badeschuh *m* bah-duh-shoe
flipper Schwimmflosse *f* shwim-flaws-suh
flood Überschwemmung *f* ew-buh-shvem-moong
floor Etage *f* eh-tah-juh
florist Blumengeschäft *n* bloo-men-guh-sheft
flounder Scholle *f* shawl-luh
flu Grippe *f* grip-puh
flying time Flugzeit *f* flook-tsight
foam mattress Isomatte *f* ee-zo-maht-tuh
fog Nebel *m* nay-bel
folk museum Volkskundemuseum *n* folks-koon-duh-moo-zay-oom
food Essen *n* es-sen
food poisoning Lebensmittelvergiftung *f* lay-bens-mit-tel-fair-ghif-toong
foot Fuß *m* foos
for seit zight
forehead Stirn *f* shteern
forest Wald *m* vahlt
forest fire Waldbrand *m* vahlt-brahnt
fork Gabel *f* gah-bel
fortress Festung *f* fes-toong
forward weiterleiten vigh-tuh-lye-ten
fountain Brunnen *m* broon-nen

fragrance-free parfümfrei
pah-<u>fewm</u>-fry
frankfurter (sausage)
Frankfurter Würstchen *n*
<u>frahnk</u>-foor-tuh <u>vewrst</u>-shen
free frei fry
free climbing Freeclimbing
n free-climing
to freeze; it's freezing frie-
ren; es friert free-ren; es
freert
French fries Pommes frites
pl pom-<u>frit</u>
fresco Fresko *n* fres-ko
fresh frisch frish
fresh-water fish
Süßwasserfisch *m* zews-
vas-suh-fish
Friday Freitag *m* fry-tahk
fried gebraten guh-<u>brah</u>-ten
fried egg Spiegelei *n*
<u>shpee</u>-gull-eye
fried potato Bratkartoffel *f*
<u>braht</u>-kah-taw-fel
friend (male) Freund *m*
froint
friend (female) Freundin *f*
froin-din
front light Vorderlicht *n*
<u>faw</u>-duh-lisht
front mezzanine erster
Rang *m* airs-tuh rahng
frontal sinus Stirnhöhle *f*
<u>steern</u>-her-luh
frost Frost *m* frawst
fruit Obst *n* ohpst
fruit and vegetable store
Obst- und
Gemüsegeschäft *n* ohpst-
unt-guh-<u>mees</u>-uh-guh-sheft
fruit juice Fruchtsaft *m*
frookt-zahft
fruit salad Obstsalat *m*
<u>ohpst</u>-zah-laht
frying pan Pfanne *f* fah-
nuh

fungal infection
Pilzinfektion *f* <u>pilts</u>-in-fek-
tsee-ohn
funnel Trichter *m* trish-tuh
fuse Sicherung *f* <u>zish</u>-air-
oong

G

gall bladder Galle *f* gahl-
luh
gallery Galerie *f* gahl-ah-<u>ree</u>
gallstone Gallenstein *m*
<u>gahl</u>-len-shtine
game Wild *n* vilt
game (match) Spiel *n* sh-
peel
garage Werkstatt *f* vairk-
shtaht
garbage can Mülleimer *m*
<u>mewl</u>-igh-muh
garden Garten *m* gah-ten
garlic Knoblauch *m*
kuh-<u>no</u>-blauwk
gas canister Gaskartusche *f*
<u>gahs</u>-kah-too-shuh
gas station Tankstelle *f*
<u>tahnk</u>-shtel-uh
gas stove Gaskocher *m*
<u>gahs</u>-kaw-khuh
gasket Dichtung *f* dish-
toong
gate Tor taw
gauze bandage Mullbinde *f*
<u>mool</u>-bin-duh
gear Gang *m* gahng
gel Gel *n* gel
generator Dynamo *m* <u>dew</u>-
nah-mo
genital Geschlechtsorgan *n*
guh-<u>shlekts</u>-aw-gahn
genuine echt esht
German measles Röteln *pl*
rer-teln

223

to get off aussteigen <u>ows</u>-shtai-ghen

to get on einsteigen <u>eye-n</u>-shtai-ghen

girl Mädchen *n* <u>made</u>-shen

girlfriend, partner Freundin *f* froin-din

glass Glas *n* glahs

glider Segelflugzeug *n* <u>zay</u>-gull-flook-tsoik

gliding Segelfliegen *n* <u>zay</u>-gull-flee-ghen

glove Handschuh *m* hahnt-shoe

glue Klebstoff *m* klayp-shtawf

to go dancing tanzen ge-hen tahn-tsen gay-en

to go out to eat essen ge-hen ess-en gay-en

to go sledding rodeln rod-eln

goal Tor *n* taw

goalkeeper Torwart *m* tor-waht

goat cheese Ziegenkäse *m* <u>tsee</u>-ghen-kay-zuh

gold Gold *n* gawlt

gold-plated vergoldet fair-<u>gawl</u>-det

golden golden gawl-den

golf (game) Golf *n* golf

golf ball Golfball *m* golf-bahl

golf club Golfschläger *m* <u>golf</u>-shlay-guh

golf course Golfplatz *m* golf-plahts

Good Friday Karfreitag *m* kah-<u>fry</u>-tahk

goose Gans *f* gahnss

gooseberry Stachelbeere *f* <u>stahk</u>-el-bair-uh

Gothic Gotik *f* go-tik

grape Weintraube *f* <u>vine</u>-trow-beh

grave Grab *n* grahp

gravy Soße *f* zo-suh

gray grau grauw

green grün grewn

grill lighter Grillanzünder *m* <u>grill</u>-ahn-tsin-duh

grilled gegrillt guh-<u>grilt</u>

grocery store Lebensmittelgeschäft *n* <u>lay</u>-bens-mit-tel-guh-sheft

ground meat Hackfleisch *n* hahk-flysh

guide dog Blindenhund *m* <u>blin</u>-den-hoont

gum infection Zahnfleischentzündung *f* <u>tsahn</u>-flysh-ent-zewnd-doong

gums Zahnfleisch *n* tsahn-flysh

gynecologist Frauenarzt *m* <u>frow</u>-en-ahtst

H

haddock Schellfisch *m* shell-fish

hail Hagel *m* hah-ghel

hair Haar *n* hah

hairband (elastic) Haargummi *m* <u>hah</u>-goom-ee

hairclip Haarklammer *f* <u>hah</u>-klah-mair

hairdresser Friseursalon *m* free-<u>zoor</u>-zah-long

hairdryer Föhn *m* fern

hairspray Haarspray *n* hah-spray

hairstyle Frisur *f* free-<u>zoor</u>

half an hour halbe Stunde *f* hahl-buh shtoon-duh

halibut Heilbutt *m* hile-boot

hall Saal *m* zahl

ham Schinken *m* shink-en

ham and eggs Spiegeleier mit Vorderschinken <u>shpee</u>-gull-eye-uh mit <u>faw</u>-duh-shink-en

hamburger Hamburger *m* <u>hahm</u>-boor-guh

hammer Hammer *m* hah-muh

hand Hand *f* hahnt

hand brake Handbremse *f* <u>hahnt</u>-brem-zuh

hand cream Handcreme *f* hahnt-krem

to hand in aufgeben <u>owf</u>-gay-ben

handbag Handtasche *f* hahnt-tah-shuh

handball Handball *m* hahnt-bahl

handmade Handarbeit *f* <u>hahnt</u>-ah-bite

hang-gliding Drachenfliegen *n* <u>drahk</u>-en-flee-ghen

hanger Kleiderbügel *m* <u>kligh</u>-duh-bew-ghel

harbor Hafen *m* hah-fen

hard-boiled hart gekocht haht guh-<u>kawkt</u>

hard cider Apfelwein *m* <u>ahp</u>-fel-vine

hard drive Festplatte *f* <u>fest</u>-plah-tuh

hardware Haushaltswaren *pl* <u>house</u>-hahlts-wah-rehn

hardware (computer) Hardware *f* hard-ware

hash browns Rösti *pl* res-tea

hat Hut *m* hoot

hat (cap) Mütze *f* mew-tsuh

to have a good head for heights schwindelfrei sein <u>shvin</u>-del-fry zeye-n

to have breakfast frühstücken <u>frew</u>-shtewk-en

to have mobility problems gehbehindert sein <u>gay</u>-buh-hin-dairt zeye-n

hay fever Heuschnupfen *m* <u>hoi</u>-shnoop-fen

hazelnut Haselnuss *f* <u>hah</u>-zel-nooss

hazy diesig dee-zish

head Kopf *m* kopf

headache pill Kopfschmerztablette *f* <u>kopf</u>-shmairts-tah-blet-tuh

headlights Scheinwerfer *m* <u>shine</u>-vair-fuh

headphones Kopfhörer *m* <u>kupf</u>-her-ruh

hearing impaired hörgeschädigt <u>her</u>-guh-shay-dikt

heart Herz *n* heirts

heart attack Herzanfall *m* <u>heirts</u>-ahn-fahl

heart problem Herzfehler *m* <u>heirts</u>-fay-luh

heartburn Sodbrennen *n* <u>zoht</u>-bren-nen

heat Heizung *f* high-tsoong

heat (temperature) Hitze *f* hit-tsuh

heatwave Hitzewelle *f* <u>hit</u>-tsuh-vel-luh

heel Ferse *f* fair-zuh

helmet Helm *m* helm

hemorrhage Blutung *f* bloo-toong

hemorrhoids Hämorrhoiden *pl* hemo-<u>ree</u>-den

herbal tea Kräutertee *m* <u>kroi</u>-tuh-tay

herbs Kräuter *pl* kroi-tuh

here hier here

hernia Leistenbruch *m* <u>lice</u>-ten-brook

herpes Herpes *m* hair-pes
herring Hering *m* hair-ring
high heels Pumps *pl*
  pumps
high tide Flut *f* floot
high-pressure area Hoch *n*
  hohk
to hike wandern
  vahn-dairn
hiking boot Bergschuh *m*
  bairk-shoe
hiking map Wanderkarte *f*
  vahn-duh-kah-tuh
hiking trail Wanderweg *m*
  vahn-duh-vayk
hill Hügel *m* hew-gull
hip Hüfte *f* hewf-tuh
homemade hausgemacht
  house-guh-mahkt
homeopathic homöopa-
  thisch ho-meh-o-pah-tish
homeopathic doctor
  Heilpraktiker *m*
  highl-prahk-tih-kuh
honey Honig *m* hoh-nig
hood Motorhaube *f*
  mo-tor-how-buh
horn Hupe *f* hoo-puh
hostel manager (female)
  Herbergsmutter *f* hair-
  bairgs-moot-tuh
hostel manager (male)
  Herbergsvater *m*
  hair-bairgs-fah-tuh
hot heiß hice
hot (spicy) scharf
  shahf
hot chocolate heiße
  Schokolade *f*
  hice-uh sho-ko-lah-duh
hot pink pink pink
hotel Hotel *n* ho-tel
hour Stunde *f* shtoon-duh
house Haus *n* house
house wine Hauswein *m*
  house-vine

husband Mann *m* mahn
hut Hütte *f* hew-tuh
hydrofoil Tragflächenboot
  n trahk-flesh-en-boht

I ⎯⎯⎯⎯⎯⎯⎯⎯

ice cream Eis *n* ice
iced coffee Eiskaffee *m*
  ice-kah-fay
ID (Personal) ausweis *m*
  (pair-zo-nahl)-ows-vice
ignition Zündung *f*
  tsewn-doong
ignition cable Zündkabel *n*
  tsewnt-kah-bel
impression Abdruck *m*
  ahp-drook
in front of vor for
in the afternoon am
  Nachmittag *m*
  ahm nahk-mit-tahk
in the evening abends
  ah-bens
in the morning morgens
  maw-ghens
in the morning vormittags
  faw-mit-tahks
in two weeks in 14 Tagen
  in feer-tsane tah-ghen
inbox Posteingang *m*
  pawst-eye-n-gahng
indigestion tablet
  Magentablette *f*
  mah-ghen-tah-blet-tuh
indoor market Markthalle *f*
  mahkt-hahl-luh
infant Säugling *m*
  zoig-ling
infection Infektion *f*
  in-fek-tsee-ohn
infectious ansteckend
  ahn-shtek-ent
inflammation Entzündung
  f ent-zewn-doong

226

inflammation of the middle ear Mittelohrentzündung f mit-tel-aw-ent-zewn-do-ong

information Auskunft f ows-koonft

ingredients Zusammensetzung f tsoo-zahm-men-zets-oong

injection Spritze f shprits-uh

injury Verletzung f fair-lets-oong

inner tube Schlauch m shlauwk

inscription Inschrift f in-shrift

insect bite Insektenstich m in-sek-ten-shtish

insect spray Insektenspray n in-zek-ten-spray

insole Einlegsohle f eye-n-layg-so-luh

insulin Insulin n in-soo-leen

insurance card Versicherungskarte f fair-sish-roongs-kah-tuh

insured package Wertpaket n vairt-pah-kate

intermission Pause f pow-zuh

internal innerlich in-air-lish

international driver's license internationaler Führerschein m in-tair-nah-tsee-o-nah-luh fur-uh-shine

internist Internist m in-tairn-ist

intersection Kreuzung f kroi-tsoong

intestine Darm m dahm

invalid ungültig oon-gewl-tish

to invite einladen eye-n-lah-den

iodine Jod n yoht

to iron bügeln bew-geln

island Insel f in-zel

J

jack Wagenheber m vah-ghen-hay-buh

jacket Jacke f yah-kuh

jam Marmelade f mah-muh-lah-duh

January Januar m yan-oo-ahr

jaw Kiefer m kee-fuh

jeans Jeans pl jeans

jeweler's Juwelier m you-vel-leer

jewelry Schmuck m shmook

Jewish jüdisch yew-dish

to jog joggen jöggen

jogging Jogging n jogging

joint Gelenk n guh-lenk

jug Kanne f kah-nuh

juice Saft m zahft

July Juli m you-lee

jumper cable Starthilfekabel n shtaht-hil-fuh-kah-bel

June Juni m you-nee

K

kayak Kajak m kah-yahk

ketchup Ketchup m ketchup

key Schlüssel m shlews-sel

kidney Niere f nee-ruh

kilometer Kilometer m kee-lo-may-tuh

king König m ker-nik

kiosk Kiosk m kee-awsk

kiwi Kiwi *f* kiwi
knee Knie *n* kuh-<u>nee</u>
kneecap Kniescheibe *f* kuh-<u>nee</u>-shigh-buh
knife Messer *n* mes-suh

L

Labor Day (May 1st) Tag der Arbeit *m* tahk dair ah-<u>bite</u>
lake See *m* zay
lamb Lamm *n* lahm
lambswool Schafwolle *f* <u>shahf</u>-vol-luh
lamp Lampe *f* lahm-puh
land excursion Landausflug *m* <u>lahnt</u>-ows-flook
landing Landung *f* lahn-doong
landscape Landschaft *f* <u>lahnt</u>-shahft
landslide Erdrutsch *m* airt-rootch
last name Familienname *m* fah-<u>meel</u>-yen-nah-muh
last stop Endstation *f* <u>end</u>-shtah-tsee-ohn
late spät shpayt
later später shpay-tuh
laundromat Waschsalon *m* <u>vash</u>-sah-long
laundry line Wäscheleine *f* <u>vesh</u>-uh-lye-nuh
laundry room Waschraum *m* vahsh-rauwm
laxative Abführmittel *n* <u>ahp</u>-fur-mit-tel
leading role Hauptrolle *f* <u>howpt</u>-raw-luh
lean mager mah-guh
leather Leder *n* lay-duh
leather goods store Lederwarengeschäft *n* <u>lay</u>-duh-vah-ren-guh-sheft

leather sole Ledersohle *f* <u>lay</u>-duh-zo-luh
to leave abreisen <u>ahp</u>-rise-en
leek Lauch *m* lauwk
left links linx
to the left nach links nahk linx
leg (animal) Keule *f* koi-luh
leg Bein *n* bine
leggings Leggins *pl* leggins
lemon Zitrone *f* tsih-<u>tro</u>-nuh
lens Objektiv *n* ohp-yek-<u>teef</u>
lentil Linse *f* lin-zeh
lettuce (Kopf)salat *m* (<u>ka</u>-<u>wpf</u>)zah-laht
level access ebenerdig <u>ay</u>-ben-air-dish
library Bibliothek *f* bib-lee-o-<u>take</u>
life jacket Schwimmweste *f* <u>shvim</u>-ves-tuh
life preserver Rettungsring *m* <u>ret</u>-toongs-ring
lifeboat Rettungsboot *n* <u>ret</u>-toongs-boat
lift pass Skipass *m* shee-pahs
light Licht lisht
light blue hellblau hell-blauw
light bulb Glühbirne *f* <u>glew</u>-beer-nuh
light food Schonkost *f* sho-ne-kawst
lighter Feuerzeug *n* <u>foi</u>-uh-tsoik
lightning Blitz *m* blits
lime Limone *f* lee-<u>mo</u>-nuh
linen Leinen *n* line-nen
lip balm Lippenpflegestift *m* <u>lip</u>-pen-flay-guh-shtift
lipstick Lippenstift *m* <u>lip</u>-pen-shtift
liqueur Likör *m* lee-<u>ker</u>

Travel Dictionary

live music Livemusik f <u>live</u>-moo-zeek
liver Leber f lay-buh
lobby Foyer n foi-<u>yay</u>
lobster Hummer m hoom-muh
local time Ortszeit f awt-tsight
local train S-Bahn f ess-bahn
locker Schließfach n shlees-fahk
logout abmelden <u>ahp</u>-mel-den
long lang lahng
long sleeve langer Ärmel m lahng-uh air-mel
to lose verlieren vair-<u>lee</u>-ren
lost and found Fundbüro n <u>foont</u>-bew-<u>ro</u>
loud laut lout
lounge Aufenthaltsraum m <u>owf</u>-ent-hahlts-rauwm
low-alcohol beer alkoholarmes Bier n ahl-ko-<u>hole</u>-ahm-ess beer
low-pressure area Tief n teef
lower back pain Hexenschuss m <u>hex</u>-en-shoos
lowfat fettarm fet-ahm
luggage Gepäck n guh-<u>pek</u>
luggage car Gepäckwagen m guh-<u>pek</u>-vah-ghen
luggage counter Gepäckannahme f guh-<u>pek</u>-ahn-nah-muh
luggage rack Gepäckträger m guh-<u>pek</u>-tray-guh
luggage ticket Gepäckschein m guh-<u>pek</u>-shine
lunch Mittagessen n <u>mit</u>-tahk-es-sen
lungs Lunge f loong-uh

M

macaroon Makrone f mah-<u>kro</u>-nuh
mackerel Makrele f mah-<u>kray</u>-luh
magazine Illustrierte f il-loo-<u>streer</u>-tuh
mask Maske f mahs-kuh
mail Post f post
to make a date sich verabreden zish fair-<u>ahp</u>-ray-den
to make reservations reservieren ray-zair-<u>veer</u>-un
malaria Malaria f mah-<u>lah</u>-ree-ah
man-made fiber Synthetik f zeen-<u>tay</u>-tik
mandarin Mandarine f mahn-dah-<u>ree</u>-nuh
map of cycling routes Radtourenkarte f <u>raht</u>-tou-ren-kah-tuh
marble Marmor m mah-mor
March März m mairts
Mardi gras Fasching m, Karneval m, Fassnacht f fah-shing <u>kah</u>-nuh-vahl fahs-nahkt
margarine Margarine f mah-guh-<u>ree</u>-nuh
marinated eingelegt, mariniert <u>eye-n</u>-guh-laygt mah-ree-<u>neert</u>
market Markt m mahkt
marmalade Orangenmarmelade f o-<u>rahng</u>-jen-mah-muh-lah-duh
married verheiratet fair-<u>high</u>-rah-tet

mascara Wimperntusche f
<u>vim</u>-pairn-too-shuh
mask Maske f mahs-kuh
massage Massage f
mah-<u>sah</u>-juh
matches Streichhölzer pl
<u>shtrysh</u>-herl-tsuh
mattress Matratze f
mah-<u>trah</u>-tsuh
mausoleum Mausoleum n
mauw-zo-<u>lay</u>-oom
May Mai m my
mayonnaise Mayonnaise f
mayo-<u>nay</u>-zuh
meal Gericht n guh-<u>risht</u>
measles Masern pl mah-
zairn
meat Fleisch n flysh
meatball Fleischklößchen n
<u>flysh</u>-klers-shen
meditation Meditation f
may-dee-tah-tsee-<u>ohn</u>
medium halbtrocken <u>hahlp</u>-
trock-en
medium (rare) medium
<u>may</u>-de-oom
to meet kennen lernen kennen lair-nen
melon Melone f mel-<u>oh</u>-
nuh
memorial Gedenkstätte f
guh-<u>denk</u>-shteh-tuh
memory card Speicherkarte
f <u>spy</u>-sher-kahr-tuh
meningitis
Hirnhautentzündung f
<u>hirn</u>-howt-ent-zewnd-doong
meringue Baiser n bay-<u>zay</u>
microfiber Mikrofaser f
<u>mee</u>-kro-fah-zuh
Middle Ages pl Mittelalter
n <u>mit</u>-tel-ahl-tuh
migraine Migräne f
mee-<u>gray</u>-nuh
milk Milch f milsh

milkshake Milchmixgetränk
n <u>milsh</u>-mix-guh-trenk
mill Mühle f mew-luh
mineral water
Mineralwasser n min-air-
<u>ahl</u>-vas-suh
miniature golf Minigolf m
mini-golf
minibar Minibar f mini-bah
minute Minute f min-oo-
tuh
mirror Spiegel m shpee-
ghel
mobility cane Taststock m
tahst-shtok
model Modell n mo-<u>del</u>
modern modern mo-<u>dairn</u>
moisturizer Tagescreme f
<u>tah</u>-ghes-krem
moisturizing mask
Feuchtigkeitsmaske f
<u>foik</u>-tih-kites-mas-kuh
to molest belästigen buh-
<u>les</u>-tee-ghen
monastery Kloster n
klohs- tuh
Monday Montag m moan-
tahk
money Geld n ghelt
month Monat m mo-naht
monument Denkmal n
denk-mahl
moon Mond m mohnt
moped Motorscooter m
<u>mo</u>-tor-scoo-tuh
morning Vormittag m <u>faw</u>-
mit-tahk
mosaic Mosaik n mo-zah-
<u>eek</u>
mosque Moschee f mo-shay
mosquito coil
Moskitospirale f maws-
<u>kee</u>-to-shpee-rahl-uh
mosquito net Moskitonetz
n maws-<u>kee</u>-to-nets

mosquito repellent
Mückenschutz m mewken-
shoots
mother Mutter f moo-tuh
motion sickness
Reisekrankheit f rise-uh-
krahnk-hight
motorbike Motorrad n mo-
tor-raht
motorboat Motorboot n
mo-tor-boat
mountain Berg m bairk
mountain climbing
Bergsteigen n
bairg-shtigh-ghen
mountain guide Bergführer
m bairg-fur-uh
mountain rescue service
Bergwacht f bairg-vahkt
mountains Gebirge n guh-
beer-guh
mousse Schaumfestiger m
shauwm-festi-guh
moustache Schnurrbart m
shnoor-baht
mouth Mund m moont
movie theater Kino n kee-
no
MP3 player MP3-Spieler m
em-pay-dry-shpee-luh
Mr. Herr m hair
Ms. Frau f frow
mucus membrane
Schleimhaut f shlighm-
howt
mud mask Fango m fahn-
go
multi-level parking garage
Parkhaus n pahk-house
mumps Mumps m moomps
mural Wandmalerei f
vahnt-mahl-uh-rye
muscle Muskel m moos-kel
museum Museum n
moo-zay-oom
mushroom Pilz m pilts

music Musik f moo-zeek
music recital Liederabend
m lee-duh-ah-bent
music store Musikgeschäft
n moo-zeek-guh-sheft
musical Musical n musical
Muslim moslemisch mos-
leh-mish
mussel Muschel f moosh-el
mustard Senf m zenf
mutton Hammel m hahm-el

N

nail file Nagelfeile f nah-
ghel-fy-luh
nail polish Nagellack m
nah-ghel-lahk
nail polish remover
Nagellackentferner m
nah-ghel-lahk-ent-fair nuh
nail scissors pl Nagelschere
f nah-ghel-shair-uh
nailbrush Nagelbürste f
nah-ghel-bewr-stuh
napkin Serviette f
zair-vee-et-tuh
narcotics Rauschgift n
rauwsh-gift
national park Nationalpark
m nah-tsee-o-nahl-pahk
National Unity Day Tag m
der Deutschen Einheit
tahk dair doi-tschen eye-n-
hite
nationality
Staatsangehörigkeit f
stahts-ahn-guh-her-ish-kite
natural fiber Naturfaser f
nah-toor-fah-zuh
nature preserve
Naturschutzgebiet n nah-
toor-shoots-guh-beet
nausea Übelkeit f ew-bel-
kite

navy blue dunkelblau
doon-kel-blauw
nearby nahe bei nah-uh by
neck (collar) Hals *m* hahls
neck (back) Nacken *m*
nahk-en
neckerchief Halstuch *n*
hahls-took
necklace Kette *f* ket-tuh
nectarine Nektarine *f* nek-
tah-ree-nuh
negative Negativ *n* neh-
gah-teef
nerve Nerv *m* nairf
neuralgia Neuralgie *f* noi-
rahl-ghee
neutral Leerlauf *m* lair-
lauwf
New Year's Day Neujahr *n*
noi-yah
New Year's Eve Silvester *m*
zil-ves-tuh
newsstand Zeitungsstand
m tsigh-toongs-shtahnt
next to neben nay-ben
next year nächstes Jahr *n*
nayx-tes yah
night Nacht *f* nahkt
night cream Nachtcreme *f*
nahkt-krem
no-parking zone Parkverbot
n pahk-fair-boat
non-alcoholic beer alkoholfreies Bier *n* ahl-ko-
hole-fry-ess beer
non-smoking Nichtraucher
m nisht-rauw-ker
non-swimmer
Nichtschwimmer *m* nisht-
shwim-muh
noodle soup Nudelsuppe *f*
noo-del-zoo-puh
Norman normannisch naw-
mahn-ish
nose Nase *f* nah-zuh

nose bleed Nasenbluten *n*
nah-zen-bloo-ten
nose drops Nasentropfen *pl*
nah-zen-trop-fen
not far nicht weit nisht vhite
novel Roman *m* ro-mahn
November November *m*
november
now jetzt yetst
nude beach FKK-Strand *m*
ef-kah-kah-shtrahnt
number Nummer *f* noo-
muh
nut Nuss *f* nooss

O

obelisk Obelisk *m* o-buh-
lisk
observatory Sternwarte *f*
shtairn-vah-tuh
occupation Beruf *m* beh-
roof
ocean Meer *n* mair
October Oktober *m* october
off-peak season Nachsaison
f nahk-say-zong
oil Öl *n* erl
oil change Ölwechsel *m*
erl-wex-el
ointment Salbe *f* zahl-buh
olive oil Olivenöl *n*
o-lee-ven-erl
olive Olive *f* o-lee-veh
omelet Omelett *n* om-let
on sale Sonderangebot *n*
zon-duh-ahn-guh-boat
onion Zwiebel *f* tsvee-bel
open geöffnet guh-erf-net
open-air theater
Freilichtbühne *f*
fry-lisht-bee-nuh
opening night Premiere *f*
prem-yair-uh
opera Oper *f* oh-pair

opera house Opernhaus *n*
oh-pairn-house
operetta Operette *f*
oh-pair-et-tuh
opposite gegenüber gay-
ghen-ew-buh
optician Optiker *m* awp-
tee-kuh
oral oral o-rahl
orange Orange *f* oh-rahng-
juh
orange juice Orangensaft
m oh-rahng-jen-zahft
orchestra Orchester *n* aw-
kest-tuh
orchestra (seating) Parkett
n pahr-kett
to order bestellen buh-
shtel-en
oregano Oregano *m* o-ray-
gahn-o
organ Orgel *f* aw-gull
original Original *n* or-ee-
ghi-nahl
original version
Originalfassung *f* aw-rig-
ee-nahl-fahs-soong
orthopedist Orthopäde *m*
or-to-pay-duh
outlet Steckdose *f*
shtek-do-zuh
outside cabin Außenkabine
f ows-sen-kah-bee-nuh
oyster Auster *f* ows-tair

P

pacemaker
Herzschrittmacher *m*
heirts-shrit-mahk-uh
pacifier Schnuller *m* sh-
nool-uh
pack Packung *f* pahk-oong
package Paket *n* pah-kate

painkiller Schmerzmittel *n*
shmairts-mit-tel
painter Maler *m* mah-luh
painting Gemälde *n*
guh-mail-duh
painting Malerei *f* mah-luh-
rye
pajamas *pl* Schlafanzug *m*
shlahf-ahn-tsook
palace Palast *m* pah-lahst
pancake Pfannkuchen *m*
fahn-kook-en
panorama Panorama *n*
pah-naw-rah-mah
panties Slip *m* slip
pants Hose *f* ho-zuh
pantyhose Strumpfhose *f*
shtroomf-ho-zuh
paper Papier *n* pah-peer
paper towels Küchenrolle *f*
kewsh-en-rol-luh
paprika Paprika *m* pah-pree-
kah
paragliding
Gleitschirmfliegen *n*
gleye-t-sheerm-flee-ghen
paraplegic
querschnittgelähmt kvair-
shnit-guh-laymt
to park parken pah-ken
park Park *m* pahk
parking disc Parkscheibe *f*
pahk-shy-buh
parking lot Parkplatz *m*
pahk-plahts
parking meter Parkuhr *f*
pahk-oor
parsley Petersilie *f* pay-tuh-
zeel-yuh
part of town Stadtteil *m*
shtaht-tile
partner Partner *m* pahrt-
nuh
partridge Rebhuhn *n* rayp-
hoon
passport Pass *m* pahss

233

pasta Nudeln *pl* noo-deln
pastry Gebäck *n* guh-<u>bek</u>
pastry shop Konditorei *f*
kone-dee-tor-<u>rye</u>
path Weg *m* vayk
to pay bezahlen buh-<u>tzah</u>-len
to pay duty verzollen
fair-<u>tsol</u>-len
to pay separately getrennt
bezahlen guh-<u>trent</u> buh-<u>tsah</u>-len
to pay together zusammen
bezahlen tsu-<u>zahm</u>-men
buh-<u>tsah</u>-len
pea Erbse *f* airp-seh
peach Pfirsich *m* feer-zish
peak season Hauptsaison *f*
<u>hauwpt</u>-say-zong
peanut Erdnuss *f* airt-nooss
pear Birne *f* beer-nuh
pearl Perle *f* pair-luh
pedal boat Tretboot *n*
trayt-boat
pedestrian zone
Fußgängerzone *f* <u>foos</u>-gheng-uh-tsoh-nuh
pediatrician Kinderarzt *m*
<u>kin</u>-duh-ahtst
pelvis Becken *n* bek-en
pencil Bleistift *m* bligh-shtift
pencil sharpener Spitzer *m*
shpits-uh
pendant Anhänger *m* <u>ahn</u>-heng-uh
peninsula Halbinsel *f*
<u>hahlp</u>-in-zel
Pentecost Pfingsten *n*
fing-sten
pepper (ground) Pfeffer *m*
fef-fuh
pepperoni Salami *f*
zah-<u>lah</u>-mee
perch Barsch *m* bahsh
perfume Parfüm *n* pah-<u>fewm</u>

perfume shop Parfümerie *f*
pah-feem-uh-<u>ree</u>
periodontal disease
Parodontose *f* pah-rah-dawn-<u>toe</u>-zuh
period Menstruation *f* men-shtroo-ah-tsee-<u>ohn</u>
pharmacy Apotheke *f* ah-po-<u>tay</u>-kuh
pheasant Fasan *m* fah-<u>zahn</u>
phone Telefon *n* tay-luh-<u>fone</u>
photo Foto *n* foh-toh
photo shop Fotogeschäft *n*
<u>foto</u>-guh-sheft
physician praktischer Arzt
m <u>prahk</u>-tish-uh ahtst
pickled eingelegt <u>eye</u>-n-guh-laygt
pickled pig's knuckle
Eisbein *n* ice-bine
pickpocket Taschendieb *m*
<u>tah</u>-shen-deep
picture Bild *n* bilt
picture book Bilderbuch *n*
<u>bil</u>-duh-bookh
piece Stück *n* shtewk
pillar Säule *f* zoi-luh
pillow Kopfkissen *n*
<u>kopf</u>-kis-sen
pilot Pilot *m* pee-lote
PIN Geheimzahl *f* guh-<u>hime</u>-tsahl
pineapple Ananas *f* <u>ah</u>-nah-nahs
pink rosa ro-zah
pipe Pfeife *f* fife-uh
pipe cleaner Pfeifenreiniger
m <u>fife</u>-en-rye-nee-guh
pistachio Pistazie *f* pis-<u>tah</u>-tsee-eh
pizza Pizza *f* pizza
place of pilgrimage
Wallfahrtsort *m*
<u>vahl</u>-fahts-awt

234

place of residence Wohnort
  m vone-ort
plane Flugzeug *n* flook-
  tsoik
planetarium Planetarium *n*
  plah-nuh-<u>tah</u>-ree-oom
plastic cup Plastikbecher *m*
  <u>plahs</u>-tik-besh-uh
plastic plate Plastikteller *m*
  <u>plahs</u>-tik-tel-luh
plastic untensils
  Plastikbesteck *n* <u>plahs</u>-tik-
  buh-shtek
plastic wrap Frischhaltefolie
  f <u>frish</u>-hahl-tuh-fol-yuh
plate Teller *m* tel-uh
platform Bahnsteig *m*
  bahn-shtaig
platinum Platin *n* plah-teen
to play spielen shpeel-en
play Theaterstück *n* tay-<u>ah</u>-
  tuh-shtewk
playground Spielplatz *m*
  shpeel-plahts
playing card Spielkarte *f*
  <u>shpeel</u>-kah-tuh
playing field Spielwiese *f*
  <u>shpeel</u>-vee-zuh
playpen Laufstall *m* lauwf-
  shtahl
please bitte bit-tuh
pliers Zange *f* tsahng-uh
plug Stecker *m* shtek-uh
plum Pflaume *f* flauw-muh
plum (green) Reineclaude *f*
  <u>ryen</u>-klo-duh
pneumonia
  Lungenentzündung *f* <u>lo</u>-
  ong-en-ent-zewnd-doong
pocket calculator
  Taschenrechner *m* <u>tah</u>-
  shen-resh-nair
pocket knife Taschenmesser
  n <u>tah</u>-shen-mes-suh
pole Skistock *m* shee-shtok
police Polizei *f* po-lee-<u>tsigh</u>

policeman Polizist *m*
  po-lee-<u>tsist</u>
policewoman Polizistin *f*
  po-lee-<u>tsis</u>-tin
polio Kinderlähmung *f* <u>kin</u>-
  duh-lay-moong
polluted verschmutzt fair-
  <u>shmootst</u>
pop concert Popkonzert *n*
  <u>pop</u>-kon-tsairt
pork Schweinefleisch *n*
  <u>shvine</u>-nuh-flysh
port Portwein *m* pawt-vine
portion Portion *f*
  paw-tsee-<u>ohn</u>
portrait Porträt *n* paw-<u>tray</u>
postcard Ansichtskarte *f*
  <u>ahn</u>-zikhts-kah-tuh
poster (large) Plakat *n*
  plah-<u>kaht</u>
poster Poster *n* poster
pot roast Schmorbraten *m*
  <u>shmor</u>-brah-ten
potato Kartoffel *f* kah-
  <u>tawf</u>-el
pottery Töpferware *f* <u>terp</u>-
  fair-vah-ruh
pottery (manufacturing)
  Töpferei *f* terp-fuh-<u>rye</u>
poultry Geflügel *n* güh-
  <u>flew</u>-gull
powder Puder *m* poo-duh,
  Pulver *n* pool-vuh
precipitation Niederschlag
  m <u>nee</u>-duh-shlahg
pregnant women
  Schwangere *f* <u>shvahng</u>-uh-
  ruh
prescription Rezept *n* ray-
  <u>tsept</u>
to print drucken drook-en
printer cartridge
  Druckerpatrone *f* <u>drook</u>-
  uh-pah-troh-nuh
production Inszenierung *f*
  in-sen-<u>eer</u>-oong

235

program Programmheft *n*
proh-<u>grahm</u>-heft
property management
Hausverwaltung *f* <u>house</u>-
fair-val-toong
Protestant protestantisch
protes-<u>tahn</u>-tish
public pool
Schwimmbad *n* shvim-
baht
pudding Pudding *m* pudding
pulled ligament
Bänderzerrung *f* <u>ben</u>-duh-
tsair-oong
pulled muscle
Muskelzerrung *f* <u>moos</u>-
kel-tsair-oong
pulled tendon
Sehnenzerrung *f* <u>zay</u>-nen-
tsair-oong
pump Luftpumpe *f* looft-
poom-puh
pumpkin Kürbis *m* kewr-
biss
purification Entschlackung
f ent-<u>shlahk</u>-oong
purple lila lee-lah
purse, handbag Handtasche
f <u>hahnt</u>-tah-shuh

Q

quail Wachtel *f* vahk-tel
queen Königin *f* <u>ker</u>-nee-
ghin

R

rabbit Kaninchen *n* kah-
<u>neen</u>-shen
radiator Kühler *m* kew-luh
radio Radio *n* <u>rah</u>-dee-oh

236

radish Radieschen *n*
rah-<u>dees</u>-shen
raft (rubber) Schlauchboot
n shlauwk-boat
raincoat Regenmantel *m*
<u>ray</u>-ghen-mahn-tel
rainy regnerisch <u>rayg</u>-nair-
ish
raisin Rosine *f* ro-zee-nuh
ramp Autobahnauffahrt *f*
<u>ow</u>-toe-bahn-owf-faht
range Herd *m* hairt
rare (steak) englisch ayng-
lish
rash Ausschlag *m* ows-
shlahk
raspberry Himbeere *f* <u>him</u>-
bair-uh
ravine Schlucht *f* shlookt
raw roh ro
razor Rasierapparat *m* rah-
<u>zeer</u>-ah-pah-raht
razor blade Rasierklinge *f*
rah-<u>zeer</u>-kling-uh
rear mezzanine zweiter
Rang *m* tsvigh-tuh rahng
rear-end collision
Auffahrunfall *m* <u>owf</u>-fah-
oon-fahl
rear-view mirror
Rückspiegel *m* <u>rewk</u>-sh-
pee-gull
receipt Quittung *f* kveet-
oong
recently vor kurzem faw
koorts-em
reception Rezeption *f* ray-
tsep-tsi-<u>ohn</u>
rectal rektal rek-<u>tahl</u>
red rot roht
red wine Rotwein *m* roht-
vine
referee Schiedsrichter *m*
<u>sheets</u>-rish-tuh

Travel Dictionary

reflexology massage Fußreflexzonenmassage *f* <u>foos</u>-reh-flex-tson-en-mah-sah-juh

refrigerator Kühlschrank *m* kewl-shrahnk

regatta Regatta *f* ray-<u>gaht</u>-tuh

relief Relief *n* rel-<u>yef</u>

religion Religion *f* reh-lig-ee-<u>ohn</u>

remains Überreste *pl* <u>ew</u>-buh-res-tuh

renaissance Renaissance *f* ren-ay-<u>sahns</u>

rent Miete *f* mee-tuh

to rent mieten mee-ten

rental fee Leihgebühr *f* <u>lye</u>-guh-bewr

repair Reparatur *f* ray-pah-rah-<u>toor</u>

to repair reparieren ray-pah-<u>reer</u>-en

to repeat wiederholen vee-duh-<u>ho</u>-len

to replace auswechseln <u>ows</u>-vex-eln

reply Antwort *f* ahnt-vawt

reserved reserviert ray-zair-<u>veert</u>

reservoir Stausee *m* shtauw-zay

restaurant Restaurant *n* rest-oh-<u>rahng</u>

restored restauriert res-tauw-<u>reert</u>

restroom Toilette *f* toi-<u>let</u>-tuh

to return zurückgeben tsoo-<u>rewk</u>-gay-ben

return flight Rückflug *m* rewk-flook

rheumatism Rheuma *n* roi-mah

rhubarb Rhabarber *m* rah-<u>bah</u>-buh

rib Rippe *f* rip-puh

ribs Rippenstück *n* <u>rip</u>-pen-stewk

rice Reis *m* rice

to ride (bicycle) fahren fah-ren

to ride (horseback) reiten rye-ten

to the right nach rechts nahk rekts

right rechts rekts

right of way Vorfahrt *f* faw-faht

ring Ring *m* ring

rinse Spülung *f* shpew-loong

river Fluss *m* floos

river rafting Rafting *n* rahfting

road Straße *f* shtrah-suh

road map Straßenkarte *f* <u>shtrahs</u>-sen-kah-tuh

roast Braten *m* brah-ten

roasted geröstet guh-<u>rers</u>-tet

rock concert Rockkonzert *n* <u>rock</u>-kon-tsairt

roll Brötchen *n* brert-shen

rolled oat Haferflocke *f* <u>hah</u>-fuh-flaw-kuh

Roman römisch rer-mish

Romanesque romanisch ro-<u>mahn</u>-ish

romantic romantisch ro-<u>mahn</u>-tish

room Zimmer *n* tsim-muh

root Wurzel *f* voor-tsel

root canal Wurzelbehandlung *f* <u>voor</u>-tsel-buh-hahnt-loong

rope Seil *n* zile

rosemary Rosmarin *m* <u>rose</u>-mah-rin

rosé Rosé *m* ro-<u>zay</u>

rough seas Seegang *m* zay-gahng

row Reihe f rye-uh
row boat Ruderboot n roo-duh-boat
rubber boot Gummistiefel m goom-ee-shtee-fel
ruins Ruine f roo-ee-nuh
rum Rum m room
RV (recreational vehicle) Wohnmobil n vone-mo-beel
rye bread Roggenbrot n raw-ghen-broht

S

saddle Sattel m zaht-tel
saddlebag Satteltasche f zaht-tel-tahsh-uh
safe Safe m safe
safety pin Sicherheitsnadel f zik-uh-hights-nah-del
to sail segeln zay-gheln
sail boat Segelboot n zay-gull-boat
salad Salat m zah-laht
sale Ausverkauf m ows-fair-cowf
salmon Lachs m lahx
salmonella poisoning Salmonellenvergiftung f zahl-mo-nel-en-fair-ghif-toong
salt Salz n zahlts
salt-water fish Seefisch m zay-fish
sand Sand m zahnt
sandal Sandale f zahn-dah-luh
sandpaper Schmirgelpapier n shmier-ghel-pah-peer
sandstone Sandstein m zahnt-shtyn
sandwich belegtes Brot n buh-layk-tes broht

sandy beach Sandstrand m zahnt-shtrahnt
sanitary napkin Binde f bin-duh
sarcophagus Sarkophag m zah-ko-fahk
sardine Sardine f zah-deen-uh
Saturday Samstag m zahms-tahk
sauce Soße f zo-suh
saucepan Topf m tawpf
sauna Sauna f sow-nah
sausage Wurst f voorst
to save speichern shpy-shairn
savings bank Sparkasse f shpah-kahs-suh
scallop Jakobsmuschel f yah-cops-moosh-el
scarf Schal m shahl
scarlet fever Scharlach m shah-lahk
schedule Fahrplan m fah-plahn
school Schule f shoo-luh
sciatica Ischias m ish-ee-ahs
scissors Schere f shay-ruh
scotch schottischer Whisky m shawt-tish-uh whisky
scrambled egg Rührei n rewr-eye
screw Schraube f shrauw-buh
screwdriver Schraubenzieher m shrauw-ben-tsee-uh
sculptor Bildhauer m bilt-how-uh
sculpture Skulptur f skoolp-toor
seafood Meeresfrüchte pl mair-es-frewsh-tuh
seasick seekrank zay-krahnk
seasoned gewürzt guh-vewtst

238

Travel Dictionary

seat Platz *m* plahts
seatbelt Sicherheitsgurt *m* <u>zisher</u>-hites-goort
second Sekunde *f* zeh-<u>koon</u>-duh
to see (someone) again (jdn.) wiedersehen (<u>yay</u>-mahn-den) <u>vee</u>-duh-zay-en
self-service Selbstbedienung *f* zelpst-buh-<u>deen</u>-oong
self-timer Selbstauslöser *m* <u>zelpst</u>-ows-ler-suh
semolina Grieß *m* grees
to send senden zen-den
to send (package) schicken shik-en
sender Absender *m* <u>ahp</u>-zen-duh
September September *m* zeptember
service (restaurant) Bedienung *f* buh-<u>deen</u>-oong
service area Raststätte *f* <u>rahst</u>-shtet-tuh
sewing needle Nähnadel *f* <u>nay</u>-nah-del
sewing thread Nähgarn *n* nay-gahn
sexually transmitted disease (STD) Geschlechtskrankheit *f* guh-<u>shlekts</u>-krahnk-hight
shade Schatten *m* shaht-ten
shallot Schalotte *f* shah-<u>lawt</u>-tuh
shampoo Shampoo *n* shahm-poo
to shave rasieren rah-<u>zee</u>-ren
shaving cream Rasierschaum *m* rah-<u>zeer</u>-shauwm
sheet Bettlaken *n* <u>bet</u>-lah-ken

shellfish Schalentier *n* <u>shahl</u>-en-teer
shell Muschel *f* moosh-el
shelter Schutzhütte *f* <u>shoots</u>-hew-tuh
Sherry Sherry *m* shair-ree
shinbone Schienbein *n* sheen-bine
ship Schiff *n* shif
ship's doctor Schiffsarzt *m* shifs-ahtst
shirt Hemd *n* hempt
shock Schock *m* shock
shock absorber Stoßdämpfer *m* <u>shtos</u>-demp-fuh
shoe polish Schuhcreme *f* shoe-krem
shoe repair shop Schuhmacher *m* <u>shoe</u>-mah-kuh
shoe store Schuhgeschäft *n* <u>shoe</u>-guh-sheft
shoelaces Schnürsenkel *m* <u>shnewr</u>-zenk-el
shoe Schuh *m* shoe
shopping center Einkaufszentrum *n* <u>eye-n</u>-cowfs-tsen-troom
short kurz koorts
short sleeve kurzer Ärmel *m* koor-tsuh air-mel
shorts Shorts *pl* shorts
shoulder Schulter *f* shool-tuh
to show zeigen tsigh-ghen
shower Dusche *f* doo-shuh
shower (rain) Regenschauer *m* <u>ray</u>-ghen-show-uh
shower gel Duschgel *n* doosh-gel
shrimp Garnele *f* gah-<u>nay</u>-luh
sick bag Spucktüte *f* <u>sh</u>-pook-tew-tuh

239

side dish Beilage _f_ <u>by</u>-lah-guh

side effect Nebenwirkung _f_ <u>nay</u>-ben-veer-koong

sight Sehenswürdigkeit _f_ <u>zay</u>-ens-weer-dish-kite

sightseeing tour Rundfahrt _f_ <u>roont</u>-faht

signature Unterschrift _f_ <u>oon</u>-tuh-shrift

silk Seide _f_ zeye-duh

silver (plated) silbern <u>zil</u>-bairn

silver Silber _n_ <u>zil</u>-buh

silverware Besteck _n_ buh-<u>shtek</u>

since seit zight

singer Sänger _m_ <u>zeng</u>-air

single Einzel- <u>eye</u>-n-tsel

single bed Einzelbett _n_ <u>eye</u>-n-tsel-bet

sink Waschbecken _n_ <u>vahsh</u>-bek-ken

sinus Nebenhöhle _f_ <u>nay</u>-ben-her-luh

sister Schwester _f_ <u>shves</u>-tuh

size Größe _f_ <u>grers</u>-suh

ski Ski _m_ shee

ski mask Skibrille _f_ <u>shee</u>-bril-uh

skiing instructor Skilehrer _m_ <u>shee</u>-lair-uh

skiing wax Skiwachs _n_ <u>shee</u>-vahx

skin Haut _f_ howt

skin diagnosis Hautdiagnose _f_ <u>howt</u>-dee-ahg-no-zuh

skirt Rock _m_ rock

skydiving Fallschirmspringen _n_ <u>fahl</u>-sheerm-shpring-en

sleeper car Schlafwagen _m_ <u>shlahf</u>-vah-ghen

sleeping bag Schlafsack _m_ <u>shlahf</u>-zahk

sleeping pill Schlaftablette _f_ <u>shlahf</u>-tah-blet-tuh

slowly langsam <u>lahng</u>-zahm

SLR camera Spiegelreflexkamera _f_ <u>shpee</u>-gull-ray-<u>flex</u>-kah-mair-ah

small package Päckchen _n_ <u>pek</u>-shen

smog Smog _m_ smog

smoked geräuchert guh-<u>roish</u>-airt

smoking compartment Raucherabteil _n_ <u>rauwk</u>-er-ahp-tile

sneaker Turnschuh _m_ <u>to</u>-orn-shoe

snorkel Schnorchel _m_ <u>shnaw</u>-shel

snow Schnee _m_ shnay

snow chain Schneekette _f_ <u>shnay</u>-ket-tuh

snow pea Zuckererbse _f_ <u>tsook</u>-kuh-airp-suh

soap Seife _f_ <u>zeye</u>-fuh

soccer ball Fußball _m_ <u>foos</u>-bahl

soccer field Fußballplatz _m_ <u>foos</u>-bahl-plahts

soccer game Fußballspiel _n_ <u>foos</u>-bahl-shpeel

socket Steckschlüssel _m_ <u>shtek</u>-shlews-sel

sock Socke _f_ <u>zaw</u>-kuh

soda Limonade _f_ lee-mo-<u>nah</u>-duh

soft drink alkoholfreies Getränk _n_ ahl-ko-<u>hol</u>-fry-es guh-trenk

sold out ausverkauft <u>ows</u>-fair-cowft

sole Seezunge _f_ <u>zay</u>-tsoong-uh

solid-color einfarbig <u>eye</u>-n-fah-bish

soloist Solist _m_ zoh-<u>list</u>

240

Travel Dictionary

something for ... etwas gegen ... et-vahs gay-ghen
sometimes manchmal mahnch-mahl
son Sohn m zone
soon bald bahlt
sore Geschwür n guh-<u>shve-wr</u>
soup Suppe f zoop-uh
sour sauer sour
souvenir shop Andenkenladen m <u>ahn-</u>denk-en-lah-den
spare gasoline can Reservekanister m ray-<u>zair</u>-vuh-kahn-is-tuh
spare part Ersatzteil n air-<u>zahts</u>-tile
spare tire Ersatzreifen m air-<u>zahts</u>-rye-fen
spark plug Zündkerze f <u>tsewnt</u>-kair-tsuh
sparkling wine Sekt m zekt
to speak sprechen shpre-shen
specialty Spezialität f sh-pets-ee-ahl-ih-<u>tayt</u>
speed Geschwindigkeit f ghe-<u>shwin</u>-dish-kite
speed (film) Empfindlichkeit f emp-<u>fint</u>-lish-kite
speedometer Tachometer m tahko-<u>may</u>-tuh
spice Gewürz n guh-<u>veerts</u>
spinach Spinat m shpih-<u>naht</u>
spine Wirbelsäule f <u>veer</u>-bel-zoi-luh
spoon Löffel m lerf-el
sporting goods store Sportgeschäft n <u>shport</u>-guh-sheft
sports jacket Sakko m zahk-ko
sprained verstaucht fair-<u>shtowkt</u>

spring Frühling m frew-ling
square Platz m plats
squash (sport) Squash n squash
squash ball Squashball m squash-bahl
squash racket Squashschläger m <u>squash</u>-shlay-guh
stadium Stadion n <u>shtah</u>-dee-on
stain remover Fleckentferner m <u>flek</u>-ent-fair-nuh
stamp Briefmarke f <u>brief</u>-mah-kuh
standing room ticket Stehplatz m shtay-plats
star Stern m stairn
start of the season Vorsaison f <u>faw</u>-say-zong
starter Anlasser m <u>ahn</u>-lahs-suh
Station Restaurant Bahnhofsgaststätte f <u>bahn</u>-hoafs-gahst-shtet-tuh
stationery store Schreibwarengeschäft n <u>shryp</u>-vah-ren-guh-sheft
statue Statue f <u>shtah</u>-too-uh
steak Steak n steak
steam bath Dampfbad n dahmpf-baht
steamed gedämpft, gedünstet guh-<u>dempft</u> guh-<u>dewns</u>-tet
steering Lenkung f lenk-oong
steward Steward m ste-ward
sting Stich m shtish
stocking Strumpf m sh-troomf
stolen gestohlen guh-<u>stoh</u>-len

241

stomach Magen *m* mah-ghen

stomach ache Magenschmerz *m* mah-ghen-shmairts

stomach ulcer Magengeschwür *n* mah-ghen-guh-shveer

stop Haltestelle *f* hahl-tuh-stel-uh

to stop halten hahl-ten

stopover Zwischenlandung *f* tsvish-en-lahn-doong

storm Sturm *m* shtoorm

storm warning Sturmwarnung *f* shtoorm-wah-noong

stormy stürmisch shtewr-mish

stove Kocher *m* kaw-kuh

straight ahead geradeaus guh-rah-duh-ows

strawberry Erdbeere *f* airt-bair-eh

street Straße *f* shtrah-suh

stroke Schlaganfall *m* shlahk-ahn-fahl

stroller Kinderwagen *m* kin-duh-vah-ghen

student Student *m* shtoo-dent

to study studieren shtoo-dee-ren

style Stil *m* shteel

styling gel Haargel *n* hah-ghel

subtitle Untertitel *m* oon-tair-tee-tel

suckling pig Spanferkel *n* shpahn-fair-kel

suede Wildleder *n* vilt-lay-duh

sugar Zucker *m* tzook-uh

suit Anzug *m* ahn-tsook

suit (for a woman) Kostüm *n* kaws-tewm

suitcase Koffer *m* kaw-fuh

summer Sommer *m* zaw-muh

summit Gipfel *m* ghip-fel

sun Sonne *f* zon-nuh

sun deck Sonnendeck *n* zon-nen-deck

sun protection factor (SPF) Lichtschutzfaktor *m* likt-shoots-fahk-tor

sunburn Sonnenbrand *m* zon-nen-brahnt

sundae Eisbecher *m* ice-besh-uh

Sunday Sonntag *m* zon-tahk

sunglasses Sonnenbrille *f* zon-nen-bril-luh

sunny sonnig zon-nik

sunrise Sonnenaufgang *m* zon-nen-owf-gahng

sunroof Schiebedach *n* she-buh-dahk

sunscreen Sonnencreme *f* zon-en-krem

sunset Sonnenuntergang *m* zon-nen-oont-uh-gahng

sunstroke Sonnenstich *m* zon-nen-shtish

suntan lotion Sonnenmilch *f* zon-en-milsh

supermarket Supermarkt *m* zoo-puh-mahkt

suppository Zäpfchen *n* tsepf-shen

surcharge Zuschlag *m* tsu-shlahk

surfboard Surfbrett *n* surf-bret

surroundings Umgebung *f* oom-gay-boong

sweater Pullover *m* pull-o-vair

sweet (wine) lieblich leep-lish

sweet süß zews

sweetener Süßstoff *m* ze-ws-shtawf
swelling Schwellung *f* sh-vel-loong
to swim schwimmen shwim-men
swimming area Strandbad *n* shtrahnt-baht
swimming pool Swimmingpool *m* swim-ming-pool
swimming trunks Badehose *f* bah-duh-ho-zuh
Swiss franc Schweizer Franken *m* shwy-tsuh frahnk-en
switch Schalter *m* shahl-tuh
swordfish Schwertfisch *m* shvairt-fish
synagogue Synagoge *f* zin-ah-go-guh

T

T-shirt T-Shirt *n* t-shirt
table Tisch *m* tish
table tennis Tischtennis *n* tish-tennis
table wine Tafelwein *m* tah-fel-vine
tablet Tablette *f* tah-blet-tuh
tail light Rücklicht *n* rewk-lisht
to take out to eat einladen eye-n-lah-den
to take photographs foto-grafieren foto-grah-feer-en
taken besetzt beh-zetst
tampon Tampon *n* tahm-pon
tangerine Mandarine *f* mahn-dah-ree-nuh

tanning salon Solarium *n* zo-lah-ree-um
tape Klebeband *n* klay-buh-bahnt
tarragon Estragon *m* es-trah-gohn
tartar Zahnstein *m* tsahn-stein
to taste schmecken shmek-en
taxi stand Taxistand *m* tahx-ee-shtahnt
tea Tee *m* tay
teabag Teebeutel *m* tay-boi-tel
team Mannschaft *f* mahn-shahft
teapot Teekanne *f* tay-kah-nuh
teaset Teeservice *n* tay-zair-vees
telephoto lens Teleobjektiv *n* tay-luh-ohp-yek-teef
temperature Temperatur *f* tem-pay-rah-toor
temple Tempel *m* temple
tendon Sehne *f* zay-nuh
tennis Tennis *n* tennis
tennis ball Tennisball *m* tennis-bahl
tennis racket Tennisschläger *m* tennis-shlay-guh
tent Zelt *n* tselt
tent peg Hering *m* hay-ring
terrace Terrasse *f* tay-rahss-uh
to thaw; it's thawing tauen; es taut tauw-en es tauwt
theater Theater *n* tay-ah-tuh
there dort dawt
thermal spa Thermalbad *n* tair-mahl-baht

thermometer
Fieberthermometer *n* fee-buh-tair-mo-may-tuh
thermos Thermosflasche *f* tair-mohs-flah-shuh
thief Dieb *m* deep
throat Hals *m* hahls
throat drops
Halsschmerztablette *f* hahls-shmairts-tah-blet-tuh
thunder Donner *m* dawn-nuh
thunderstorm Unwetter *n* oon-vet-tuh
Thursday Donnerstag *m* dawn-airs-tahk
thyme Thymian *m* tew-mee-ahn
thyroid gland Schilddrüse *f* shilt-dree-zuh
tick bite Zeckenbiss *m* tsek-en-biss
ticket Fahrkarte *f* fah-kah-tuh
ticket machine
Fahrkartenautomat *m* fah-kah-ten-ow-toe-maht
ticket validation machine
Entwerter *m* ent-vair-tuh
tie Krawatte *f* kruh-vaht-tuh
tight eng ehng
time Zeit tsight
tip Trinkgeld *n* trink-ghelt
tire Reifen *m* rye-fen
tire pressure Reifendruck *m* rye-fen-drook
tissue (paper)
Papiertaschentuch *n* pah-peer-tash-en-tookh
toast Toast *m* toast
tobacconist Tabakladen *m* tah-bahk-lah-den
toboggan run Rodelbahn *f* ro-del-bahn
today heute hoi-tuh
244

toe Zehe *f* tsay-uh
toilet paper Toilettenpapier *n* toi-let-ten-pah-peer
toilet/restroom Toilette *f* toi-let-tuh
toll Maut *f* mauwt
toll booth Mautstelle *f* mauwt-shtel-uh
tomato Tomate *f* to-mah-tuh
tomorrow morgen maw-ghen
tongue Zunge *f* tsoong-uh
tonic water Tonic *n* tonic
tonight heute Abend hoi-tuh ah-bent
tonsillitis Madelentzündung *f* mahn-del-ent-zewn-doong
tonsils Mandeln *pl* mahn-deln
tools Werkzeug *n* vairk-tsoik
tooth Zahn *m* tsahn
toothbrush Zahnbürste *f* tsahn-bewr-stuh
toothpaste Zahnpasta *f* tsahn-pahs-tuh
toothpick Zahnstocher *m* tsahn-shtawk-uh
torn ligament Bänderriss *m* ben-duh-riss
tour boat Ausflugsboot *n* ows-flooks-boat
tour group Reisegruppe *f* rise-uh-groo-puh
tourist guide
Fremdenführer *m* frem-den-fur-uh
tourist office
Fremdenverkehrsamt *n* frem-den-vair-kairs-ahmt
tow rope Abschleppseil *n* ahp-shlep-zile
tow truck Abschleppwagen *m* ahp-shlep-vah-ghen

towel Handtuch n
hahn-tookh
tower Turm m
toorm
town Stadt f
shtaht
town center Innenstadt f
in-nen-shtaht
town gate Stadttor n
shtaht-taw
town hall Rathaus n
raht-house
town wall Stadtmauer f
shtaht-mauw-uh
toy Spielzeug n
shpeel-tsoik
track pants Jogginghose f
jogging-ho-zuh
track Gleis n glys
tracksuit Jogginganzug m
jogging-ahn-tsook
traffic lights Ampel f
ahm-pel
trail Loipe f loi-puh
trailer Wohnwagen m
vone-vah-ghen
train Zug m tsook
train station Bahnhof m
bahn-hoaf
tranquilizer
Beruhigungsmittel n
buh-roo-ih-goongs-mit-tel
to transfer umsteigen
oom-sty-ghen
transfer Überweisung f ee-
buh-vize-oong
transmission Getriebe n
guh-tree-buh
trash Abfall m ahp-fahl
travel bag Reisetasche f
rise-uh-tah-shuh
travel guide Reiseführer m
rise-uh-fee-ruh
treasury Schatzkammer f
shahts-kahm-muh

trip Überfahrt f
ew-buh-faht
trout Forelle f faw-rel-luh
Tuesday Dienstag m
deens-tahk
tumur Tumor m
too-maw
tuna Thunfisch m toon-fish
turkey Pute f, Truthahn m
poo-tuh troot-hahn
turn signal Blinklicht n
blink-lisht
turnip Rübe f rew-buh
turquoise türkis
tewr-kees
TV Fernseher m
fairn-zay-uh
TV room Fernsehraum m
fairn-zay-rauwm
tweezers Pinzette f
pin-tset-tuh

U ────────────

ulcer Geschwür n
guh-shvewr
umpire Schiedsrichter m
sheets-rik-tuh
undershirt Unterhemd n
oon-tuh-hempt
to understand verstehen
fair-shtay-en
underwear Unterwäsche f
oon-tuh-vesh-uh
university Universität f
oon-ih-vair-see-tate
until bis bis
up the steps die Treppe f
hinauf dee trep-puh hin-
owf
urologist Urologe m
oor-o-lo-guh
UV filter UV-Filter m
oo-fauw-fil-tuh

V

vacation Urlaub *m*
oor-<u>lauwp</u>
vacation apartment/rental
Ferienwohnung *f*
<u>fair</u>-ee-en-<u>vo</u>-noong
vacation home Ferienhaus
n <u>fair</u>-ee-en-house
vaccination card Impfpass
m impf-pahs
valid gültig gewl-tik
to validate entwerten
ent-<u>vair</u>-ten
valley Tal *n* tahl
valve Ventil *n* ven-<u>teel</u>
variable wechselhaft
<u>vex</u>-el-hahft
variety show Varieté *n*
vah-ree-ay-<u>tay</u>
VAT (value added tax)
Mehrwertsteuer *f*
<u>mair</u>-vert-shtoi-uh
vault Gewölbe *n*
guh-<u>verl</u>-buh
veal Kalbfleisch *n*
kahlp-flysh
vegetables Gemüse *n*
guh-<u>mew</u>-zuh
vegetarian vegetarisch
vay-guh-<u>tah</u>-rish
vehicle registration
Kfz-Schein *m*
kah-ef-<u>tset</u>-shine
venison Reh *n* ray
vertebrae Wirbel *m* veer-
bel
vest Weste *f* ves-tuh
veterinarian Tierarzt *m*
teer-ahtst
victory Sieg *m* zeek
video camera Videokamera
f <u>video</u>-kah-mair-ah
video cassette
Videokassette *f*
<u>video</u>-kahs-set-tuh

view Aussicht *f* ows-zisht
vinegar Essig *m* es-sish
to visit besichtigen buh-
<u>zish</u>-tee-ghen
visored cap Schirmmütze *f*
<u>sheerm</u>-mewts-uh
volleyball (game) Volleyball
n volley-bahl
voltage elektrische
Spannung *f* ay-<u>lek</u>-trish-uh
<u>shpahn</u>-oong
vomiting Erbrechen *n*
air-<u>bresh</u>-en

W

to wait warten vah-ten
waiter Kellner *m* kel-nuh
waiting room Wartesaal *m*
<u>vah</u>-tuh-zahl
waitress Kellnerin *f*
<u>kel</u>-nuh-rin
walkers' map Wanderkarte
f <u>vahn</u>-duh-kah-tuh
walking shoe Wanderschuh
m <u>vahn</u>-duh-shoe
walking stick Wanderstock
m <u>vahn</u>-duh-shtok
wall Mauer *f* mauw-uh
wallet Portemonnaie *n*
pawt-mo-<u>nay</u>
walnut Walnuss *f*
vahl-nooss
wardrobe Schrank *m*
shrahnk
to wash waschen
vahsh-en
washcloth Waschlappen *m*
<u>vahsh</u>-lahp-pen
washing machine
Waschmaschine *f*
<u>vahsh</u>-muh-shee-nuh
watch Uhr *f* oor
watch shop Uhrmacher *m*
<u>oor</u>-mah-kuh

watchband Uhrarmband n
  <u>oor</u>-ahm-bahnt
water Wasser n vahs-suh
water quality
  Wasserqualität f
  <u>vahs</u>-suh-kvah-lee-tate
water ski Wasserski m
  <u>vas</u>-suh-shee
watercolor Aquarell n
  ah-kvah-<u>rel</u>
watercress (Brunnen)Kresse
  f (<u>broon</u>-nen)-kres-suh
waterfall Wasserfall m
  <u>vas</u>-suh-fahl
watermelon Wassermelone
  f <u>vas</u>-suh-mel-o-nuh
wave Welle f vel-luh
wave pool Wellenbad n
  <u>vel</u>-len-baht
Wednesday Mittwoch m
  mit-vawk
week Woche f vaw-kuh
well done durchgebraten
  <u>doorsh</u>-guh-brah-ten
wet nass nahss
wheel Rad n raht
wheel brace Kreuzschlüssel
  m <u>kroits</u>-shlews-sel
wheelchair lift Hebebühne
  f <u>hay</u>-buh-bee-nuh
whisky Whisky m whisky
white weiß vice
white bread Weißbrot n
  vice-broht
white wine Weißwein m
  vice-vine
whole grain bread
  Vollkornbrot n
  <u>fol</u>-korn-broht
whooping cough
  Keuchhusten m
  <u>koish</u>-hoos-ten
wide-angle lens
  Weitwinkelobjektiv n
  <u>vite</u>-vink-el-ohp-yek-teef
wife Frau f frow

to win gewinnen
  guh-<u>vin</u>-en
wind Wind m vint
window Fenster n fens-tuh
window display
  Schaufenster n
  <u>shauw</u>-fen-stuh
windshield wipers
  Scheibenwischer m
  <u>shy</u>-ben-vish-uh
wine Wein m vine
winter Winter m vinter
wiper blade
  Scheibenwischerblatt n
  <u>shy</u>-ben-vish-uh-blaht
wipe feuchtes Tuch n
  foish-tes tookh
wire Draht m draht
wisdom tooth
  Weisheitszahn m
  <u>vice</u>-hights-tsahn
witness Zeuge m tsoi-guh
wood Wald m vahlt
wool Wolle f vol-luh
works Werk n vairk
wound Wunde f voon-duh
wrench Schraubenschlüssel
  m <u>shrauw</u>-ben-shlews-sel
wrinkle-free bügelfrei
  <u>bew</u>-ghel-fry
writing pad Schreibblock m
  shryb-lawk
writing paper Briefpapier n
  <u>breef</u>-pah-pee-uh

Y

year Jahr n yah
yellow gelb gelp
yesterday gestern
  ghes-tairn
yoga Yoga n yo-gah
yogurt Joghurt m yogurt

youth hostel
 Jugendherberge *f* <u>you</u>-
 ghent-hair-bair-guh
youth hostel ID
 Jugendherbergsausweis
 m <u>you</u>-ghent-hair-bairgs-
 auws-vice

Z ────────

zip code Postleitzahl *f*
 <u>post</u>-light-tsahl
zipper Reißverschluss *m*
 <u>rice</u>-fair-shloos
zoo Zoo *m* tsoh
zoom lens Zoomobjektiv *n*
 <u>zoom</u>-ohp-yek-teef
zucchini Zucchini *pl* zoo-
 <u>kee</u>-nee

A

Abend *m* evening
Abfahrt *f* departure
Abflug *m* departure *(airplane)*
Achtung! Caution!
Adresse *f* address
Ankunft *f* arrivals
Auf Wiedersehen! Good bye!
Auffahrt *f* ramp
Ausfahrt *f* driveway;
– **freihalten!** Do not block
driveway!
Ausgang *m* exit
Auskunft *f* information
Ausland *n* abroad
Auslandsflüge *mpl*
international flights
Autobahn *f* motorway;
freeway
Autovermierung *f* car rental

B

Bäckerei *f* bakery
Bank *f* bank
Bedarfshaltestelle *f* request
stop
Benzin *n* petrol; gasoline
berühren to touch; **Bitte nicht
–!** Please do not touch!
besetzt occupied; taken
Besichtigung *f* tour
Betreten verboten! Keep out!
No trespassing!
Bitte einordnen Get in lane
bleifrei unleaded
Briefe *mpl* letters
Briefmarken *fpl* stamps
Brücke *f* bridge
Bücher *npl* books
Buchhandlung *f* bookstore
Bus *m* bus
Busspur *f* bus lane

C

Campingplatz *m* campsite
Cent *m* cent

D

Damen *fpl* ladies; ladies' room
deutsch German
Dienstag *m* Tuesday
Diesel *m* diesel
Donnerstag *m* Thursday
drücken press; push
Durchgangsstraße *f* through
road

E

Einbahnstraße *f* one-way
street
Einfahrt *f* driveway; – **freihal-
ten!** Do not block driveway!
Eingang *m* entrance; **Kein –!**
No entry!
einschließlich including
eintreten to enter; **Bitte –!**
Please enter!
Eintritt *m* admission; – **frei** free
admission; **Kein –!** No entry!
Einzel(fahrkarte) *f* single
(ticket)
englisch English
Erdgeschoss *n* ground floor
Ermäßigung *f* reduction *(price)*
Erwachsene *mpl* adults; **nur
für –** adults only
etwa about; circa
Euro *m* euro
Europa *n* Europe

F

Fahrrad *n* bicycle;
-vermietung *f* bicycles for
rent
Fahrspur *f* lane

Feiertag *m* holiday
Feuer *n* fire
Feuerlöscher *m* fire
  extinguisher
Feuerwehr *f* fire department
Fischgeschäft *n* fishmonger's
Fleischer *m* butcher
Flug *m* flight
Flughafen *m* airport
Fotogeschäft *n* photostore
frei vacant; free
freihalten keep clear
Freitag *m* Friday
Frisör *m* hairdresser
Führung *f* guided tour;
  nächste –
  next guided tour

G

Gefahr! Danger!
Geldwechsel *m* money
  exchange
geöffnet open
geradeaus straight ahead
geschlossen closed
Geschwindigkeitsbegrenzung
  f speed limit
gestrichen painted; **frisch –**
  wet paint
Gottesdienst *m* religious
  service
gratis free of charge
Gruppe *f* group
gültig valid; **Ab 9.30 h –** valid
  from 9.30 a.m.

H

Hafen *m* harbor
Halt! Stop!
Haltestelle *f* (bus/subway) stop
Halteverbot *n* no stopping or
  standing
Handelsmesse *f* trade fair
handgemacht handmade

Hauptpost *f* main post office
heiß hot *(temperature)*
Herein! Come in!
Herren *mpl* men; men's room
Herrenfriseur *m* barber
hier here
Hilfe *f* help; **erste –** first aid
hinauslehnen to lean out;
  nicht – do not lean out
Höchstgeschwindigkeit *f* top
  speed
Hotel *n* hotel
Hund *m* dog

I

inbegriffen included
Inland *n* domestic; national
Inlandsflüge *mpl* domestic
  flights;

J

Jugendherberge *f* youth hostel
Juwelier *m* jeweller's

K

kalt cold
Karte *f* ticket; card; map
Kasse *f* cash register
Kaution *f* deposit
keine Geldrückgabe no
  change given
Kinder children *npl*
Kirche *f* church
Kleingeld *n* change *(money)*
Kreuzung *f* crossroads;
  intersection

L

langsam (fahren) (drive) slowly
letzte / letzter / letztes last
links left; **– abbiegen**
  verboten no left turn

M

Mahlzeit *f* meal
Markt(platz) *m* (outdoor) market
Markthalle *f* (indoor) market
Meer *n* sea; ocean
Menü *n* set menu
Messe *f* trade fair
Metzger *m* butcher
Minute *f* minute
mittags at lunchtime
Mittagszeit *f* lunchtime
Mittwoch *m* Wednesday
Montag *m* Monday
Morgen *m* morning; **Guten –!** Good morning!
morgen tomorrow
morgens in the morning; a.m.
Münze *f* coin

N

nachmittags afternoons
nächste Leerung next (mail) collection
Nacht *f* night; **Gute –!** Good night!
nachts at night
national national
Nichtraucher *m* non smoker; non smoking
Norden *m* north
Notausgang *m* emergency exit
Notfall *m* emergency
Notruf *m* emergency number

O

Obst- und Gemüse *n* fruit and vegetables
Öffnungszeiten *fpl* opening times
Optiker *m* optician
Osten *m* east

P

Parken nur mit Berechtigungsschein parking by permit holders only
Parkplatz *m* car park; parking lot
Pension *f* bed & breakfast
Personalausweis *m* ID; passport
Pfund *n* pound
Polizei *f* police
Postamt *n* post office
postlagernd in care of *(mail)*
privat private

R

Rasen *m* grass; lawn **Den – nicht betreten!** Keep off the gras!
Rathaus *n* town hall; city hall
rauchen to smoke; – **verboten!** No smoking!
Raucher *m* smoker; smoking
rechts right; – **abbiegen verboten!** no right turn!
Reinigung *f* dry-cleaner
Reisebüro *n* tavel agency
Reisepass *m* passport
Rettungsdienst *m* rescue service
Rezeption *f* reception
Richtung *f* direction
Rolltreppe *f* escalator
Rückfahrkarte *f* return ticket
Ruhe bewahren keep calm
Ruhe bitte! Quiet, please!

S

Samstag *m* Saturday
Schlussverkauf *m* end of season sale
Schnellstraße *f* (4-lane) expressway

Schritt fahren drive at walking speed
Schuhmacher *m* shoe repairs
Schüler *m* student; pupil
Selbstbedienung *f* self-service
Senioren *mpl* senior citizens
Sonderangebot *n* on sale; special offer
Sonnabend *m* Saturday
Sonntag *m* Sunday
Speisekarte *f* menu
Stockwerk *n* floor
Straße *f* road; street
Straßenarbeiten *fpl* roadworks
Straßenverengung *f* road narrows
Student *m* student *(college/university)*
Stunde *f* hour
Süden *m* south
Supermarkt *m* supermarket

T

Tabakwarenladen *m* tobacconist
Tag *m* day; **Guten –!** Hello!
Tagesgericht *n* menu of the day
Tageskarte *f* one-day ticket; daily menu
Taxi *n* taxi
Terminal *m (airport)* terminal
Tiefparterre *n* basement
Toiletten *fpl* restrooms
Touristeninformation *f* tourist information
Trinkgeld *n* tip (service)
Trinkwasser *n* potable water; **Kein –!** Water not potable!

U

U-Bahn *f* underground; subway
Umkleidekabinen *fpl* fitting rooms
Umleitung *f* detour
Unterschrift *f* signature

V

verboten prohibited
verkaufen to sell; **zu –** for sale
Verkehr *m* traffic
vermieten to let; to rent; **zu –** to let; for rent
Verspätung *f* delay
Vorfahrt (be)achten yield to traffic
vormittags in the morning; a.m.
Vorschicht! Caution! Danger! **– bissiger Hund!** Beware of the dog!
Vorverkauf *m* advance bookings

W

Waschsalon *m* laundromat
WC *m* restrooms
Wechselgeld *n* change *(money)*
Westen *m* west
wochentags weekdays
Wohnsitz *m* residence; **ständiger –** permanent residence

Z

Zentrum *n* center
ziehen pull
Zimmer *n* room; **– frei** vacancy
Zoll *m* customs
Zoo *m* zoo

A

accident 51, 53, 170
address 23, 51, 168
airmail 168
airport 42, 57
alcohol 91, 99
ambulance III, 51, 176
appetizer 96, 99
appointment 148
area code 70
arm 62, 138, 180
arts and crafts 115

B

bank 166, 167
bar 74, 99, 164
bathroom 26, 28, 33
battery 122, 127, 129
beach 118, 136, 138, 139
bed 26, 27, 28, 31, 34, 36
beer 91, 94, 110
bicycle 61, 145
bill 30, 34, 97, 166
boat 47, 136, 138, 139, 146, 160
book 63, 64, 132, 134
bottle 62, 63, 99, 125
box office 162
breakfast 26, 27, 28, 99
bus 32, 38, 46, 55, 56

C

cabin 47, 48
café 71, 74
cake 87, 99, 110
camera 128, 129, 130
car 28, 33, 38, 45, 46, 48, 49, 51, 52, 53, 61
check 34, 42, 106, 166
cheese 86, 110
cigarette 133, 134
city 57
clock 122, 127
coffee 34, 93, 94, 111
color 116, 128
concert 161, 163
consulate 170
contact lens 128
credit card 104, 106, 167
cup 94, 100, 126

D

date 193
deckchair 48, 136
dentist 175, 176, 187, 188
departure 42, 45, 57
diabetic 95, 178
dining room 28
dinner 19, 27, 98, 100
discount 27, 43, 60, 156, 161
doctor 175, 176, 177, 179

E
e-mail 71, 72
electronics 107
engine 52
evening lll,16,71,164,191
events 154, 160
exit 35, 42, 45

F
fabric 116
family 156, 186
ferry 47, 48
field 139, 142
first-aid kit 174
first-aid station 137
fish 81, 100, 107, 111
flight 41, 42
fruit 88, 100, 107, 111

G.
game 141, 142
garage 52, 54
gas station 50
glass 35, 100, 115, 126
glasses 127, 162
golf 141
grocery 108
guided tour 156

H
hair 137, 149
hairdresser 108
harbor 158

herbs 111
hiking 120, 144
hotel 26, 67

I
information 95
injury 184
insurance 49, 52, 54, 170
invitation 99

J
jewelry 115, 122
juice 92, 93, 110, 112

K
key 29, 31

L
leg 67, 181
lift 68, 147, 148
light 29, 35, 53, 54, 55, 100,
   118, 126, 145, 146
liter 50, 109
locker 40, 137
luggage 28, 30, 39, 40, 45,
   68

M
mail 72, 168
mailbox 167
menu 62, 75, 94
message 29, 70

money 107, 166
month 191, 192, 193
movie 161
movie theater 163
music 108, 131, 163

N
newspaper 131
night 26, 27, 124, 163,
    191, 192
noise 199
non-smoking 43, 45, 74
number 48, 52, 56, 71, 167
nuts 112

O
ointment 175
optician 108, 127
organ 159

P
package 168
passport 129, 147, 166
pharmacy 108, 172
picture 64
pill 174, 175, 186
play 140, 142, 163
police 51, 169
post office 167
postcard 133, 167, 168
poultry 80, 113
present 106, 114, 122
price 49

R
repair 53, 108, 127, 129,
    145, 187
restaurant 74, 95, 101
restroom 33, 66, 74
road 38, 39, 49, 52
room 26, 27, 28, 29, 32, 35,
    36, 45, 60, 68, 138, 162

S
salad 101
sauna 143, 152
season 35, 36, 106
seat 41, 43, 53, 61, 67, 74,
    145, 162, 163, 164
ship 48
shoe 108, 120, 121, 143,
    144
shower 29, 36, 124, 139,
    198
sightseeing tour 48, 154, 155
skin 150, 151, 181
soup 102
souvenir 108, 114, 122
spices 113
sports 119
square 31, 38, 160
stamp 168
stationery 108
store 107, 108
street 38
subway 38, 55, 56, 154
suitcase 40
sweet 102

T

table 36, 63, 74, 102, 142
tablets 174, 175
taxi 30, 57, 58, 68
theft 169
ticket 40, 41, 43, 46, 47, 56, 58, 155, 161, 162
time 19, 42, 71, 190, 192
tire 50, 54, 146
tobacco 134
tour 160
tourist information 26, 154
tow truck 51
town 131, 154, 159, 160
trail 143, 144, 148
train 42, 43, 44, 58
train station 57

V

vegetable 83, 102, 107, 114

W

watch 108, 122
water 34, 36, 45, 63, 92, 93, 101, 102, 112, 140, 199, 200
weather 196
wheelchair 66, 67, 68
wine 90, 95, 102, 113, 114

Y

year 192

Colors and Fabrics